the Unofficial Guide® to Disneyland
1999

Also available from Macmillan Travel:

The Unofficial Disney Companion: The Inside Story of Walt Disney World and the Man Behind the Mouse, by Eve Zibart

The Unofficial Guide to Atlanta, by Fred Brown and Bob Sehlinger

The Unofficial Guide to Branson, Missouri, by Bob Sehlinger and Eve Zibart

The Unofficial Guide to Chicago, by Joe Surkiewicz and Bob Sehlinger

The Unofficial Guide to Cruises, by Kay Showker and Bob Sehlinger

The Unofficial Guide to the Great Smoky and Blue Ridge Mountains, by Bob Sehlinger and Joe Surkiewicz

The Unofficial Guide to Las Vegas, by Bob Sehlinger

The Unofficial Guide to Miami and the Keys, by Bob Sehlinger and Joe Surkiewicz

The Unofficial Guide to New Orleans, by Eve Zibart with Bob Sehlinger

The Unofficial Guide to New York City, by Eve Zibart and Bob Sehlinger with Jim Leff

The Unofficial Guide to San Francisco, by Joe Surkiewicz and Bob Sehlinger with Richard Sterling

The Unofficial Guide to Skiing in the West, by Lito Tejada-Flores, Peter Shelton, Seth Masia, and Bob Sehlinger

The Unofficial Guide to Walt Disney World, by Bob Sehlinger

The Unofficial Guide to Washington, D.C., by Bob Sehlinger and Joe Surkiewicz with Eve Zibart

Mini-Mickey: The Pocket-Sized Unofficial Guide to Walt Disney World, by Bob Sehlinger

the Unofficial Guide® to Disneyland 1999

Bob Sehlinger

Macmillan • USA

Every effort has been made to ensure the accuracy of information throughout this book. Bear in mind, however, that prices, schedules, etc., are constantly changing. Readers should always verify information before making final plans.

Macmillan Travel
A Simon & Schuster Macmillan Company
1633 Broadway
New York, New York 10019-6785

Produced by Menasha Ridge Press
Design by Barbara E. Williams

ISBN 0-02-862615-X

ISSN 1053-248X

Manufactured in the United States of America

10 9 8 7 6 5 4 3 2 1

1999 edition

CONTENTS

ACKNOWLEDGMENTS

Special thanks to our field research team, who rendered a Herculean effort in what must have seemed like a fantasy version of Sartre's *No Exit* to the tune of "It's a Small World." We hope you all recover to tour another day.

Many thanks also to Molly Burns and Clay White, who kept the schedule, to Barbara Williams for design and production, and to Sarah Nawrocki and Laura Poole for editorial work on this book. Caroline Carr earned our appreciation by keeping tight deadlines in providing the typography. Cartography was created by Brian Taylor. The index was prepared by Ann Cassar.

Peals of laughter and much appreciation to nationally renowned cartoonist Tami Knight for her brilliant and insightful work.

Grace Walton, Clay White, Patt Palmer, and Mike Jones all contributed energetically to shaping this latest edition. Sue Katz is to be credited with pushing everybody to try harder. Dr. Karen Turnbow, Dr. Gayle Janzen, and Dr. Joan Burns, psychologists, provided much insight into the experiences of small children at Disneyland.

—*Bob Sehlinger*

For Shane, my California girl.

Introduction

How Come "Unofficial"?

DECLARATION OF INDEPENDENCE

The author and researchers of this guide specifically and categorically declare that they are and always have been totally independent of the Walt Disney Company, Inc., of Disneyland, Inc., of Walt Disney World, Inc., and of any and all other members of the Disney corporate family not listed.

The material in this guide originated with the authors and researchers and has not been reviewed, edited, or in any way approved by the Walt Disney Company, Inc., Disneyland, Inc., or Walt Disney World, Inc.

This guidebook represents the first comprehensive critical appraisal of Disneyland. Its purpose is to provide the reader with the information necessary to tour the theme park with the greatest efficiency and economy and with the least amount of hassle and standing in line. The researchers of this guide believe in the wondrous variety, joy, and excitement of the Disney attractions. At the same time, we recognize realistically that Disneyland is a business, with the same profit motivations as businesses the world over.

In this, the "unofficial" guide, we have elected to represent and serve you, the consumer. The contents were researched and compiled by a team of evaluators who were, and are, completely independent of Disneyland and the Walt Disney Company, Inc. If a restaurant serves bad food, if a gift item is overpriced, or if a certain ride isn't worth the wait, we can say so; in the process, we hope we can make your visit more fun, efficient, and economical.

THE IMPORTANCE OF BEING GOOFY

A group of Disney executives, clean-shaven (because of a company policy banning all facial hair) and impeccably attired in dark suits, is gathered around a polished black walnut table. There is an almost palpable tension.

Everyone speaks in hushed tones, carefully measuring their words:

"I don't want to be blindsided by this at the shareholders' meeting."

"No one's raised the issue yet. Let's just sit on it. The last thing we want is to stir something up."

"Too late; I've heard the *Post* is working on a story. There are even rumors about a paternity suit."

"What's Donald saying?"

"He's stonewalling. Won't return my calls."

"Well, he's going to have to come clean. Our people need to know what to tell the press."

"Right. And we need to know, too. If he doesn't have a brother and he doesn't have a sister, where *did* Huey, Dewey, and Louie come from?"

And so it goes . . .

What really makes writing about Disneyland fun is that the Disney people take everything so seriously. Day to day they debate momentous decisions with far-ranging consequences: Do you think Goofy would look swishy in a silver cape? Have we gone too far with the Little Mermaid's cleavage? At a time when the whole nation is concerned about the drug problem, can we afford to have a dwarf named "Dopey"?

Unofficially, we think having a sense of humor is pretty important. This guidebook has a sense of humor, and it is probably necessary that you do, too. . . . Not to use this book, but more significantly, to have fun at Disneyland. Disneyland (in the popular phrasing) is the mother of all tourist attractions. A certain amount of levity is required simply to survive. Think of the *Unofficial Guide* as a private trainer to help get your sense of humor in shape. It will help you understand the importance of being Goofy.

The Death of Spontaneity

One of our all-time favorite letters is from a man in Chapel Hill, North Carolina; he writes:

> *Your book reads like the operations plan for an amphibious landing. . . . Go here, do this, proceed to Step 15. . . . You must think that everyone [who visits Disneyland] is a hyperactive, Type-A, theme-park commando. Whatever happened to the satisfaction of self-discovery or the joy of spontaneity? Next you will be telling us when to empty our bladders.*

As it happens, we at the *Unofficial Guide* are a pretty existential crew. We are big on self-discovery when walking in the woods or watching birds. Some of us are able to improvise jazz without reading music, while others can whip up a mean pot of chili without a recipe. When it comes to Disneyland, however, we all agree that you either need a good plan or a frontal lobotomy. The operational definition of self-discovery and spontaneity at Disneyland is the "pleasure" of heat prostration and the "joy" of standing in line.

It's easy to spot the free spirits at Disneyland, particularly at opening time. While everybody else is stampeding to Splash Mountain or Indiana Jones, they are the ones standing in a cloud of dust puzzling over the park map. Later, they are the people running around like chickens in a thunderstorm trying to find an attraction with less than a 40-minute wait. Face it, Disneyland is not a very existential place. In many ways it's the quintessential system, the ultimate in mass-produced entertainment, the most planned and programmed environment imaginable. Spontaneity and self-discovery work about as well at Disneyland as they do on your tax return.

We're not saying you can't have a great time at Disneyland. Bowling isn't very spontaneous either, but lots of people love it. What we *are* saying is that you need a plan. You don't have to be compulsive or inflexible about it, just think about what you want to do before you go. Don't delude yourself by rationalizing that the information in this modest tome is only for the pathological and super-organized. Ask not for whom the tome tells, Bubba, it tells for thee.

How This Guide Was Researched and Written

While much has been written concerning Disneyland, very little has been comparative or evaluative. In preparing this guide, nothing was taken for granted. The theme park was visited at different times throughout the year by a team of trained observers who conducted detailed evaluations, rating the theme park along with all of its component rides, shows, exhibits, services, and concessions according to a formal, pretested rating instrument. Interviews with attraction patrons were conducted to determine what tourists of all age groups enjoyed most and least during their Disneyland visit.

While our observers are independent and impartial, we do not claim special expertise or scientific background relative to the types of exhibits, performances, or attractions viewed. Like you, we visit Disneyland as tourists, noting our satisfaction or dissatisfaction. Disneyland offerings are marketed to the touring public, and it is as the public that we have experienced them.

The primary difference between the average tourist and the trained evaluator is in the evaluator's professional skills in organization, preparation, and observation. The trained evaluator is responsible for much more than simply observing and cataloging. While the tourist is being entertained and delighted by the *Enchanted Tiki Room,* the professional evaluator seated nearby is rating the performance in terms of theme, pace, continuity, and originality. He is also checking out the physical arrangements: is the sound system clear and audible without being overpowering; is the audience shielded from the sun or rain; is seating adequate; can everyone in the audience clearly see the staging area? Similarly, detailed and relevant checklists are prepared and applied by observer teams to rides, exhibits, concessions, and to the theme park in general. Finally, observations and evaluator ratings are integrated with audience reactions and the opinions of patrons to compile a comprehensive quality profile of each feature and service.

In compiling this guide, we recognize the fact that a tourist's age, gender, background, and interests will strongly influence his/her taste in Disneyland offerings and will account for his/her preference of one ride or feature over another. Given this fact, we make no attempt at comparing apples with oranges. How indeed could a meaningful comparison be made between the serenity and beauty of the Storybook Land Canal Boats and the wild roller coaster ride of Space Mountain? Instead, our objective is to provide the reader with a critical evaluation and enough pertinent data to make knowledgeable decisions according to individual tastes.

The essence of this guide, then, consists of individual critiques and descriptions of each feature of Disneyland, supplemented with some maps to help you get around and several detailed touring plans to help you avoid bottlenecks and crowds. Because so many Disneyland guests also visit Universal Studios Hollywood, we have included comprehensive coverage and touring plans for that park as well.

LETTERS, COMMENTS, AND QUESTIONS FROM READERS

Many of those who use *The Unofficial Guide to Disneyland* write to us asking questions, making comments, or sharing their own strategies for visiting Disneyland. We appreciate all such input, both positive and critical, and encourage our readers to continue writing. Readers' comments and observations are frequently used in revised editions of the *Unofficial Guide,* and have contributed immeasurably to its improvement. Please write to:

Bob Sehlinger
The Unofficial Guide to Disneyland
P.O. Box 43059
Birmingham, AL 35243

When you write, be sure to put a return address on your letter as well as the envelope; sometimes envelopes and letters get separated. It's also a good idea to include your phone number. And remember, our work often requires that we be out of the office for long periods of time, so forgive us if our response is a little slow.

Questions from Readers

Questions frequently asked by our readers are listed and answered in an appendix at the end of the *Unofficial Guide*.

Reader Survey

At the end of this guide, you will find a short questionnaire that can be used to express your opinions about your Disneyland visit. The questionnaire is designed so that each member of your party, regardless of age, can tell us what he or she thinks. Clip out the questionnaire along the dotted line and mail to:

Reader Survey
The Unofficial Guide to Disneyland
P.O. Box 43059
Birmingham, AL 35243

Disneyland: An Overview

If you are selecting among the tourist attractions of California, the question is not whether to visit Disneyland but how to see the best of the various Disney offerings with some economy of time, effort, and finances.

Make no mistake: there is nothing quite like Disneyland. Incredible in its scope, genius, beauty, and imagination, it is a joy and wonderment for people of all ages. A fantasy, a dream, and a vision all rolled into one, it transcends simple entertainment, making us children and adventurers, freeing us for an hour or a day to live the dreams of our past, present, and future.

Disneyland, even more than its Florida counterpart, embodies that quiet, charming spirit of nostalgia that so characterized Walt Disney himself. Disneyland is vast, yet intimate, etched in the tradition of its founder, yet continually changing. A visit to Disneyland is fun, but it is also a powerful and moving experience, a living testimony to the achievements and immense potential of the loving and life-embracing side of man's creativity.

Certainly we are critics, but it is the responsibility of critics to credit that which is done well as surely as to remark negatively on that which is done poorly. The Disney attractions are special, a quantum leap beyond and above any man-made entertainment offering we know of. It is incredible to us that anyone could visit southern California and bypass Disneyland.

WHAT DOES DISNEYLAND CONSIST OF?

Disneyland was opened in 1955 on a 107-acre tract surrounded almost exclusively by orange groves, just west of the sleepy, and little-known, southern California community of Anaheim. Constrained by finances and ultimately enveloped by the city it helped create, Disneyland operated on that same modest parcel of land until just recently. On what amounts to a huge city block resides the Disneyland theme park, its backlot and service area, and its ample visitor parking lot.

The Disneyland theme park is a collection of adventures, rides, and shows symbolized by the Disney cartoon characters and the Sleeping Beauty Castle. Disneyland is divided into eight sub-areas or "lands" arranged around a central hub. First encountered is Main Street, U.S.A., which connects the Disneyland entrance with the central hub. Moving clockwise around the hub, the other lands are Adventureland, Frontierland, Fantasyland, and Tomorrowland. Two major lands, Critter Country and New Orleans Square, are accessible via Adventureland and Frontierland but do not connect directly with the central hub. A newer land, Mickey's Toontown, connects to Fantasyland. All eight lands will be described in detail later.

Located across West Street and connected to the theme park by the Disneyland Monorail system is the Disneyland Hotel, and next door, the Disneyland Pacific Hotel. Some visitors expect to be able to tour the Walt Disney Company's studio while at Disneyland. The studio, alas, is some miles distant, in Burbank, California, and does not offer tours.

GROWTH AND CHANGE AT DISNEYLAND

Growth and change at Disneyland (until 1996) had been internal, in marked contrast to the ever-enlarging development of spacious Walt Disney World near Orlando, Florida. Until recently, when something new was added at Disneyland, something old had to go. The Disney engineers, to their credit, however, have never been shy about disturbing the status quo. Patrons of the park's earlier, more modest years are amazed by the transformation. Gone are the days of the "magical little park" with the Monsanto House of the Future, flying saucer–style bumper cars, and Captain Hook's Pirate Ship. Substituted in a process of continuous evolution and modernization are "state of the art" fourth-, fifth-, and sixth-generation attractions and entertainment. To paraphrase Walt Disney, Disneyland will never stop changing as long as there are new ideas to explore.

THE INCREDIBLE EXPANDING MOUSE

The Disneyland theme park was arguably Walt Disney's riskiest venture. It was developed on a shoestring budget made possible only through Disney's relationship with ABC Television and a handful of brave corporate sponsors. The capital available was barely sufficient to acquire the property and build the park; there was nothing left over for the development of hotels or the acquisition and improvement of property adjoining the park. Even the Disneyland Hotel, connected to the theme park by Monorail, was owned and operated by a third party until less than a decade ago.

Disneyland's success spawned a wave of development that rapidly surrounded the theme park with mom and pop motels, souvenir stands, and fast-food restaurants. Disney, still deep in debt, looked on in abject shock, powerless to intervene. In fact, the Disneyland experience was etched so deeply into the Disney corporate consciousness that Walt purchased 27,500 acres and established his own autonomous development district in Florida (unaccountable to any local or county authority) when he was ready to launch Walt Disney World.

Though the Florida project gave Disney the opportunity to develop a destination resort in a totally controlled environment, the steady decline of the area encircling Disneyland continued to rankle him. After tolerating the blight for 30 years, the Walt Disney Company (finally flush with funds and ready for a good fight) set about putting Disneyland right. Quietly at first, then aggressively, Disney began buying up the mom and pop motels, as well as the few remaining orange and vegetable groves near the park.

In June 1993, the City of Anaheim adopted a Disney plan that called for the development of a new Disney destination resort, including a second theme park situated in the current Disneyland parking lot; a Disney-owned hotel district with 4,600 hotel rooms (of which 1,000 are existing rooms in the Disneyland Hotel); two new parking facilities; and improvements, including extensive landscaping of the streets that provide access to the complex. City of Anaheim, Orange County, and State of California infrastructure changes required to support the expanded Disney presence include the widening of I-5, the building of new interchanges, the moving of a major power line, new sewer systems, and expanded utilities capacity.

DISNEY'S CALIFORNIA ADVENTURE

The new park, expected to open in 2001, will be called Disney's California Adventure and will draw on California's natural, historical, and cultural heritage for its theme. Though still in the design stage, the park is expected to have three main "entertainment districts" or "lands." The Golden State district will celebrate California's natural beauty and diversity. Attractions will include a whitewater raft ride and a hang-glider thrill ride over Yosemite. An adjacent district, yet to be named, will focus on the state's seashore and surfing tradition and will feature an old-fashioned boardwalk, and improbably, a pirate ship playground for children. The third major district is inspired by Hollywood and will be a scaled-down version of the Disney-MGM Studios theme park at Walt Disney World. Key attractions planned for the Hollywood section are an introduction to the art of animation and a replica of Walt Disney's original garage studio. The "Main

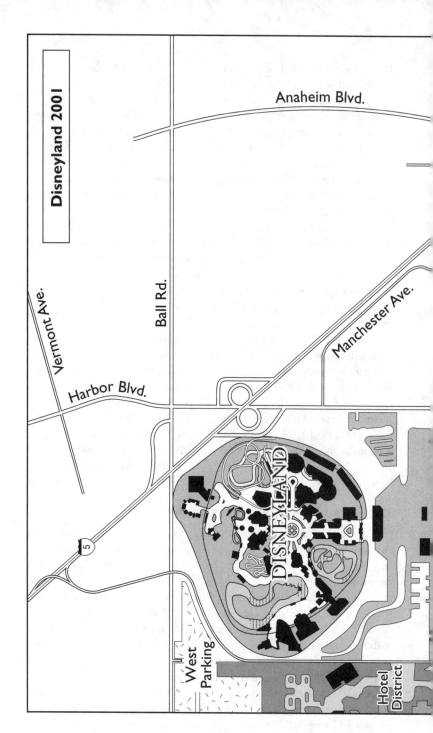

Disneyland 2001

Anaheim Blvd.

Vermont Ave.

Ball Rd.

Manchester Ave.

Harbor Blvd.

5

DISNEYLAND

West Parking

Hotel District

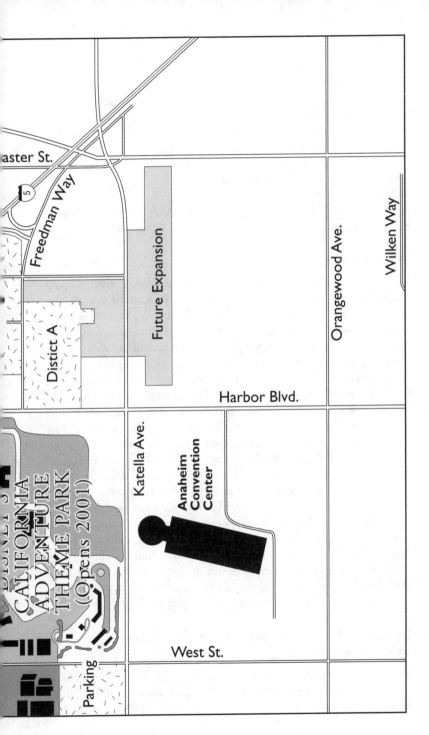

aster St.

5

Freedman Way

Future Expansion

Distict A

DISNEY'S
CALIFORNIA
ADVENTURE
THEME PARK
(Opens 2001)

Parking

Katella Ave.

Anaheim
Convention
Center

West St.

Harbor Blvd.

Orangewood Ave.

Wilken Way

Street" of the Hollywood section will be a Disneyfied version of Rodeo Drive. In a departure from traditional Disney practice, a 750-room luxury hotel (The Grand Californian) will actually be situated inside the park, adjacent to the Golden State district.

The main entrance to Disney's California Adventure will face the existing Disneyland park across a tree-lined pedestrian plaza that runs from Harbor Boulevard on the east to a new entertainment, shopping, and dining venue called Disneyland Center on the west. Beyond Disneyland Center will be the hotel district made up of the existing Disneyland and Disneyland Pacific hotels and a new Magic Kingdom Hotel. The existing Monorail will connect Disneyland Center with the two theme parks.

PLEASE EXCUSE OUR DUST

You can reasonably expect that the area surrounding the Disneyland park will be in a state of turmoil for the next several years. As of this writing, sewers are being enlarged and extensive modifications and improvements are being made to I-5. Because the new theme park is to be located within the boundaries of the existing parking lot, a new parking facilities must be completed before construction on the new theme park can begin. The new (west) parking facility, in turn, requires the completion of an additional I-5 feeder interchange, as well as a two-lane overpass over Ball Road. In addition, almost all of the surface streets bordering Disneyland will be widened, have medians added, be renamed, and/or (as in one case) be rerouted. The bottom line is that the whole area will be torn up for quite a while. There will be substantial noise and, until work on the freeway and surface streets is finished, major traffic congestion. Construction is planned to proceed in phases so that everything is not uprooted at once. Even so, it is impossible to predict how the overall project will affect your visit.

When you make hotel reservations, consider properties south of Katella Avenue or east of Harbor Boulevard. In our chapter covering lodging we have added a number of hotels near Anaheim Stadium (about one mile away) that will not be impacted by the disruption. If you are not staying in the immediate area, contact Disneyland Information the day before your visit for advice on traffic conditions and preferred routing.

SHOULD I GO TO DISNEYLAND IF I'VE SEEN WALT DISNEY WORLD?

Disneyland is roughly comparable to the Magic Kingdom theme park at Walt Disney World near Orlando, Florida. Both are arranged by "lands" accessible from a central hub and connected to the entrance by a Main

Street. Both parks feature many rides and attractions with the same name: Space Mountain, Jungle Cruise, Pirates of the Caribbean, It's a Small World, and Dumbo, the Flying Elephant, to name a few. Interestingly, however, the same name does not necessarily connote the same experience. Pirates of the Caribbean at Disneyland is much longer and more elaborate than its Walt Disney World counterpart. Big Thunder Mountain is more elaborate in Florida, and Dumbo is about the same in both places.

Disneyland is more intimate than the Magic Kingdom, not having the room for expansion enjoyed by the Florida park. Pedestrian thoroughfares are narrower, and everything from Big Thunder Mountain to the Castle is scaled down somewhat. Large crowds are more taxing at Disneyland because there is less room for them to disperse. At Disneyland, however, there are dozens of little surprises, small unheralded attractions tucked away in crooks and corners of the park, which give Disneyland a special charm and variety that the Magic Kingdom lacks. And, of course, Disneyland has the stamp of Walt Disney's personal touch.

To allow for a meaningful comparison, we have provided a summary of those features found only at Disneyland, followed by a critical look at the attractions found at both parks.

Attractions Found Only at Disneyland	
Main Street:	"Great Moments with Mr. Lincoln" *The Walt Disney Story*
Adventureland:	Indiana Jones Adventure
Frontierland:	Sailing Ship *Columbia* *Fantasmic!*
New Orleans Square:	The Disney Gallery
Fantasyland:	Pinocchio's Daring Journey Casey Jr. Circus Train Storybook Land Canal Boats Alice in Wonderland Matterhorn Bobsleds Sleeping Beauty Castle Diorama
Tomorrowland:	Rocket Rods Submarine Voyage
Mickey's Toontown:	Roger Rabbit's Car Toon Spin Goofy's Bounce House Chip 'n' Dale's Treehouse Jolly Trolley

Critical Comparison of Attractions Found at Both Parks

Main Street

WDW/Disneyland Railroad	The Disneyland Railroad is far more entertaining by virtue of the Grand Canyon Diorama and the Primeval World components not found at the Magic Kingdom

Adventureland

Jungle Cruise	More realistic AudioAnimatronic (robotic) animals and longer ride at Walt Disney World
Enchanted Tiki Room	Walt Disney World's version recently upgraded
Swiss Family Treehouse	Larger at the Magic Kingdom

New Orleans Square

Pirates of the Caribbean	Far superior and more politically correct at Disneyland
Haunted Mansion	Slight edge to the Magic Kingdom version

Critter Country

Country Bear Jamboree/ Country Bear Playhouse	Same production with a much shorter wait at Disneyland
Splash Mountain	Drier at Walt Disney World

Frontierland

Various river cruises (canoes, boats, etc.)	More interesting sights at the Magic Kingdom
Tom Sawyer Island	Comparable, but a little more elaborate with better food service at the Magic Kingdom
Big Thunder Mountain Railroad	About the same; sights and special effects are better at the Magic Kingdom

Fantasyland

Snow White's Scary Adventures	New Magic Kingdom version is better
Peter Pan's Flight	Better at Disneyland
Mr. Toad's Wild Ride	Better at Disneyland

Critical Comparison of Attractions Found at Both Parks	
Dumbo, the Flying Elephant	About the same at both parks
Carousels	About the same at both parks
Castles	Far larger and more beautiful at the Magic Kingdom
Mad Tea Party	The same at both parks
It's a Small World	About the same at both parks
Tomorrowland	
Autopia/Tomorrowland Speedway	About the same at both parks
AstroOrbiter	About the same at both parks
Space Mountain	Better in terms of special effects at the Magic Kingdom, better ride at Disneyland
Honey, I Shrunk the Audience	About the same at both parks

Part One

Planning Before You Leave Home

Gathering Information

In addition to this guide, we recommend that you obtain copies of the following publications:

1. The Disney Travel Company California Brochure This full-color booklet describes Disneyland in its entirety and lists rates for the Disneyland Hotel. Also described are Disneyland package vacations with lodging options at more than 25 nearby hotels. The brochure is available from most full-service travel agents, or it can be obtained by calling the Walt Disney Travel Company at (800) 605-1234. If you are in a hurry, a two-page fax brochure is also available.

2. Disneyland Guidebook for Guests with Disabilities If members of your party are sight- or hearing-impaired, or partially or wholly non-ambulatory, you will find this small guide very helpful. To receive a copy, call (714) 781-4560.

3. California Traveler Discount Guide Another good source of lodging, restaurant, and attraction discounts throughout the state of California, the California Traveler Discount Guide can be obtained by calling (352) 371-3948, Monday–Friday, 8 a.m. to 5 p.m., EST. Published by Exit Information Guide, the discount guide is free, but you will be charged $3 for postage and handling. Similar guides to other states are available at the same number.

Disneyland Main Information Address & Phone This address is for general information. Inquiries may be expedited by using addresses specific to the nature of the inquiry (other addresses are listed in this chapter).

Disneyland Guest Relations
P.O. Box 3232
1313 Harbor Boulevard
Anaheim, CA 92803-3232
(714) 781-4565 for recorded information
(714) 781-4560 for live information

The Phone from Hell Sometimes it is virtually impossible to get through to the Disneyland information numbers listed above. You will get a recording that offers various information options. If none of the recorded options answer your question, you will have to hold on for a live person. Eat before you call: you may have a long wait. If, after repeated attempts, you get tired of a busy signal in your ear or, worse, 20 minutes' worth of mice singing "Cindarellie" in an alto falsetto while you wait on hold, call the Disneyland Hotel at (714) 956-MICKEY.

Cyber Disney Disneyland now maintains a World Wide Web site that offers brief information on everything from lodging and transportation to new rides and the weekly weather forecast. Like many similar Web sites, the most exciting aspect of Disneyland's is the color graphics. Disneyland's URL is **www.disneyland.com.**

Additional information concerning Disneyland can be obtained at the public library and through travel agencies.

ADMISSION OPTIONS

One-day, two-day, and three-day admission passes are available for purchase for both adults (age 12 years and up) and children (age 3 to 11 years inclusive). All rides, shows, and attractions (except the Frontierland Shooting Exposition) are included in the price of admission. Multiday passes do not have to be used on consecutive days.

Admission prices, not unexpectedly, increase from time to time. For planning your budget, however, the following provides a fair estimate:

One-Day Passport—Adult	About $38
One-Day Passport—Child (3–11)	About $28
One-Day Passport—Senior (60+)	About $36
Two-Day Passport—Adult	About $68
Two-Day Passport—Child (3–11)	About $51
Flex Signature Passport—Adult	About $68
Flex Signature Passport—Child (3–11)	About $51
Disney's Passport Plus—Adult	About $76
Disney's Passport Plus—Child (3–11)	About $59

Three-Day Passport—Adult	About $95
Three-Day Passport—Child (3–11)	About $75
Annual Passport	About $99–199

Flex Signature Passports: Important Information

The Flex Signature Passport costs the same as the regular Two-Day Passport, but it is good for five consecutive days' admission. The five-day countdown begins on the day the Flex Pass is first used (regular multiday passports do not have to be used on consecutive days). More important, however, is that Flex Signature Passport holders are eligible for early entry to the park on one of the five consecutive days.

Until recently, Flex Signature Passports were available only to guests who purchased Walt Disney Travel Company vacation packages. Now Flex Signature Passports can be purchased à la carte, but *not* at Disneyland. Flex Signature Passports can be obtained in advance through your travel agent, from the Walt Disney Travel Company, or in Anaheim at the Disneyland Hotel. Most Disney Stores in shopping malls are now able to order Flex Signature Passports. If you purchase your Flex Signature Passports from a mall store, be sure to order them at least three weeks before you leave.

A similar five consecutive days' admission, which does not include early admission, can be purchased at the concierge desks of the Anaheim Marriott, Howard Johnson, and other hotels. For an extra $5 per morning, the pass can be upgraded to include early entry privileges.

If you buy through your travel agent from the Walt Disney Travel Company, you will be offered a special Flex Signature Passport called Disney's Passport Plus, with a breakfast included on your early entry day and a discount coupon book for area attractions, hotels, and restaurants. Disney's Passport Plus runs about $76 for adults and $59 for children. Because the whole point of getting into the park early is to enjoy the attractions before they get crowded, we suggest you buy the basic Flex Pass without the breakfast.

Finally, be aware that Disney constantly experiments with admission options and that the Flex Signature Passport may be discontinued or evolve into something different at any time. For the moment, however, the à la carte purchase of a Flex Signature Passport represents the only way you can obtain early entry privileges without staying in the Disneyland Hotel or buying a Walt Disney Travel Company vacation package.

Regular admission passes (i.e., not Flex Signature Passes) can be ordered through the mail by writing:

Disneyland Ticket Mail Order
P.O. Box 61061
Anaheim, CA 92803-6161

The Disneyland Ticket Mail Order accepts personal checks and money orders. Mail orders take three to four weeks to process. Call (714) 999-4565 for an exact computation of charges and tax. To order tickets by telephone, call (714) 781-4043, Monday–Friday, 8:30 a.m. to 5 p.m. PST.

In addition to the Ticket Mail Order, regular Disneyland admissions can be purchased in advance at Disney Stores throughout the United States.

Admission and Disneyland Hotel Discounts

Disney Shareholder Discounts   The discount program for Walt Disney Company shareholders was effectively dismantled in 1993. At present, shareholders are simply offered the option of buying a two-year Magic Kingdom Club Card for about $50, an option also available to non-shareholders for around $15 more. For additional information call the Walt Disney Company Shareholder Relations office at (714) 781-1550.

Magic Kingdom Club Member Discounts   The Magic Kingdom Club is offered as a benefit by employers, credit unions, and organizations. Membership entitles you to a 10–20% discount on Disney lodging, a 10% discount on merchandise at Disney Stores, and a 5% discount on theme park tickets, among other things. Almost all state and federal government employees are Magic Kingdom Club members (although a lot of them don't know it). If you work for a large company or organization, ask your personnel department if the Magic Kingdom Club benefit is provided.

Individuals whose employer does not provide Magic Kingdom Club benefits can join for about $65 for a two-year membership under the Magic Kingdom Club Gold Card program. There is practically no difference between the Magic Kingdom Club and the Magic Kingdom Club Gold Card. For information call (714) 781-1550 or write:

Magic Kingdom Club
Gold Card
P.O. Box 3850
Anaheim, CA 92803-3850

Organizations and Auto Clubs   As Disney has become more aggressive about selling guest rooms, it has developed time-limited programs with a number of auto clubs and other organizations. Recently, for instance, AAA members were offered 15% savings on Walt Disney resorts and a 20% discount on Disney package vacations. While these deals come and go, the market suggests that there will be more coming than going for the next year. If you are a member of AARP, AAA, or any travel or auto club, check to see if your association has a program before shopping elsewhere.

RIDES AND SHOWS CLOSED FOR REPAIRS OR MAINTENANCE

Rides and shows at Disneyland are sometimes closed for maintenance or repairs. If there is a certain attraction that is important to you, call (714) 781-4565 before your visit to make sure it will be operating. A mother from Dover, Massachusetts, wrote us, lamenting:

We were disappointed to find Space Mountain, Swiss Family Treehouse, and the Riverboat closed for repairs. We felt that a large chunk of the [park] was not working, yet the tickets were still full price and expensive!

HOW MUCH DOES IT COST TO GO TO DISNEYLAND FOR A DAY?

Let's say we have a family of four, Mom and Dad, Tim (age 12), and Tami (age 8), driving their own car. Since they plan to be in the area for a few days they intend to buy the Two-Day Passports. A typical day would cost $298.25, excluding lodging and transportation.

How Much Does a Day Cost?	
Breakfast for four at Denny's with tax & tip	$22.75
Disneyland parking fee	7.00
One day's admission on a Two-Day Passport	
Dad: Adult, Two-Day with tax = $68 divided by 2 (days)	34.00
Mom: Adult, Two-Day with tax = $68 divided by 2 (days)	34.00
Tim: Adult, Two-Day with tax = $68 divided by 2 (days)	34.00
Tami: Child, Two-Day with tax = $51 divided by 2 (days)	25.50
Morning break (soda or coffee)	7.00
Fast-food lunch (burger, fries, soda), no tip	25.50
Afternoon break (soda and popcorn)	13.50
Dinner in park at full-service restaurant with tax & tip	59.00
Souvenirs (Mickey T-shirts for Tim and Tami) with tax*	36.00
One-day total (not including lodging and transportation)	$298.25

*Cheer up, you won't have to buy souvenirs every day.

Timing Your Visit

SELECTING THE TIME OF YEAR FOR YOUR VISIT

Crowds are largest at Disneyland during the summer (Memorial Day to Labor Day) and during specific holiday periods during the rest of the year. The busiest time of all is Christmas Day through New Year's Day. Thanksgiving weekend, the week of Washington's Birthday, spring break for colleges, and the two weeks around Easter are also extremely busy. To give you some idea of what *busy* means at Disneyland, more than 77,000 people have toured the park on a single day! While this level of attendance is far from typical, the possibility of its occurrence should prevent all but the ignorant and the foolish from challenging this mega-attraction at its busiest periods.

The least busy time of all is from after the Thanksgiving weekend until the week before Christmas. The next slowest times are September through the weekend preceding Thanksgiving, January 4 through the first week of March, and the week following Easter through Memorial Day. At the risk of being blasphemous, our research team was so impressed with the relative ease of touring in the fall and other "off" periods that we would rather take

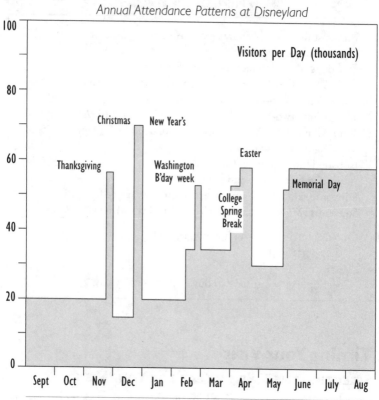

Annual Attendance Patterns at Disneyland

Visitors per Day (thousands)

(Attendance figures represent weekly averages)

our children out of school for a few days than do battle with the summer crowds. Though we strongly recommend going to Disneyland in the fall or in the spring, it should be noted that there are certain trade-offs. The park often closes earlier on fall and spring days, sometimes early enough to eliminate evening parades and other live entertainment offerings. Also, because these are slow times of the year at Disneyland, you can anticipate that some rides and attractions may be closed for maintenance or renovation. Finally, if Disneyland opens late and closes early, it's tough to see everything even if the crowds are light.

Given the choice, however, we would never go to Disneyland in the summer or during a holiday period. To us, small crowds, bargain hotel rates, and stress-free touring are well worth risking colder weather or a couple of attractions being out of service.

Most readers who have tried Disney theme parks at varying times during the year agree. A gentleman from Ottawa, Ontario, who toured in early December, wrote:

> *It was the most enjoyable trip I have ever had, and I can't imagine going [back to Disneyland] when it is crowded. Even without the crowds we were still very tired by afternoon. Fighting crowds certainly would have made a hellish trip. We will never go again at any other time.*

SELECTING THE DAY OF THE WEEK FOR YOUR VISIT

The crowds at Walt Disney World in Florida are comprised of mostly out-of-state visitors. Not necessarily so at Disneyland, which, along with Six Flags Magic Mountain, serves as an often-frequented recreational resource to the greater Los Angeles and San Diego communities. To many southern Californians, Disneyland is less of a tourist attraction than it is their private theme park. Yearly passes are available at less cost than a year's membership to the YMCA, and the Disney management has intensified its efforts to appeal to the local market.

What all this means is that weekends are usually packed. Saturday is the busiest day of the week. Sunday, particularly Sunday morning, is the best bet if you have to go on a weekend, but it is nevertheless extremely busy.

During the summer, Monday and Friday are very busy; Wednesday and Tuesday are usually less so; and Thursday is normally the slowest day of all. During the "off season" (September–May, holiday periods excepted) Thursday is usually the least crowded day, followed by Tuesday.

The Impact of the Early Admission/ Magic Morning Program

A major factor when considering which day of the week to visit Disneyland is the early admission/Magic Morning program. On designated days of the week, guests at the Disneyland Hotel, guests from other hotels on Disneyland package vacations, as well as holders of Flex Signature Passports and Disney's Passport Plus, are invited to enter the park 60 to 90 minutes before it is opened to the general public. If you are eligible for the early entry program, be sure to take advantage of it. If you plan to visit Disneyland during the summer when the crowds are heavy, you would be well advised to consider a Disneyland package with early entry privileges, or alternatively to purchase a Flex Signature Passport or Disney's Passport Plus (described under Admission Options).

Disney's Passport Plus and some Disneyland package vacations include early entry and a breakfast in the park. If these features are included in your package, skip the breakfast. The main advantage of getting into the park early is to beat the crowd to the most popular attractions. Don't blow your advantage by sitting in a restaurant.

If you are not eligible for early entry, try to avoid visiting on those days when early entry is in effect. During the slower times of year, the park schedules early entry three or four times a week. During the summer, however, early entry is often scheduled every day of the week except two (usually Wednesday and Sunday). What this means, if you are not eligible, is that no matter how early you arrive, Disneyland will already be packed when you get there. This, we believe, is manifestly unfair to the general public ("day guests" in Disneyspeak). In our opinion, every guest should have an equal opportunity to be among the first admitted to the park.

OPERATING HOURS

It cannot be said that the Disney folks are not flexible when it comes to hours of operation for the park. They run a dozen or more different operating schedules during the year, making it advisable to call (714) 781-4565 the day before you arrive for the exact hours of operation.

PACKED PARK COMPENSATION PLAN

The thought of teeming, jostling throngs jockeying for position in endless lines under the baking Fourth of July sun is enough to wilt the will and ears of the most ardent Mouseketeer. Why would anyone go to Disneyland on a summer Saturday or during a major holiday period? Indeed, if you have never been to Disneyland, and you thought you would just drop in for a few rides and a little look-see on such a day, you might be better off shooting yourself in the foot. The Disney folks, however, being Disney folks, feel kind of bad about those interminably long lines and the basically impossible touring conditions on packed days and compensate their patrons with a no less than incredible array of first-rate live entertainment and happenings.

Throughout the day the party goes on with shows, parades, concerts, and pageantry. In the evening there is so much going on that you have to make some tough choices. Big-name music groups perform on the River Stage in Frontierland and at the Fantasyland Theatre. Other concerts are produced concurrently at the Golden Horseshoe Stage and in Tomorrowland. There are always parades, sometimes fireworks, and the Disney characters make frequent appearances. Stage shows and rock concerts are

presented at the Plaza Gardens (off the central hub) and at Tomorrowland Terrace. No question about it, you can go to Disneyland on the Fourth of July (or any other extended-hours, crowded day), never get on a ride, and still get your money's worth. Admittedly, it's not the ideal situation for a first-timer who really wants to see the park, but for anyone else it's one heck of a good party.

If you decide to go on one of the park's "big" days, we suggest that you arrive an hour and 20 minutes before the stated opening time. Use the Disneyland touring plan of your choice until about 1 p.m. and then take the Monorail to the Disneyland Hotel for lunch and relaxation. Southern Californian visitors often chip in and rent a room for the group (make reservations well in advance) in the Disneyland Hotel, thus affording a place to meet, relax, have a drink, or change clothes before enjoying the pools at the hotel. A comparable arrangement can be made at other nearby hotels as long as they furnish a shuttle service to and from the park. After an early dinner, return to the park for the evening's festivities, which really get cranked up about 8 p.m.

Getting There

ANAHEIM/DISNEYLAND TRAFFIC

At Walt Disney World in Florida, automobile traffic enters and exits via four-lane expressways that connect directly to interstate highways. At Disneyland, unfortunately, automobile access, for the time being at least, is not so streamlined. To begin with, Disneyland is close to, but not directly connected to, Interstate 5 (Santa Ana Freeway). Exit signs on the freeway give the impression that one exit provides as easy an access to Disneyland as the next. In fact, there is no way at present to access Disneyland parking without either multiple turns or a number of traffic signals.

The freeways themselves are capricious in the extreme, with congestion and bumper-to-bumper traffic likely to erupt at almost any hour of the day. Add to this prevailing confusion the crunch of rush-hour traffic, and you have the best reason imaginable for choosing a hotel as close to Disneyland as possible. Our research team once lodged in Laguna Beach and commuted to the park each day. Driving the same distance on every trip, our transportation time to the park ranged from 25 minutes to two-and-a-half hours. Disney employees have devised complex routes through subdivisions and city streets in order to beat the freeway mess and be at work on time.

For the next several years, freeway and surface street improvements as well as the construction of Disney's California Adventure theme park will compound traffic problems throughout the Disneyland area. Though roadwork

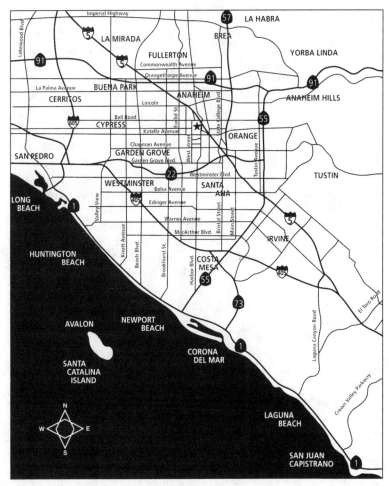

Anaheim and Surrounding Areas

Source: Anaheim/Orange County Travel Agent Guide, 1994. Reproduced courtesy of the Anaheim Area Visitor & Convention Bureau.

and other projects will be conducted in phases, the number of streets torn up at any one time will be more than sufficient to try the patience of saints. If you have been thinking about visiting Walt Disney World in Florida, the next couple of years will be an ideal time. If Walt Disney World is not in the cards, or if only Disneyland will satisfy, be prepared for some delays.

If the foregoing did not get your attention, try this: When the park opens early or closes early, Anaheim rush-hour traffic and Disneyland rush-hour traffic literally meet head on, tying up the streets and freeways surrounding the park for miles. Early (6 p.m.) closings create the greatest confusion. Park patrons depart en masse and attempt to fight their way out of the parking lot and onto city streets and freeways jammed with local commuters. This congestion is so horrendous that insiders claim Disneyland removed the Skyway attraction because guests were able to see the freeway snarl from the ride and were consequently departing the park early.

Help is on the way, however, including at least one Disneyland parking complex that connects with I-5. The bad news is that the complex will not become operational until late 1998 at the earliest. By the year 2001, however, I-5 will be widened and new interchanges will allow Disney patrons to drive directly into and out of parking facilities without becoming enmeshed in surface street traffic.

Until the new parking facilities are complete, don't expect the same Disney efficiency in emptying the parking lot as in filling it. There will be lots of Disney employees to help you park in the morning, but virtually none to help you get out in the evening.

If you visit in late 1998 or 1999 you will probably park in the new lot on the northwest corner of Katella Avenue and West Street. To reach the lot from the I-5, exit at Katella and go west. You can also exit onto Harbor Boulevard and then turn right (west) onto Katella. Once you have parked, a Disney tram will haul you (depending on the state of construction) to the park entrance or to a tram loading area connected to the park entrance by a pedestrian corridor.

To make the most of an almost intolerable traffic situation, we make the following recommendations:

1. Stay as close to Disneyland as possible, but make pointed inquiries about how construction noise and congestion will affect the hotel you are considering. Insist on a room on an upper level away from the street. If you are within walking distance, leave your car at the hotel and walk to the park. If your hotel provides efficient shuttle service (i.e., will get you to the park at least a half-hour before opening), use the shuttle.

2. If your hotel is more than five miles from Disneyland and you

intend to drive your car, leave for the park extra early, say an hour or more. If you get lucky and don't encounter too many problems you can relax over breakfast at a restaurant near Disneyland while you wait for the park to open.

3. If you must use the Santa Ana Freeway (I-5), give yourself lots of extra time. If you are traveling south, exit onto Harbor Boulevard. If you are traveling north, take the Katella Avenue exit.

4. If you must use the Garden Grove Freeway, exit onto Euclid Street, turn right onto Ball Road, and finally right onto Harbor Boulevard. This will take you into the Disneyland lot without any left turns.

5. If your hotel does not offer a shuttle service and is not within walking distance, try to avoid Disneyland on days when the park closes at 6 p.m. If your schedule allows no alternative, either leave before 4:30 p.m. (you will be able to get out of the parking lot, but you will almost certainly get stuck in the local rush-hour traffic) or stay in the park until Main Street closes (half an hour after the rest of the park) and steel yourself for some major-league problems getting out of the parking lot.

6. Anytime you leave the park just before, at, or just after closing time, you can expect considerable congestion in the parking lot and in the loading area for hotel shuttles. The easiest way to return to your hotel (if you do not have a car in the Disneyland parking lot) is to take the Monorail (or walk) to the Disneyland Hotel, and from there take a cab to your hotel. While cabs in Anaheim are a little pricey, they are usually available in ample numbers at the Disneyland Hotel and at the pedestrian entrance on Harbor. When you consider the alternatives of fighting your way onto a hotel shuttle or trudging back to your hotel on worn-out feet, spending a couple of bucks for a cab often sounds pretty reasonable.

7. If you walk or use a hotel shuttle to get to the park and are then caught in a monsoon, the best way to return to your hotel without getting soaked is to take the Monorail to the Disneyland Hotel, and catch a taxi from there.

8. Finally, be aware that the Orange County Transit District provides very efficient bus service to Disneyland with three different lines. Running approximately every 30 minutes during the day and evening, service begins at 5 a.m. and concludes between 6:30 and 10:55 p.m., depending on the season. Buses drop off and pick up passengers at the Disneyland Hotel. From there guests can take a Disney tram to the park entrance. Trams run approximately every six minutes. Bus fare is about $1 and the tram is free. For additional information on buses call (714) 636-7433.

TAKING A TRAM OR SHUTTLE BUS FROM YOUR HOTEL

Trams and shuttle buses are provided by many hotels and motels in the vicinity of Disneyland. They represent a fairly carefree alternative for getting to and from the theme park, letting you off near the entrance and saving you the cost of parking. The rub is that they might not get you there as early as you desire (a critical point if you take our touring advice) or be available at the time you wish to return to your lodging. Also, some shuttles are direct to Disneyland, while others make stops at other motels and hotels in the vicinity. Each shuttle service is a little bit different, so check out the particulars before you book your hotel. If the shuttle provided by your hotel runs regularly throughout the day to and from Disneyland and if you have the flexibility to tour the park over two or three days, the shuttle provides a wonderful opportunity to tour in the morning and return to your lodging for lunch, a swim, or perhaps a nap; then you can head back to Disneyland refreshed in the early evening for a little more fun.

Be forewarned that most hotel shuttle services do not add additional vehicles at park opening or closing times. In the mornings, your biggest problem is that you might not get a seat. At closing time, however, and sometimes following a hard rain, you can expect a mass exodus from the park. The worst-case scenario in this event is that more people will be waiting for the shuttle to your hotel than the bus will hold and that some will be left. While most (but not all) hotel shuttles return for stranded guests, you may suffer a wait of 15 minutes to an hour. Our suggestion, if you are depending on hotel shuttles, is to exit the park at least 45 minutes before closing. If you stay in the park until closing and lack the energy to deal with the shuttle or hike back to your hotel, try taking the Monorail to the Disneyland Hotel and catching a cab from there. There is also a cab stand adjacent to the Harbor Boulevard pedestrian entrance.

A new shuttle loading area is now open on the Harbor Boulevard side of Disneyland's main entrance. The loading area connects to a pedestrian corridor that leads to the park entrance. Each hotel's shuttle bus is color coded yellow, blue, red, silver, or white. Signs of like color designate where the shuttles load and unload.

WALKING TO DISNEYLAND FROM NEARBY HOTELS

While it is true that many Disneyland area hotels provide shuttle service and that the Disneyland Hotel is accessible by Monorail, it is equally true that an ever-increasing number of guests walk to Disneyland from their hotels. Shuttles are not always available when needed, and parking in the Disneyland lot has become pretty expensive. In early 1998, Disneyland opened a new pedestrian walkway from Harbor Boulevard that provides safe access to Disneyland for guests on foot. Eventually, this pedestrian corridor will extend from Harbor Boulevard all the way to the Disneyland Hotel, connecting Disneyland, Disney's California Adventures theme park, and all of the Disney entertainment and shopping venues.

A Word about Lodging

While this guide is not about lodging, we have found lodging to be a primary concern of those visiting Disneyland. Traffic around Disneyland, and in the Anaheim–Los Angeles area in general, is so terrible that we advocate staying in accommodations within two or three miles of the park. Included in this radius are, of course, many expensive hotels as well as a goodly number of moderately priced establishments and a small number of bargain motels.

When Walt Disney built Disneyland, he did not have the funding to include hotels or to purchase the property surrounding his theme park. Even the Disneyland Hotel was owned by outside interests until a few years ago. Consequently, the area around the park developed in an essentially uncontrolled manner. Many of the hotels and motels near Disneyland were built in the early '60s, and they are small and unattractive by today's standards. Quite a few motels adopted adventure or fantasy themes in emulation of Disneyland. As you might imagine, these themes from three decades ago seem hokey and irrelevant today. There is a disquieting number of seedy hotels near Disneyland, and even some of the chain properties fail to live up to their national standards.

If you consider a non–Disney-owned hotel in Anaheim, check its quality as reported by a reliable independent rating system such as those offered by the *Unofficial Guide,* AAA Directories, Mobil Guides, or Frommer's *America on Wheels.* Checking two or three independent sources is better than depending on one. Also, before you book, ask how old the hotel is and when the guest rooms were last refurbished. Additionally, ask how new park construction and roadwork will impact the hotel during your stay. Locate the hotel on a local street map to verify its proximity to Disneyland. If you will not have a car, make sure the hotel has a shuttle service that will satisfy your needs.

Package tours are routinely available that include lodging, park admission, and other features. Some of these are very good deals if you make use of the features you are paying for.

Finally, a good source of information is:

Anaheim/Orange County Visitor and Convention Bureau
Department C
P.O. Box 4270
Anaheim, CA 92803
(714) 999-8999

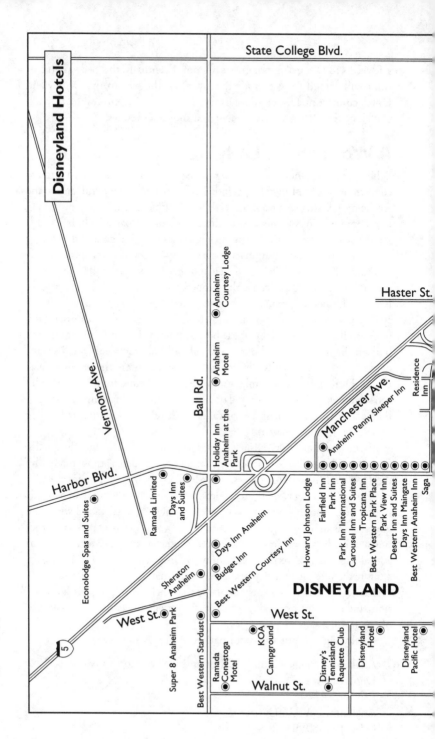

State College Blvd.

Disneyland Hotels

Haster St.

Vermont Ave.

Ball Rd.

Anaheim Courtesy Lodge

Anaheim Motel

Manchester Ave.

Residence Inn

Holiday Inn Anaheim at the Park

Anaheim Penny Sleeper Inn

Harbor Blvd.

Ramada Limited

Days Inn and Suites

Econolodge Spas and Suites

Howard Johnson Lodge

Fairfield Inn

Park Inn

Park Inn International

Carousel Inn and Suites

Tropicana Inn

Best Western Park Place

Park View Inn

Desert Inn and Suites

Days Inn Maingate

Best Western Anaheim Inn

Saga

Days Inn Anaheim

Budget Inn

Best Western Courtesy Inn

Sheraton Anaheim

DISNEYLAND

West St.

Super 8 Anaheim Park

Best Western Stardust

West St.

Ramada Conestoga Motel

KOA Campground

Disney's Tennisland Raquette Club

Disneyland Hotel

Disneyland Pacific Hotel

Walnut St.

5

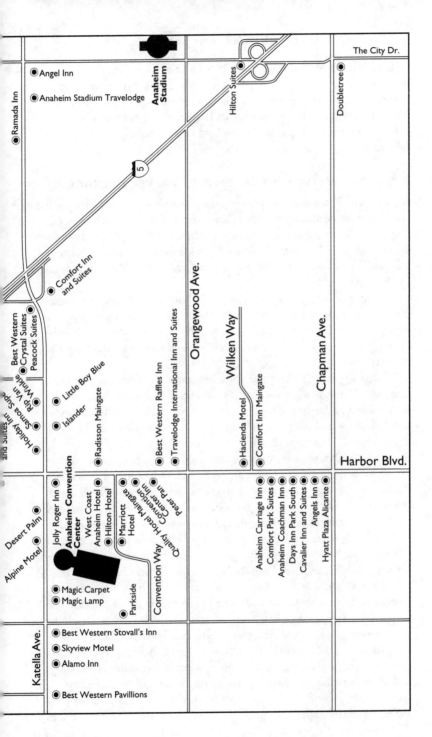

The City Dr.

⦿ Angel Inn

⦿ Anaheim Stadium Travelodge

Anaheim Stadium

⦿ Ramada Inn

⦿ Hilton Suites

⦿ Doubletree

5

⦿ Comfort Inn and Suites

Orangewood Ave.

Wilken Way

Chapman Ave.

⦿ Best Western Crystal Suites

⦿ Peacock Suites

⦿ Rip Van Winkle

⦿ Samoa Super

Holiday Inn Suites and

⦿ Little Boy Blue

⦿ Islander

⦿ Radisson Maingate

⦿ Best Western Raffles Inn

⦿ Travelodge International Inn and Suites

⦿ Hacienda Motel

⦿ Comfort Inn Maingate

Harbor Blvd.

⦿ Desert Palm

⦿ Alpine Motel

⦿ Jolly Roger Inn

Anaheim Convention Center

⦿ West Coast Anaheim Hotel

⦿ Hilton Hotel

⦿ Marriott Hotel

⦿ Quality Hotel Maingate

⦿ Convention Center Inn

⦿ Peter Pan

Convention Way

⦿ Magic Carpet

⦿ Magic Lamp

⦿ Parkside

⦿ Anaheim Carriage Inn

⦿ Comfort Park Suites

⦿ Anaheim Coachman Inn

⦿ Days Inn Park South

⦿ Cavalier Inn and Suites

⦿ Angels Inn

⦿ Hyatt Plaza Alicante

Katella Ave.

⦿ Best Western Stovall's Inn

⦿ Skyview Motel

⦿ Alamo Inn

⦿ Best Western Pavillions

31

If your travel plans include a stay in the area of more than two or three days, lodge near Disneyland only before and on the days you visit the park. The same traffic you avoid by staying close to the park will eat you alive when you begin branching out to other Los Angeles–area attractions. Also, the area immediately around Disneyland is uninspiring, and there is a marked scarcity of decent restaurants.

How to Evaluate a Disneyland Travel Package

Hundreds of Disneyland package vacations are offered to the public each year. Some are created by the Walt Disney Travel Company, others by airline touring companies, and some by independent travel agents and wholesalers. Almost all Disneyland packages include lodging at or near Disneyland and theme park admission. Packages offered by the airlines include air transportation.

Package prices vary seasonally, with mid-June to mid-August and holiday periods being most expensive. Off season, forget packages: There are plenty of empty rooms and you can negotiate great discounts (at non-Disney properties) yourself. Similarly, airfares and rental cars are cheaper at off-peak times.

Almost all package ads feature a headline stating "Disneyland for 3 Days from $298" or some such wording. The key word in the ads is "from." The rock-bottom package price connotes the least desirable hotel accommodations. If you want better or more conveniently located digs, you'll have to pay more, often much more.

At Disneyland, packages offer a wide selection of hotels. Some, like the Disney-owned Disneyland Hotel, are very good. Others unfortunately run the quality gamut. Packages with lodging in non-Disney hotels are much less expensive. On the flip side, guests staying in the Disneyland Hotel and the Disney Pacific Hotel are accorded special privileges such as free parking and being able to enter the theme park an hour before the general public on selected days. Early entry privileges are also available at non-Disney hotels if the package is purchased from the Walt Disney Travel Company.

Packages should be a win/win proposition for both the buyer and the seller. The buyer only has to make one phone call and deal with a single salesperson to set up the whole vacation: transportation, rental car, admissions, lodging, meals, and even golf and tennis. The seller, likewise, only has to deal with the buyer one time, eliminating the need for separate sales, confirmations, and billing. In addition to streamlining selling, processing, and administration, some packagers also buy airfares in bulk on contract, like a broker playing the commodities market. Buying a large number of airfares in advance allows the packager to buy them at a significant savings from posted fares. The same practice is applied also to hotel rooms. Because selling vacation packages is an efficient way of doing business, and because the packager can often buy individual package components (airfare, lodging, etc.) in bulk at a discount, savings in operating expenses realized by the seller are sometimes passed on to the buyer so that, in addition to convenience, the package is also an exceptional value. In any event, that is the way it is supposed to work.

All too often, in practice, the seller realizes all of the economies and passes on nothing in the way of savings to the buyer. In some instances, packages are loaded with extras that cost the packager next to nothing, but run the retail price of the package sky-high. As you might expect, the savings to be passed along to customers are still somewhere in Fantasyland.

When considering a package, choose one that includes features you are sure to use. Whether you use all the features or not, you will most certainly pay for them. Second, if cost is of greater concern than convenience, make a few phone calls and see what the package would cost if you booked its individual components (airfare, rental car, lodging, etc.) on your own. If the package price is less than the à la carte cost, the package is a good deal. If the costs are about the same, the package is probably worth it for the convenience.

If you buy a package from Disney, do not expect Disney reservationists to offer suggestions or help you sort out your options. As a rule they will not volunteer information, but will only respond to specific questions you pose, adroitly ducking any query that calls for an opinion. A reader from North Riverside, Illinois, wrote to the *Unofficial Guide,* complaining:

I have received various pieces of literature from [Disney] and it is very confusing to try and figure everything out. My wife made two telephone calls and the [Disney] representatives were very courteous. However, they only answered the questions posed and were not very eager to give advice on what might be most cost effective. [The Disney] reps would not say if we would be better off doing one thing over the other. I feel a person could spend eight hours on the telephone with [Disney] reps and not have any more input than you get from reading the literature.

Another reader, also from Illinois, had this to say:

I called Disney's reservations number and asked for availability and rates. . . . [Because] of the Unofficial Guide *warning about Disney reservationists answering only the questions posed, I specifically asked, "Are there any special rates or discounts for that room during the month of October?" She replied, "Yes, we have that room available at a special price . . ." [For] the price of one phone call, I saved $440.*

If you cannot get the information you need from the Disney people, try a good travel agent. Chances are the agent will be more forthcoming in helping you sort out your options.

Information Needed for Evaluation   For quick reference and to save on phone expenses, write or call Walt Disney Travel Company at (800) 605-1234 and ask that you be mailed a current Walt Disney Travel Company California Brochure containing descriptions and room rates for all Disneyland lodging properties. Summarized information sheets on lodging are available by fax. Also ask for a rate sheet listing admission options and prices for the theme park. With this in hand, you are ready to evaluate any package that appeals to you. Remember that all packages are quoted on a per person basis, two to a room (double occupancy). Good luck.

GETTING A GOOD DEAL ON YOUR HOTEL ROOM

Below are some tips and strategies for getting a good deal on a hotel room near Disneyland. Though the following list may seem a bit intimidating and may refer to players in the travel market that are unfamiliar to you, acquainting yourself with the concepts and strategies will serve you well in the long run. Simply put, the tips we provide for getting a good deal near Disneyland will work equally well at just about any other place where you need a hotel. Once you have invested a little time and have experimented with these strategies, you will be able to routinely obtain rooms at the best hotels and at the lowest possible rates.

1. Exit Information Guide   A company called EIG (Exit Information Guide) publishes a book of discount coupons for bargain rates at hotels throughout California. These books are available free of charge in many restaurants and motels along the main interstate highways in and leading to California. Since most folks make reservations before leaving home, picking up the coupon book en route does not help much. For $3 ($5 Canadian), however, EIG will mail you a copy before you make your reservations. You can use a credit card or send a money order or check. The guide is free; the charge is for the postage. Write or call:

Exit Information Guide
4205 NW 6th Street
Gainesville, FL 32609
(352) 371-3948

2. Special Weekend Rates   If you are not averse to about an hour drive to Disneyland, you can get a great weekend rate on rooms in downtown Los Angeles. Most hotels that cater to business, government, and convention travelers offer special weekend discounts that range from 15% to 40% below normal weekday rates. You can find out about weekend specials by calling the hotel or by consulting your travel agent.

3. Getting Corporate Rates Many hotels offer discounted corporate rates (5–20% off rack). Usually you do not need to work for a large company or have a special relationship with the hotel to obtain these rates. Simply call the hotel of your choice and ask for their corporate rates. Many hotels will guarantee you the discounted rate on the phone when you make your reservation. Others may make the rate conditional on your providing some sort of *bona fides*—for instance, a fax on your company's letterhead requesting the rate, or a company credit card or business card at check-in. Generally, the screening is not rigorous.

4. Half-Price Programs The larger discounts on rooms (35–60%), in the Disneyland area or anywhere else, are available through half-price hotel programs, often called travel clubs. Program operators contract with an individual hotel to provide rooms at a deep discount, usually 50% off rack rate, on a "space available" basis. Space available, in practice, generally means that you can reserve a room at the discounted rate whenever the hotel expects to be at less than 80% occupancy. A little calendar sleuthing to help you avoid high season, big conventions at the Anaheim Convention Center, holidays, and special events will increase your chances of choosing a time when the discounts are available.

Most half-price programs charge an annual membership fee or directory subscription price of $25 to $125. Once enrolled, you receive a membership card and a directory listing all the hotels participating in the program. On examining the directory, you will notice immediately that there are a lot of restrictions and exceptions. Some hotels, for instance, "black out" certain dates or times of year. Others may offer the discount only on certain days of the week or require you to stay a certain number of nights. Still others may offer a much smaller discount than 50% off rack rate.

Some programs specialize in domestic travel, some in international travel, and some in both. The more established operators offer members between one and four thousand hotels to choose from in the United States. All of the programs have a heavy concentration of hotels in California and Florida, and most have a very limited selection of participating properties in New York City and Boston. Offerings in other cities and regions of the United States vary considerably. The programs with the largest selection of hotels in the Disneyland area are Encore, at (800) 638-0930, and National Hotel & Dining Directory (Entertainment Publications), at (800) 285-5525.

One problem with half-price programs is that not all hotels offer a full 50% discount. Another slippery problem is the base rate against which the discount is applied. Some hotels figure the discount on an exaggerated rack rate that nobody would ever have to pay. A few participating hotels may deduct the discount from a supposed "superior" or "upgraded" room rate, even though the room you get is the hotel's standard accommodation. Though specific numbers are hard to pin down, the majority of participating properties base discounts on the published rate in the *Hotel & Travel Index* (a quarterly reference work used by travel agents) and work within the spirit of their agreement with the program operator. As a rule, if you travel several times a year, you will more than pay for your program membership in room rate savings.

A noteworthy addendum to this discussion is that deeply discounted rooms through half-price programs are not commissionable to travel agents. In practical terms, this means that you must ordinarily make your own inquiry calls and reservations. If you travel frequently, however, and run a lot of business through your travel agent, he/she will probably do your legwork despite the lack of commission.

5. Preferred Rates   If you cannot book the hotel of choice through a half-price program, you and your travel agent may have to search for a lesser discount, often called a preferred rate. A preferred rate could be a discount made available to travel agents to stimulate their booking activity or a discount initiated to attract a certain class of traveler. Most preferred rates are promoted through travel industry publications and are often accessible only through an agent. We recommend sounding out your travel agent about possible deals. Be aware, however, that the rates shown on travel agents' computerized reservations systems are not always the lowest rates obtainable. Zero in on a couple of hotels that fill your needs in terms of location and quality of accommodations, and then have your travel agent call for the latest rates and specials. Hotel reps are almost always more responsive to travel agents, because travel agents represent a source of additional business. Again, there are certain specials that hotel reps will disclose *only* to travel agents. Travel agents also come in handy when the hotel you want is supposedly booked. A personal appeal from your agent to the hotel's director of sales and marketing will get you a room more than half of the time.

6. Wholesalers, Consolidators, and Reservation Services   If you do not want to join a program or buy a discount directory, you can take advantage of the services of a wholesaler or consolidator. Wholesalers and consolidators buy rooms, or options on rooms (room blocks), from hotels at a low negotiated rate. They then resell the rooms at a profit through travel agents, through tour packagers, or directly to the public. Most wholesalers and consolidators have a provision for returning unsold rooms to participating hotels, but they are disinclined to do so. The wholesaler's or consolidator's relationship with any hotel is predicated on volume. If they return rooms unsold, the hotel might not make as many rooms available to them the next time around. Thus wholesalers and consolidators often offer rooms at bargain rates, anywhere from 15–50% off rack, occasionally sacrificing profit margin in the process, to avoid returning the rooms to the hotel unsold.

When wholesalers and consolidators deal directly with the public, they frequently represent themselves as "reservation services." When you call, you can ask for a rate quote for a particular hotel or, alternatively, ask for their best available deal in the area where you prefer to stay. If there is a maximum amount you are willing to pay, say so. Chances are the service will find something that will work for you, even if they have to shave a dollar or two off their own profit. Sometimes you will have to prepay for your room with your credit card when you make your reservation. Most often, you will pay when you check out. Listed below are two services that frequently offer substantial discounts in the Anaheim area:

California Reservations	(800) 576-0003
Hotel Reservations Network	(800) 964-6835

7. If You Make Your Own Reservation   As you poke around trying to find a good deal, there are several things you should know. First, always call the hotel in question as opposed to the hotel chain's national toll-free number. Quite often, the reservationists at the national numbers are unaware of local specials. Always ask about specials before you inquire about corporate rates. Do not be reluctant to bargain. If you are buying a hotel's weekend package, for example, and want to extend your stay into the following week, you can often obtain at least the corporate rate for the extra days. Do your bargaining before you check in, however, preferably when you make your reservations. Work far enough in advance to receive a faxed or mailed confirmation.

8. Internet Deals   Many hotels, airlines, cruise lines, and other travel vendors offer special deals on their Internet home pages. The same goes for a growing number of wholesalers, packagers, and other travel industry middle men. Selling on the Web allows travel providers to reach a wide audience, move a time-sensitive product at the last minute, and avoid paying travel agent commissions. The downside of looking for deals on the Web is that comparative shopping is difficult, and unless you have a specific hotel or airline (for instance) in mind, you may be in for a numbing amount of browsing. If, however, surfing the Web is something you enjoy and you are willing to put in the time, there are a fair number of bargains to be found.

Hotels and Motels: Rated and Ranked

WHAT'S IN A ROOM?

Except for cleanliness, state of repair, and decor, most travelers do not pay much attention to hotel rooms. There is, of course, a discernible standard of quality and luxury that differentiates Motel 6 from Holiday Inn, Holiday Inn from Marriott, and so on. In general, however, hotel guests fail to appreciate that some rooms are better engineered than others.

Contrary to what you might suppose, designing a hotel room is (or should be) a lot more complex than picking a bedspread to match the carpet and drapes. Making the room usable to its occupants is an art, a planning discipline that combines both form and function.

Decor and taste are important, certainly. No one wants to spend several days in a room where the decor is dated, garish, or even ugly. But beyond the decor, there are variables that determine how "livable" a hotel room is. In Anaheim, for example, we have seen some beautifully appointed rooms that are simply not well designed for human habitation. The next time you stay in a hotel, pay attention to the details and design elements of your room. Even more than decor, these are the things that will make you feel comfortable and at home.

It takes the *Unofficial Guide* researchers up to 40 minutes to inspect a hotel room. Here are a few of the things we check that you may want to start paying attention to:

Room Size   While some smaller rooms are cozy and well designed, a large and uncluttered room is generally preferable, especially for a stay of more than three days.

Temperature Control, Ventilation, and Odor   The guest should be able to control the temperature of the room. The best system, because it's so quiet, is central heating and air conditioning, controlled by the room's own thermostat. The next best system is a room module heater and air conditioner, preferably controlled by an automatic thermostat, but usually by manually operated button controls. The worst system is central heating and air without any sort of room thermostat or guest control.

The vast majority of hotel rooms have windows or balcony doors that have been permanently secured shut. Though there are some legitimate safety and liability issues involved, we prefer windows and balcony doors that can be opened to admit fresh air. Hotel rooms should be odor-free and smoke-free and should not feel stuffy or damp.

Room Security   Better rooms have locks that require a plastic card instead of the traditional lock and key. Card and slot systems essentially allow the hotel to change the combination or entry code of the lock with each new guest who uses the room. A burglar who has somehow acquired a room key to a conventional lock can afford to wait until the situation is right before using the key to gain access. Not so with a card and slot system. Though larger hotels and hotel chains with lock and key systems usually rotate their locks once each year, they remain vulnerable to hotel thieves much of the time. Many smaller or independent properties rarely rotate their locks.

In addition to the entry lock system, the door should have a dead bolt, and preferably a chain that can be locked from the inside. A chain by itself is not sufficient. Doors should also have a peephole. Windows and balcony doors, if any, should have secure locks.

Safety   Every room should have a fire or smoke alarm, clear fire instructions, and preferably a sprinkler system. Bathtubs should have a nonskid surface, and shower stalls should have doors that either open outward or slide side to side. Bathroom electrical outlets should be high on the wall and not too close to the sink. Balconies should have sturdy, high rails.

Noise   Most travelers have been kept awake by the television, partying, the amorous activities of people in the next room, or by traffic on the street outside. Better hotels are designed with noise control in mind. Wall and ceiling construction are substantial, effectively screening out routine noise. Carpets and drapes, in addition to being decorative, also absorb and muffle sounds. Mattresses mounted on stable platforms or sturdy bed frames do not squeak even when challenged by the most passionate and acrobatic lovers. Televisions enclosed in cabinets, and with volume governors, rarely disturb guests in adjacent rooms.

In better hotels, the air conditioning and heating system is well maintained and operates without noise or vibration. Likewise, plumbing is quiet and positioned away from the sleeping area. Doors to the hall and to adjoining rooms are thick and well fitted to better keep out noise.

Darkness Control   Ever been in a hotel room where the curtains would not quite come together in the middle? Thick, lined curtains that close completely in the center and extend beyond the dimensions of the window or door frame are required. In a well-planned room, the curtains, shades, or blinds should almost totally block light at any time of day.

Lighting   Poor lighting is an extremely common problem in American hotel rooms. The lighting is usually adequate for dressing, relaxing, or watching television, but not for reading or working. Lighting needs to be bright over tables and desks and alongside couches or easy chairs. Because so many people read in bed, there should be a separate light for each person. A room with two queen beds should have individual lights for four people. Better bedside reading lights illuminate a small area, so if you want

to sleep and someone else prefers to stay up and read, you will not be both-
ered by the light. The worst situation by far is a single lamp on a table
between beds. In each bed, only the person next to the lamp will have sufficient light to read. This deficiency is often compounded by light bulbs of
insufficient wattage.

In addition, closet areas should be well lit, and there should be a switch
near the door that turns on lights in the room when you enter. A seldom
seen, but desirable, feature is a bedside console that allows a guest to control all or most lights in the room from bed.

Furnishings   At bare minimum, the bed(s) must be firm. Pillows should
be made with nonallergenic fillers and, in addition to the sheets and
spread, a blanket should be provided. Bedclothes should be laundered with
a fabric softener and changed daily. Better hotels usually provide extra
blankets and pillows in the room or on request, and sometimes use a second topsheet between the blanket and the spread.

There should be a dresser large enough to hold clothes for two people
during a five-day stay. A small table with two chairs or a desk with one chair
should be provided. The room should be equipped with a luggage rack and
a three-quarter- to full-length mirror.

The television should be cable-connected and color; ideally it should
have a volume governor and remote control. It should be mounted on a
swivel base and preferably enclosed in a cabinet. Local channels should be
posted on the set, and a local TV program guide should be supplied.

The telephone should be touchtone and conveniently situated for bedside use, and it should have on or near it easily understood dialing instructions and a rate card. Local white and yellow pages should be provided. Better hotels have phones in the bath and equip room phones with long cords.

Well-designed hotel rooms usually have a plush armchair or a sleeper
sofa for lounging and reading. Better headboards are padded for comfortable reading in bed, and there should be a nightstand or table on each side
of the bed(s). Nice extras in any hotel room include a small refrigerator, a
digital alarm clock, and a coffeemaker.

Bathroom   Two sinks are better than one, and you cannot have too much
counter space. A sink outside the bath is a great convenience when one person bathes as another dresses. Sinks should have drains with stoppers.

Better bathrooms have both a tub and shower with nonslip bottoms.
Faucet controls should be easy to operate. Adjustable shower heads are preferred. The bath needs to be well lit and should have an exhaust fan and a
guest-controlled heater. Bath towels should be large, soft, fluffy, and provided in generous quantities, as should hand towels and washcloths. There
should be an electrical outlet for each sink, conveniently and safely placed.

Complimentary shampoo, conditioner, soap, and lotion are a plus, as are robes and bathmats. Better hotels supply their bathrooms with tissues and extra toilet paper. Luxurious baths feature a phone, a hair dryer, and sometimes a small television or even a jacuzzi.

Vending There should be complimentary ice and a drink machine on each floor. Welcome additions include a snack machine and a sundries (combs, toothpaste) machine. The latter are seldom found in large hotels that have 24-hour restaurants and shops.

ROOM RATINGS

To separate properties according to the relative quality, tastefulness, state of repair, cleanliness, and size of their standard rooms, we have grouped the hotels and motels into classifications denoted by stars. Star ratings in this guide apply to Anaheim properties only, and do not necessarily correspond to ratings awarded by Mobil, AAA, or other travel critics. Because stars have little relevance when awarded in the absence of commonly recognized standards of comparison, we have tied our ratings to expected levels of quality established by specific American hotel corporations.

Star ratings apply to *room quality only,* and describe the property's standard accommodations. For most hotels and motels a "standard accommodation" is a hotel room with either one king bed or two queen beds. In an all-suite property, the standard accommodation is either a one- or two-room suite. In addition to standard accommodations, many hotels offer luxury rooms and special suites that are not rated in this guide. Star ratings for rooms are assigned without regard to whether a property has restaurant(s), recreational facilities, entertainment, or other extras.

In addition to stars (which delineate broad categories), we also employ a numerical rating system. Our rating scale is 0–100, with 100 as the best

Room Star Ratings		
★★★★★	*Superior Rooms*	Tasteful and luxurious by any standard
★★★★	*Extremely Nice Rooms*	What you would expect at a Hyatt Regency or Marriott
★★★	*Nice Rooms*	Holiday Inn or comparable quality
★★	*Adequate Rooms*	Clean, comfortable, and functional without frills— like a Motel 6
★	*Super Budget*	

possible rating, and zero (0) as the worst. Numerical ratings are presented to show the difference we perceive between one property and another. Rooms at the Hyatt Plaza Alicante, Peacock Suites, and Park Inn International are all rated as three and one-half stars (★★★½). In the supplemental numerical ratings, the Hyatt Plaza Alicante is rated an 80, the Peacock is rated an 81, and the Park Inn International a 75. This means that within the three-and-a-half-star category the Hyatt and Peacock Suites are comparable, and both have slightly nicer rooms than the Park Inn International.

HOW THE HOTELS COMPARE

Cost estimates are based on the hotel's published rack rates for standard rooms. Each "$" represents $40. Thus a cost symbol of "$$$" means a room (or suite) at that hotel will be about $120 a night (it may be less for weekdays or more on weekends).

Following is a hit parade of the nicest rooms in town. We've focused strictly on room quality and have excluded any consideration of location, services, recreation, or amenities. In some instances, a one- or two-room suite can be had for the same price or less than that of a hotel room.

If you used an earlier edition of this guide, you will notice that many of the ratings and rankings have changed. In addition to the inclusion of new properties, these changes are occasioned by such positive developments as guest room renovation or improved maintenance and housekeeping. A failure to properly maintain guest rooms or a lapse in housekeeping standards can negatively affect the ratings.

Finally, before you begin to shop for a hotel, take a hard look at this letter we received from a couple in Hot Springs, Arkansas:

We cancelled our room reservations to follow the advice in your book [and reserved a hotel highly ranked by the Unofficial Guide]. *We wanted inexpensive, but clean and cheerful. We got inexpensive, but dirty, grim, and depressing. I really felt disappointed in your advice and the room. It was the pits. That was the one real piece of information I needed from your book! The room spoiled the holiday for me aside from our touring.*

Needless to say, this letter was as unsettling to us as the bad room was to our reader. Our integrity as travel journalists, after all, is based on the quality of the information we provide to our readers. Even with the best of intentions and the most conscientious research, however, we cannot inspect every room in every hotel. What we do, in statistical terms, is take a sample: we check out several rooms selected at random in each hotel and base our ratings and rankings on those rooms. The inspections are conducted anonymously and without the knowledge of the property's management. Although it would be unusual, it is certainly possible that the rooms we randomly inspect are not representative of the majority of rooms at a particular hotel. Another possibility is that the rooms we inspect in a given hotel are representative but that by bad luck a reader is assigned to an inferior room. When we rechecked the hotel our reader disliked so intensely, we discovered that our rating was correctly representative but that he and his wife had unfortunately been assigned to one of a small number of threadbare rooms scheduled for renovation.

The key to avoiding disappointment is to do some advance snooping around. We recommend that you ask to get a photo of a hotel's standard guest room before you book, or at least a copy of the hotel's promotional brochure. Be forewarned, however, that some hotel chains use the same guest room photo in their promotional literature for all hotels in the chain, and that the guest room in a specific property may not resemble the photo in the brochure. When you or your travel agent call, ask how old the property is and when the guest room you are being assigned was last renovated. If you arrive and are assigned a room inferior to that which you had been led to expect, demand to be moved to another room.

How the Hotels Compare

Hotel	Room Star Rating	Room Quality Rating	Cost ($=$40)	Phone A/C (714)
Disneyland Hotel	★★★★	88	$$$$$–	956-6425
Universal City Hilton and Towers *	★★★★	87	$$$$–	(818) 506-2500
Hilton Suites	★★★★	85	$$$$+	938-1111
Sheraton Universal *	★★★★	85	$$$$+	(818) 980-1212
Disney Pacific Hotel	★★★★	84	$$$$$–	956-6425
Doubletree	★★★★	84	$$$+	634-4500
Marriott Hotel (Main)	★★★★	84	$$$$$–	750-8000
Sheraton Anaheim Hotel	★★★★	83	$$$+	778-1700
Marriott Hotel (North)	★★★½	82	$$$$$–	750-8000
Summerfield Suites West Hollywood *	★★★½	81	$$$$$$+	(310) 657-7400
Hilton Hotel	★★★½	81	$$$$$$+	750-4321
Peacock Suites	★★★½	81	$$$–	535-8255
Hyatt Plaza Alicante	★★★½	80	$$$$–	750-1234

* Within driving distance of Universal Studios Hollywood; about one hour from Disneyland.

How the Hotels Compare (continued)

Hotel	Room Star Rating	Room Quality Rating	Cost ($=$40)	Phone A/C (714)
Hilton Burbank Airport*	★★★½	80	$$$$$−	(818) 843-6000
Residence Inn	★★★½	78	$$$$$−	533-3555
Best Western Crystal Suites	★★★½	76	$$$+	535-7773
Westcoast Anaheim Hotel	★★★½	76	$$$$	750-1811
Howard Johnson Lodge	★★★½	75	$$+	776-6120
Park Inn International	★★★½	75	$$−	635-7275
Carousel Inn & Suites	★★★	72	$$−	758-0444
Comfort Park Suites	★★★	72	$$+	971-3553
Jolly Roger Inn	★★★	72	$$+	772-7621
Ramada Inn	★★★	71	$$−	978-8088
Candy Cane Inn	★★★	73	$$+	774-5284
Radisson Maingate	★★★	70	$$$−	750-2801
Holiday Inn Hollywood*	★★★	70	$$$$$−	(213) 462-7181
Fairfeild Inn	★★★	69	$$+	772-6777
Holiday Inn Burbank*	★★★	68	$$$−	(818) 841-4770
Quality Hotel Maingate	★★★	67	$$$−	750-3131
Best Western Stoval's Inn	★★★	66	$$−	778-1880
Comfort Inn & Suites	★★★	66	$$−	772-8713
Desert Inn & Suites	★★★	66	$$−	772-5050
Best Western Park Place Inn	★★★	65	$$$−	776-4800
Best Western Raffles Inn	★★★	65	$$−	750-6100
Best Western Stardust Motel	★★★	65	$$	774-7600
Colony Inn Budget Host N. Hollywood*	★★½	64	$$−	(818) 763-2787
Anaheim Plaza Hotel	★★½	63	$$−	772-5900
Best Western Pavillions	★★½	63	$$+	776-0140
Holiday Inn Anaheim at the Park	★★½	63	$$$−	758-0900
Holiday Inn Express	★★½	62	$$+	772-7755

* Within driving distance of Universal Studios Hollywood; about one hour from Disneyland.

How the Hotels Compare (continued)

Hotel	Room Star Rating	Room Quality Rating	Cost ($=$40)	Phone A/C (714)
Ramada Conestoga Hotel	★★½	63	$$+	535-0300
Best Western Hollywood Plaza Inn *	★★½	63	$$$–	(213) 851-1800
Best Western Anaheim Inn	★★½	62	$$$–	774-1050
Castle Inn & Suites	★★½	62	$$+	774-8111
Travelodge Anaheim Stadium	★★½	62	$$–	634-1920
Desert Palm Inn & Suites	★★½	61	$$+	535-1133
Days Inn Anaheim	★★½	61	$$–	520-0101
Ramada Limited	★★½	61	$$–	999-0684
Best Western Courtesy Inn	★★½	60	$$–	772-2470
Motel 6	★★½	60	$+	520-9696
Anaheim Angel Inn	★★½	59	$+	634-9121
Days Inn Park South	★★½	59	$$–	703-1220
Days Inn Maingate	★★½	58	$$–	635-3630
Tropicana Inn	★★½	58	$$–	635-4082
Abbey's Anaheimer Inn	★★½	57	$+	774-0211
Econolodge Spas & Suites	★★½	57	$+	535-7878
Travelodge International Inn & Suites	★★½	56	$$–	971-9393
Days Inn & Suites	★★½	56	$$–	533-8830
Ramada Maingate Saga Inn	★★½	56	$$–	772-0440
Anaheim Carriage Inn	★★	55	$+	740-1440
Anaheim Coachman Inn	★★	55	$+	971-5556
Cavalier Inn & Suites	★★	55	$$$–	750-1000
Comfort Inn Maingate	★★	55	$$–	750-5211
Super 8 Anaheim Park	★★	54	$+	778-0350
Alpine Motel	★★	53	$+	535-2186
Anaheim Courtesy Lodge	★★	53	$+	533-2570

* Within driving distance of Universal Studios Hollywood; about one hour from Disneyland.

How the Hotels Compare (continued)

Hotel	Room Star Rating	Room Quality Rating	Cost ($=$40)	Phone A/C (714)
Alamo Inn	★★	52	$−	635-8070
Anaheim Motel	★★	52	$+	774-3882
Magic Lamp Motel	★★	52	$+	772-7242
Anaheim Penny Sleeper Inn	★★	51	$$−	991-8100
Samoa Super 8	★★	51	$+	778-6900
Budget Inn	★★	50	$+	535-5524
Convention Center Inn	★★	49	$+	740-2500
Park View Inn	★★	48	$$−	772-5721
Magic Carpet Motel	★★	48	$+	772-9450
Peter Pan Motor Lodge	★★	48	$	750-0232
Angels Inn	★★	47	$−	971-0255
Hacienda Motel	★½	46	$+	750-2101
Samoa Motel	★½	41	$	776-2815
Rip Van Winkle's	★½	40	$−	776-6210
Islander	★½	38	$+	778-6565
Parkside	★	37	$−	971-5511
Skyview Motel	★	34	$+	533-4505
Arena Inn	½	26	$−	533-7040
Little Boy Blue	½	25	$+	635-2781

THE TOP 30 BEST DEALS

Having listed the nicest rooms in town, let's take a look at the best combinations of quality and value in a room. As before, the rankings are made without consideration of location or the availability of restaurant(s), recreational facilities, entertainment, or amenities. The Disneyland Hotel, you may notice, is not one of the best deals. This is because you can get more for your money at other properties. The Disneyland Hotel, however, is one of the most popular hotels in the area, and many guests are willing to pay a higher rate for the convenience, service, and amenities.

We recently had a reader complain to us that he had booked one of our top-ranked rooms for value and had been very disappointed in the room. On checking we noticed that the room the reader occupied had a quality rating of ★★ ½. We would remind you that the value ratings are intended to give you some sense of value received for your lodging dollar spent. A

★★½ room at $35 may have the same value rating as a ★★★★ room at $85, but that does not mean the rooms will be of comparable quality. Regardless of whether it's a good deal or not, a ★★½ room is still a ★★½ room.

Listed below are the top 30 room buys for the money, regardless of location or star classification, based on rack rates. Note that sometimes a suite can cost less than a hotel room.

	The Top 30 Best Deals			
Hotel	Room Star Rating	Room Quality Rating	Cost ($=$40)	Phone A/C (714)
1. Park Inn International	★★★½	75	$$–	635-7275
2. Anaheim Angel Inn	★★½	59	$+	634-9121
3. Days Inn Park South	★★½	59	$$–	703-1220
4. Motel 6	★★½	60	$+	520-9696
5. Howard Johnson Lodge	★★★½	75	$$+	776-6120
6. Alamo Inn	★★	52	$–	635-8070
7. Abbey's Anaheimer Inn	★★½	57	$+	774-0211
8. Carousel Inn & Suites	★★★	72	$$–	758-0444
9. Ramada Inn	★★★	71	$$–	978-8088
10. Econolodge Spas & Suites	★★½	57	$+	535-7878
11. Doubletree	★★★★	84	$$$+	634-4500
12. Candy Cane Inn	★★★	73	$$+	774-5284
13. Sheraton Anaheim Hotel	★★★★	83	$$$+	778-1700
14. Best Western Stovall's Inn	★★★	66	$$–	778-1880
15. Desert Inn & Suites	★★★	66	$$–	772-5050
16. Universal City Hilton and Towers *	★★★★	87	$$$$–	(818) 506-2500
17. Magic Lamp Motel	★★	52	$+	772-7242
18. Best Western Park Place Inn	★★★	65	$$$–	776-4800
19. Best Western Raffles Inn	★★★	65	$$–	750-6100
20. Fairfeild Inn	★★★	69	$$+	772-6777
21. Ramada Limited	★★½	61	$$–	999-0684
22. Best Western Stardust Motel	★★★	65	$$	774-7600
23. Sheraton Universal *	★★★★	85	$$$$+	(818) 980-1212

* Within driving distance of Universal Studios Hollywood; about one hour from Disneyland.

Hotel	Room Star Rating	Room Quality Rating	Cost ($=$40)	Phone A/C (714)
24. Jolly Roger Inn	★★★	72	$$+	772-7621
25. Colony Inn Budget Host N. Hollywood *	★★½	64	$$–	(818) 763-2787
26. Angels Inn	★★	47	$–	971-0255
27. Disney Pacific Hotel	★★★★	84	$$$$$–	956-6425
28. Quality Hotel Maingate	★★★	67	$$$–	750-3131
29. Holiday Inn Anaheim at the Park	★★½	63	$$$–	758-0900
30. Peacock Suites	★★★½	81	$$$–	535-8255

The Top 30 Best Deals (continued)

Making the Most of Your Time

ALLOCATING TIME

The Disney people recommend a day and a half to three full days at Disneyland. While this may seem a little self-serving, it is not without basis. Disneyland is *huge,* with something to see or do crammed into every conceivable space. In addition, touring requires a lot of walking and often a lot of waiting in lines. Moving in and among large crowds all day is exhausting, and often the unrelenting southern California sun zaps even the most hardy, making tempers short. During our many visits to Disneyland we observed, particularly on hot summer days, a dramatic transition from happy, enthusiastic touring on arrival to almost zombie-like plodding along later in the day. Visitors who began their day enjoying the wonders of Disney imagination ultimately lapsed into an exhausted production mentality ("We've got two more rides in Fantasyland, then we can go back to the hotel").

OPTIMUM TOURING SITUATION

The optimum touring situation would call for having three days of touring time at your disposal. Buy a Flex Signature Passport or the regular Three-Day Passport. Both entitle you to admission plus unlimited use of attractions. The Flex Passport is good for 5 consecutive days, while the regular Three-Day Passport is good for any 3 days within a 14-day period.

Day One   Tour Disneyland early in the morning, when the lines are short and the day is cooler, following Day One of Two-Day Touring Plan A provided in this guide to help you avoid long lines. At about noon go back to your hotel for lunch and maybe a swim or a nap—whatever you feel like.

If the park closes early (6 to 8 p.m.), return refreshed about two hours before closing and continue your visit in the relative cool and diminished crowds of the evening. Eat dinner somewhere outside of Disneyland after the park closes.

If Disneyland closes late (after 8 p.m.), take a relaxing dinner break outside the park and return refreshed to enjoy yourself until closing time. Evenings on a late-closing night are special at Disneyland. We recommend this time for taking in special events and live performances. If you stay until almost closing time, you will find the lines for the more popular rides vastly diminished.

Day Two Arrive early in the morning and follow Day Two of Two-Day Touring Plan A provided in this guide.

If the park closes early, stick around for the afternoon parade and some of the other live performances around the park. Visit Tom Sawyer Island before dusk. If you enjoy shopping, this is a good time to explore the shops.

If the park remains open late, eat an early dinner outside Disneyland and return around 7:30 p.m. to enjoy the evening festivities.

Day Three Arrive early and experience again those rides and attractions that you enjoyed most from the first two mornings. Catch any of the shows or rides you missed on the previous days.

The essence of the "Optimum Touring Situation" is to see the various attractions of Disneyland in a series of shorter, less exhausting visits during the cooler, less crowded parts of the day, with plenty of rest and relaxation in between visits. Since the "Optimum Touring Situation" calls for leaving and returning to Disneyland on most days, it obviously makes for easier logistics if you stay fairly close to the park (i.e., two miles or less to your hotel). If you are lodged too far away for a great deal of coming and going, try relaxing during the heat of the day in the lounges or at the pools of the Disneyland Hotel complex.

SEEING DISNEYLAND ON A TIGHT SCHEDULE

Many visitors do not have three days to devote to Disneyland. Some are en route to other California destinations, while others wish to spend time sampling other attractions. For these visitors, efficient, time-effective touring is a must. They cannot afford long waits in line for rides, shows, or meals.

Even the most efficient touring plan will not allow the visitor to cover Disneyland in one day without making some choices. The basic trade-off is between enjoying the rides or catching specially scheduled live entertainment such as parades, concerts, and so on. If the park closes late (after 8 p.m.), you can, with a little organization, have the best of both worlds. If, however, the park closes early, you will probably have to give up seeing some of the attractions.

ONE-DAY TOURING

Comprehensively touring Disneyland in one day is possible but requires a knowledge of the park, good planning, and no small reserve of energy and endurance. One-day touring does not leave much time for leisurely meals in sit-down restaurants, prolonged browsing in the many shops, or lengthy rest breaks. Even so, one-day touring can be a fun and rewarding experience.

Successful one-day touring hinges on *three cardinal rules:*

1. Determine in Advance What You Really Want to See.

What rides and attractions most appeal to you? Which additional rides and attractions would you like to experience if you have any time left? What are you willing to forgo?

To help you establish your touring priorities, we have described every attraction in detail. In each description we include the author's critical evaluation of the attraction as well as the opinions of Disneyland guests expressed as star ratings. Five stars is the highest (best) rating possible.

Finally, because Disneyland attractions range in scope from midway-type rides and horse-drawn trolleys to colossal, high-tech extravaganzas spanning the equivalent of whole city blocks, we have developed a hierarchy of categories for attractions to give you some sense of their order of magnitude:

Super Headliners   The best attractions the theme park has to offer. They are mind-boggling in size, scope, and imagination and represent the cutting edge of modern attraction technology and design.

Headliners   Full-blown, multimillion-dollar, full-scale, themed adventure experiences and theater presentations. They are modern in their technology and design and employ a full range of special effects.

Major Attractions   Themed adventure experiences on a more modest scale, but incorporating state-of-the-art technologies. Or, larger scale attractions of older design.

Minor Attractions   Midway-type rides, small "dark rides" (spook house–type rides), small theater presentations, transportation rides, and elaborate walk-through attractions.

Diversions   Exhibits, both passive and interactive. Also includes playgrounds, video arcades, and street theater.

Though not every Disneyland attraction fits neatly into the above categories, the categories provide a relative comparison of attraction size and scope. Remember, however, that bigger and more elaborate does not always mean better. Peter Pan's Flight, a minor attraction, continues to be one of the park's most beloved rides. Likewise, for many small children, there is no attraction, regardless of size, that can surpass Dumbo.

2. Arrive Early! Arrive Early! Arrive Early!

This is the single most important key to touring efficiently and avoiding long lines. With your admission pass in hand, be at the gate ready to go 30 minutes before the theme park's stated opening time. There are no lines and relatively few people first thing in the morning. The same four rides you can experience in one hour in the early morning will take more than three hours to see after 11 a.m. Have breakfast before you arrive so you will not have to waste prime touring time sitting in a restaurant. If you visit Disneyland during the summer, make every attempt to take advantage of a travel package that offers early entry or buy a Flex Signature Passport.

3. Avoid Bottlenecks.

Helping you avoid bottlenecks is what this guide is all about. Bottlenecks occur as a result of crowd concentrations and/or less-than-optimal traffic engineering. Concentrations of hungry people create bottlenecks at restaurants during the lunch and dinner hours; concentrations of people moving toward the exit near closing time create bottlenecks in the gift shops en route to the gate; concentrations of visitors at new and unusually popular rides create bottlenecks and long waiting lines; rides slow to load and unload passengers create bottlenecks and long waiting lines. Avoiding bottlenecks involves being able to predict where, when, and why they occur. To this end we provide field-tested **Touring Plans** to keep you ahead of the crowd or out of its way. In addition, we provide **Critical Data** on all rides and shows, which help you to estimate how long you may have to wait in line, which compare rides in terms of their capacity to accommodate large crowds, and which rate the rides according to our opinions and the opinions of other Disneyland visitors.

TRAFFIC PATTERNS INSIDE DISNEYLAND

When we began our research on Disneyland, we were very interested in traffic patterns throughout the park, specifically:

1. What attractions and which sections of the park do visitors head for when they first arrive? When guests are admitted to the various lands, the flow of people to Adventureland (Indiana Jones) and Tomorrowland (Star Tours and Space Mountain) is heaviest. The next most crowded land is Fantasyland, followed by Critter Country, Mickey's Toontown, New Orleans Square, and Frontierland. In our research we tested the assertion, often heard, that most people turn right into Tomorrowland and tour Disneyland in an orderly, counterclockwise fashion, and found it without basis. As the park fills, visitors appear to head for specific favored attractions that they wish to ride before the lines get long. This more than any other factor determines traffic patterns in the mornings and accounts for the relatively equal distribution of visitors throughout Disneyland. Attractions that are heavily attended in the early morning are:

Tomorrowland	Star Tours
	Space Mountain
Adventureland	Jungle Cruise
	Indiana Jones
Critter Country	Splash Mountain
Fantasyland	Dumbo
	Matterhorn Bobsleds
Mickey's Toontown	Car Toon Spin

In addition to the above, Mickey's Toontown, the park's newest "land" (1993), attracts many families with small children early in the morning.

On days when early entry is in effect, certain attractions open 90 minutes before the general public is admitted. Attractions scheduled to open early are subject to change, but often include those in Fantasyland and Tomorrowland as well as Indiana Jones.

2. How long does it take for the park to reach peak capacity for a given day? How are the visitors dispersed throughout the park?   There is a surge of "early birds" who arrive before or around opening time but are quickly dispersed throughout the empty park. After the initial onslaught is absorbed, there is a bit of a lull that lasts until about an hour after opening. Following the lull, the park is inundated with arriving guests for about two hours, peaking between 10 and 11 a.m. Guests continue to arrive in a steady but diminishing stream until around 2 p.m.

On days when the early entry program is in effect, a large number of Disneyland Hotel and Disneyland package vacation guests are admitted to the park 90 minutes early. Particularly during the summer and on Saturdays all year, this program adds significant numbers of guests to the early morning crowd.

Sampled lines reached their longest length between noon and 2 p.m., indicating more arrivals than departures into the early afternoon. For general touring purposes, most attractions develop substantial lines between 9:30 and 11 a.m. In the early morning, Adventureland, Tomorrowland,

Critter Country, and Fantasyland fill up first. By late morning and into early afternoon, attendance is fairly equally distributed through all of the "lands." Mickey's Toontown, because it is new and comparatively small, stays mobbed from about 11 a.m. on. By midafternoon, however, we noted a concentration of visitors in Fantasyland, New Orleans Square, and Adventureland and a slight decrease of visitors in Tomorrowland. This pattern did not occur consistently day to day, but happened often enough for us to suggest Tomorrowland as the best bet for midafternoon touring.

In the late afternoon and early evening, attendance is normally more heavily distributed in Tomorrowland, Critter Country, and Fantasyland. Though Star Tours, Space Mountain, and Splash Mountain remain inundated throughout the day, most of the other attractions in Tomorrowland and Critter Country have reasonable lines. In New Orleans Square, the Haunted Mansion, the Pirates of the Caribbean, and the multitudes returning from nearby Critter Country keep traffic brisk. Frontierland and Adventureland (except for the Indiana Jones ride) become less congested as the afternoon and evening progress.

3. How do most visitors go about touring the park? Is there a difference in the touring behavior of first-time visitors and repeat visitors?
Many first-time visitors accompany friends or relatives who are familiar with Disneyland and who guide their tour. These tours sometimes do and sometimes do not proceed in an orderly (clockwise or counterclockwise) touring sequence. First-time visitors without personal touring guidance tend to be more orderly in their touring. Many first-time visitors, however, are drawn to Sleeping Beauty Castle on entering the park and thus commence their rotation from Fantasyland. Repeat visitors usually proceed directly to their favorite attractions or to whatever is new. (At the moment, the newer attractions are the Indiana Jones ride in Adventureland and *Honey, I Shrunk the Audience* and Rocket Rods in Tomorrowland.)

4. What effect do special events, such as parades, fireworks, and *Fantasmic!* have on traffic patterns?   Special events such as parades, fireworks, and *Fantasmic!* pull substantial numbers of visitors from the lines for rides, especially when *Fantasmic!* and a parade are staged at the same time. Unfortunately, however, the left hand taketh what the right hand giveth. A parade and *Fantasmic!* kicking off simultaneously snarls traffic flow throughout Disneyland so much that guests find themselves captive wherever they are. Attraction lines in Tomorrowland, Mickey's Toontown, Adventureland, and Fantasyland (behind the castle) diminish dramatically, making Star Tours, Space Mountain, the Jungle Cruise, the Indiana Jones Adventure, Peter Pan's Flight, and Snow White's Scary Adventures particularly good choices during the evening festivities. The remainder of the park (Critter Country, New Orleans Square, Frontierland, Main Street) is so congested with guests viewing the parade and *Fantasmic!* that it is almost impossible to move.

5. What are the traffic patterns near to and at closing time? On our sample days, recorded in and out of season, park departures outnumbered arrivals beginning in midafternoon, with a substantial number of guests leaving following the afternoon parade. Additional numbers of visitors departed during the late afternoon as the dinner hour approached. When the park closed early, there were steady departures during the two hours preceding closing, with a mass exodus of remaining visitors at closing time.

When the park closed late, departures were distributed throughout the evening hours, with waves of departures following the evening parade(s), fireworks, and *Fantasmic!* performances. Though departures increased exponentially as closing time approached, a huge throng was still on hand when the park finally shut down. The balloon effect of this last throng at the end of the day generally overwhelmed the shops on Main Street, the parking lot (including the hotel shuttle loading zone), and the exits onto adjoining Anaheim streets. In the hour before closing in the lands other than Main Street, touring conditions were normally uncrowded except at the Indiana Jones attraction in Adventureland.

SAVING TIME IN LINE BY UNDERSTANDING THE RIDES

There are many different types of rides in Disneyland. Some rides, like It's a Small World, are engineered to carry several thousand people every hour. At the other extreme, rides such as Dumbo, the Flying Elephant, can only accommodate around 500 people in an hour. Most rides fall somewhere in between. Lots of factors figure into how long you will have to wait to experience a particular ride: the popularity of the ride, how it loads and unloads, how many people can ride at one time, how many units (cars, rockets, boats, flying elephants, or whatever) of those available are in service at a given time, and how many staff personnel are available to operate the ride. Let's take them one by one:

1. How Popular Is the Ride? Newer rides like Indiana Jones and Rocket Rods attract a lot of people, as do longtime favorites such as the Jungle Cruise. If you know a ride is popular, you need to learn a little more about how it operates to determine when might be the best time to ride. But a ride need not be especially popular to form long lines: the lines can be the result of less-than-desirable traffic engineering; that is, it takes so long to

load and unload that a line builds up anyway. This is the situation at the Mad Tea Party and Dumbo, the Flying Elephant. Only a small percentage of the visitors to Disneyland (mostly children) ride Dumbo, for instance, but because it takes so long to load and unload that this ride can form long waiting lines.

2. How Does the Ride Load and Unload?   Some rides never stop. They are like a circular conveyor belt that goes around and around. We call these "continuous loaders." The Haunted Mansion is a continuous loader. The more cars or ships or whatever on the conveyor, the more

people can be moved through in an hour. The Haunted Mansion has lots of cars on the conveyor belt and consequently can move more than 2,400 people an hour.

Other rides are "interval loaders." This means that cars are unloaded, loaded, and dispatched at certain set intervals (sometimes controlled manually and sometimes by a computer). Matterhorn Bobsleds is an interval loader. It has two separate tracks (in other words, the ride has been duplicated in the same facility). Each track can run up to 10 sleds, released at 23-second or greater intervals (the bigger the crowd, the shorter the interval). In another kind of interval loader, like the Jungle Cruise, empty boats return to the starting point, where they line up waiting to be reloaded. In a third type of interval loader, one group of riders enters the vehicle while the last group of riders departs. We call these "in and out" interval loaders. Indiana Jones is a good example of an "in and out" interval loader. As a troop transport pulls up to the loading station, those who have just completed their ride exit to the left. At almost the same time, those waiting to ride enter the troop transport from the right. The troop transport is released to the dispatch point a few yards down the line where it is launched according to whatever second interval is being used. Interval loaders of both types can be very efficient at moving people if (1) the release (launch) interval is relatively short, and (2) the ride can accommodate a large number of vehicles in the system at one time. Since many boats can be floating through Pirates of the Caribbean at a given time and the release interval is short, almost 2,300 people an hour can see this attraction. Submarine Voyage is an "in and out" interval loader, but it can only run a maximum of eight submarines at a time. Thus, Submarine Voyage can only handle up to 1,700 people an hour.

A third group of rides are "cycle rides." Another name for these same rides is "stop and go" rides; those waiting to ride exchange places with those who have just ridden. The main difference between "in and out" interval rides and cycle rides is that with a cycle ride the whole system shuts down when loading and unloading is in progress. While one boat is loading and unloading in It's a Small World, many other boats are proceeding through the ride. But when Dumbo, the Flying Elephant touches down, the whole ride is at a standstill until the next flight is launched. Likewise, with the AstroOrbiter (formerly the Rocket Jets), all riders dismount and the space capsules stand stationary until the next group is loaded and ready to ride. In discussing a cycle ride, the amount of time the ride is in motion is called "ride time." The amount of time that the ride is idle while loading and unloading is called "load time." Load time plus ride time equals "cycle time," or the time expended from the start of one run of the ride until the start of the succeeding run. Cycle rides are the least efficient of all the Disneyland rides in terms of traffic engineering.

3. How Many People Can Ride at One Time?   This figure is defined in terms of "per-ride capacity" or "system capacity." Either way, the figures refer to the number of people who can be riding at the same time. Our discussion above illustrates that the greater the carrying capacity of a ride (all other things being equal), the more visitors it can accommodate in an hour.

4. How Many "Units" Are in Service at a Given Time? A "unit" is simply a term for the vehicle you sit in during your ride. At the Mad Tea Party the unit is a teacup; at the Submarine Voyage it's a submarine; and at Alice in Wonderland it's a caterpillar. On some rides (mostly cycle rides), the number of units in operation at a given time is fixed. Thus there are always 16 flying elephant units operating on the Dumbo ride, 72 horses on King Arthur Carrousel, and so on. What this fixed number of units means to you is that there is no way to increase the carrying capacity of the ride by adding more units. On a busy day, therefore, the only way to carry more people each hour on a fixed-unit cycle ride is to shorten the loading time (which, as we will see in section 5 below, is sometimes impossible) or by decreasing the riding time, the actual time the ride is in motion. The bottom line on a busy day for a cycle ride is that you will wait longer and be rewarded for your wait with a shorter ride. This is why we try to steer you clear of the cycle rides unless you are willing to ride them early in the morning or late at night. The following rides are cycle rides:

Fantasyland	Dumbo, the Flying Elephant
	King Arthur Carrousel
	Mad Tea Party
Tomorrowland	AstroOrbiter
Mickey's Toontown	Gadget's Go-Coaster
	Goofy's Bounce House
	Chip 'n' Dale's Acorn Ball Crawl

Other rides at Disneyland can increase their carrying capacity by adding units to the system as the crowds build. The Big Thunder Mountain Railroad is a good example. If attendance is very light, Big Thunder can start the day by running one of five available mine trains. When lines start to build, more mine trains can be placed into operation. At full capacity, a total of five trains can carry about 2,400 people an hour. Likewise, Pirates of the Caribbean can increase its capacity by adding more boats, and Snow White's Scary Adventures by adding more mine cars. Sometimes a long line will disappear almost instantly when new units are brought on line. When an interval-loading ride places more units into operation, it usually shortens the dispatch interval, so more units are being dispatched more often.

5. How Many Staff Personnel Are Available to Operate the Ride? Allocation of additional staff to a given ride can allow extra units to be placed in operation, or additional loading areas or holding areas to be opened. Pirates of the Caribbean and It's a Small World can run two separate waiting lines and loading zones. Haunted Mansion has a short "preshow," which is staged in a "stretch room." On busy days a second stretch room can be activated, thus permitting a more continuous flow of visitors to the actual loading area. Additional staff make a world of difference on some cycle rides. Often, if not usually, one attendant will operate the Mad Tea Party. This single person must clear the visitors from the ride just completed, admit and seat visitors for the upcoming ride, check that all teacups are properly secured (which entails an inspection of each teacup), return to the control panel, issue instructions to the riders, and finally, activate the ride (whew!). A second attendant allows for the division of these responsibilities and has the effect of cutting loading time by 25 to 50%.

SAVING TIME IN LINE BY UNDERSTANDING THE SHOWS

Many of the featured attractions at Disneyland are theater presentations. While not as complex from a traffic engineering viewpoint as rides, a little enlightenment concerning their operation may save some touring time.

Most of the theater attractions at Disneyland operate in three distinct phases:

1. First, there are the visitors who are in the theater viewing the presentation.
2. Next, there are the visitors who have passed through the turnstile into a holding area or waiting lobby. These people will be admitted to the theater as soon as the current presentation is concluded. Several attractions offer a preshow in their waiting lobby to entertain the crowd until they are admitted to the main show.
3. Finally, there is the outside line. Visitors waiting here will enter the waiting lobby when there is room and then move into the theater when the audience turns over (is exchanged) between shows.

The theater capacity and popularity of the presentation, along with the level of attendance in the park, determine how long the lines will be at a given theater attraction. Except for holidays and other days of especially heavy attendance, the longest wait for a show usually does not exceed the length of one complete performance.

Since almost all Disneyland theater attractions run continuously, only stopping long enough for the previous audience to leave and the waiting audience to enter, a performance will be in progress when you arrive. If a show at the *Country Bear Playhouse* lasts 15 minutes, the wait under normal circumstances should be 15 minutes if you were to arrive just after the show began.

All Disneyland theaters (except the Main Street Cinema and some amphitheater productions) are very strict when it comes to controlling access. Unlike a regular movie theater, you cannot just walk in during the middle of a performance; you will always have at least a short wait.

HOW TO DEAL WITH OBNOXIOUS PEOPLE

At every theater presentation at Disneyland, visitors in the preshow area elbow, nudge, and crowd one another in order to make sure they are admitted to the performance. Not necessary—if you are admitted through the turnstile into the preshow area a seat has automatically been allocated for you in the theater. When it is time to proceed into the theater don't rush; just relax and let other people jam the doorways. When the congestion has been relieved simply stroll in and take a seat.

Attendants at many theaters will instruct you to enter a row of seats and move completely to the far side, filling every seat so that each row can be completely filled. And invariably some inconsiderate, pea-brained thunderhead will plop down right in the middle of the row, stopping traffic or forcing other visitors to climb over him. Take our word for it—there is no such thing as a bad seat. All of the Disney theaters have been designed to provide a nearly perfect view from every seat in the house. Our recommendation is to follow instructions and move to the far end of the row.

The Disney people also ask that visitors not use flash photography in the theaters (the theaters are too dark for the pictures to turn out, plus the flash is disruptive to other viewers). Needless to say, this admonition is routinely ignored. Flashers are more difficult to deal with than row-blockers. You can threaten to turn the offenders over to Disney Security, or better yet, simply hold your hand over the lens (you have to be quick) when they raise their cameras.

Part Two

Basic Essentials

The Bare Necessities

CREDIT CARDS

American Express, MasterCard, VISA, JCB, and Discover are accepted for theme park admission. No credit cards are accepted in the theme park at vending carts. Disneyland shops, fast-food and counter-service restaurants, sit-down restaurants, and the Disneyland Hotel accept American Express, MasterCard, VISA, JCB, and Discover credit cards.

RAIN

If it rains, go anyway; the bad weather will diminish the crowds. Additionally, most of the rides and attractions in Disneyland are under cover. Likewise, all but a few of the waiting areas are protected from inclement weather. If you get caught in an unexpected downpour, rain gear of varying sorts can be purchased at a number of Disneyland shops.

VISITORS WITH SPECIAL NEEDS

Disabled Visitors   Rental wheelchairs are available if needed. Most rides, shows, attractions, rest rooms, and restaurants are engineered to accommodate the disabled. For specific inquiries or problems call (714) 781-4560. If you are in Disneyland and need some special assistance, go to City Hall on Main Street. Close-in parking is available for the disabled; inquire when you pay your parking fee.

Visitors with Dietary Restrictions   Visitors on special or restricted diets, including those requiring kosher meals, can arrange for assistance at City Hall on Main Street. For Disneyland Hotel restaurants, call the restaurant one day in advance for assistance.

Foreign Language Assistance   Available to non–English-speaking guests. Inquire by calling (714) 781-4560 or by stopping in at City Hall or at Guest Relations to the right of the main entrance.

Lost Adults   Arrange a plan for regrouping with those in your party should you become separated (the *Unofficial Guide* crew regroups at the Refreshment Corner at the central hub end of Main Street). Failing this, you can leave a message at City Hall for your missing person. For information concerning lost children, see page 90.

Messages   Can be left at City Hall.

Car Trouble   If you elected to decrease the chance of losing your keys by locking them in your car, or decided that your car might be easier to find if you left your lights on you may have a little problem to deal with when you return to the parking lot at the end of your visit. Fortunately, the security patrols that continually cruise the parking lots are equipped to handle these types of situations and can quickly put you back in business.

Lost and Found   If you lose (or find) something, the lost and found office is located in the same place where lockers are available (walk down Main Street toward the castle and go to the end of the first cul-de-sac street on the right). If you do not discover your loss until you have left the park, call (714) 781-4765.

Excuse Me, But Where Can I Find . . .

Someplace to Put All These Packages?   Lockers are available down Main Street one block from the entrance (as you walk toward the castle) and to the right. A more convenient solution, if you plan to spend a minimum of two more hours in the park, is to have the salesperson forward your purchases to Package Pick-Up. When you leave the park they will be there waiting for you. Package Pick-Up is located at the News Stand, to the right of the main entrance as you exit the park. If you are staying at the Disneyland Hotel, you can have your purchases delivered directly to your room.

A Mixed Drink or Beer?   If you are in Disneyland you are out of luck. You will have to exit the park and try one of the hotels.

Some Rain Gear?   If you get caught in a rare California monsoon, here's where you can find something to cover up with:

Main Street:	The Emporium
Tomorrowland:	The Star Trader
Fantasyland:	Mad Hatter
Frontierland:	Davy Crockett's Pioneer Mercantile

At Disneyland, rain gear is readily available but not always displayed. As the Disney people say, it is sold "under the counter." In other words, you have to ask for it. If you are caught without protection on a rainy day, don't slog around dripping. Rain gear is one of the few shopping bargains at Disneyland. Ponchos can be had for less than $6, and umbrellas are $9 and up.

A Cure for This Headache?   Aspirin and various other sundries can be purchased on Main Street at the Emporium (they keep them behind the counter, so you have to ask).

A Prescription Filled?   Unfortunately, there is no place in Disneyland to have a prescription filled.

Suntan Lotion?   Suntan lotion and various other sundries can be purchased on Main Street at the Emporium (they keep them behind the counter, so you have to ask).

A Smoke?   Cigarettes are readily available throughout Disneyland.

Feminine Hygiene Products?   Feminine hygiene products are available in most of the women's rest rooms at Disneyland.

Cash?   The Bank of Main Street offers the following services:

- Personal checks may be cashed for $100 or less if drawn on U.S. banks; presentation of a valid driver's license and a major credit card is required.
- Cash for traveler's checks.
- Exchange of foreign currency for dollars.
- In addition, cash advances on MasterCard and VISA credit cards (25¢ fee, with a maximum equaling the patron's credit limit) are available at Starcade in Tomorrowland.

If the cashier is closed, there are Automatic Teller Machines (ATMs) at these locations:

- Outside the main entrance.
- On Main Street, next to *The Walt Disney Story* at the Town Square end.
- At the entrance to Frontierland on the left.
- Near the Fantasyland Theater at Meeko's.

A Place to Leave My Pet?   Cooping up an animal in a hot car while you tour can lead to disastrous results. Additionally, pets are not allowed in Disneyland (except for Seeing Eye dogs). Kennels and holding facilities are provided for the temporary care of your pets and are located to the right of the main entrance. If you are adamant, the folks at the kennels will accept custody of just about any type of animal. Owners of pets, exotic or otherwise, must themselves place their charge in the assigned cage. Small pets (mice, hamsters, birds, snakes, turtles, alligators, etc.) must arrive in their own escape-proof quarters. Kennels cost $10 a day.

In addition to the above, there are several other details you may need to know:

- Advance reservations for animals are not accepted.
- No horses, llamas, or cattle are accepted.
- Kennels open 30 minutes before the theme park opens and close 30 minutes after the theme park closes.
- Pets may not be boarded overnight.

- Guests leaving exotic pets should supply food for their pet.

- On busy days there is a one- to two-hour bottleneck at the kennel, beginning a half-hour before the park opens. If you need to use the kennel on such a day, arrive at least an hour before the park's stated opening time.

- Pets are fed on request only, and there is no additional charge for food.

Cameras and Film? If you do not have a camera, you can buy a disposable one, with or without a flash, at the Camera Center on Main Street. You can buy film throughout the park. Finally, photo tips, including recommendations for settings and exposures, are provided in the Disneyland map brochure, available free when you enter the park.

Part Three

Disneyland with Kids

The Agony and the Ecstasy

The national media and advertising presence of Disney is so overwhelming that any child who watches TV or shops with Mom is likely to get all revved up about going to Disneyland. Parents, if anything, are even more susceptible. Almost every parent has brightened with anticipation at the prospect of guiding their children through the wonders of this special place: "Imagine little Tami's expression when she first sees Mickey Mouse. Think of her excitement and awe as she crosses the moat to Sleeping Beauty's Castle, or her small arms around me when Dumbo takes off." Are these not the treasured moments we long to share with our children?

While dreams of visiting Disneyland are tantamount to nirvana for a three-year-old and dear enough to melt the heart of any parent, the reality of actually taking that three-year-old (particularly during the summer) is usually a lot closer to the "agony" than the "ecstasy."

A mother from Dayton, Ohio, describes taking her five-year-old to the Magic Kingdom in Walt Disney World, but it could just as easily be Disneyland:

> I felt so happy and excited before we went. I guess it was all worth it, but when I look back I think I should have had my head examined. The first day we went to Disney World [the Magic Kingdom] and it was packed. By 11 in the morning we had walked so far and stood in so many lines that we were all exhausted. Kristy cried about going on anything that looked or even sounded scary, and was frightened by all of the Disney characters (they are so big!) except Minnie and Snow White.
>
> We got hungry about the same time as everyone else but the lines for food were too long and my husband said we would have to wait.

By 1 in the afternoon we were just plugging along, not seeing anything we were really interested in, but picking rides because the lines were short, or because whatever it was was air-conditioned. We rode Small World three times in a row and I'll never get that song out of my head (Ha!). At around 2:30 we finally got something to eat, but by then we were so hot and tired that it felt like we had worked in the yard all day. Kristy insisted on being carried and we had 50 fights about not going on rides where the lines were too long. At the end, we were so P.O.'d and uncomfortable that we weren't having any fun. Mostly by this time we were just trying to get our money's worth.

Before you stiffen in denial, let us assure you that the Ohio family's experience is fairly typical. Most small children are as picky about the rides as they are about what they eat, and more than 50% of preschoolers are intimidated by the friendly Disney characters. Few humans (of any age), moreover, are mentally or physically equipped to march all day in a throng of 40,000 people under the California sun. Finally, would you be surprised to learn that almost 52% of preschoolers said the thing they liked best about their Disneyland vacation was the hotel swimming pool?

REALITY TESTING: WHOSE DREAM IS IT?

Remember when you were little and you got that nifty electric train for Christmas, the one your dad wouldn't let you play with? Did you ever wonder who that train was really for? Ask yourself the same question about your vacation to Disneyland. Whose dream are you trying to make come true, yours or your child's?

Small children are very adept at reading their parents' emotions. When you ask, "Honey, how would you like to go to Disneyland?" your child will be responding more to your smile and excitement, and the idea of doing something with Mom and Dad, than to any notion of what Disneyland is all about. The younger the child in question, the more this is true. For many preschoolers you could elicit the same enthusiastic response by asking, "Honey, how would you like to go to Cambodia on a dogsled?"

So, is your warm, fuzzy fantasy of introducing your child to the magic of Disney a pipe dream? Not necessarily, but you will have to be practical and open to a little reality testing. For instance, would you increase the probability of a happy, successful visit by holding off a couple of years? Is your child spunky and adventuresome enough to willingly sample the variety of Disneyland? Will your child have sufficient endurance and patience to cope with long waits in line and large crowds?

RECOMMENDATIONS FOR MAKING THE DREAM COME TRUE

When contemplating a Disneyland vacation with small children, anticipation is the name of the game. Here are some of the things you need to consider:

Age Although the color and festivity of Disneyland excite children of all ages, and while there are specific attractions that delight toddlers and preschoolers, the Disney entertainment mix is generally oriented to older kids and adults. We believe that children should be a fairly mature seven years old to *appreciate* Disneyland.

Time of Year to Visit If there is any way you can swing it, avoid the hot, crowded summer months. Try to go in October, November (except Thanksgiving), early December, March, and April (except Easter and spring break). If your kids are preschoolers, don't even think about going during the summer. If you have children of varying ages and your school-age kids are good students, take the older ones out of school so you can visit during the cooler, less congested off-season. Arrange special study assignments relating to the many educational aspects of Disneyland. If your school-age children are not great students and cannot afford to miss any school, take your vacation as soon as the school year ends in late May or early June. Nothing, repeat, nothing will enhance your Disneyland vacation as much as avoiding summer months and holiday periods.

Building Naps and Rest into Your Itinerary   Disneyland is huge. If your schedule allows, try to spread your visit over at least two days. Tour in the early morning and return to your hotel around 11:30 a.m. for lunch, a swim, and a nice nap. Even during the off-season, when the crowds are smaller and the temperature more pleasant, the sheer size of the park will exhaust most children under age eight by lunchtime. Go back to the park in the late afternoon or early evening and continue your touring.

Where to Stay   The time and hassle involved in commuting to and from Disneyland will be somewhat reduced if you can afford to stay at the Disneyland Hotel or at another hotel within easy striking range. But even if, for financial or other reasons, you lodge relatively far away, it remains imperative that you get small children out of the park each day for a few hours to rest and recuperate. Neglecting to relax and unwind is the best way we know to get the whole family in a snit and ruin the day (or the entire vacation).

Relief from the frenetic pace of the theme park, even during the off-season, is indispensable. While it's true that you can gain some measure of peace by retreating to the Disneyland Hotel for lunch or by finding a quiet spot or restaurant in the theme park, there is really no substitute for returning to the familiarity and security of your own hotel. Regardless of what you may have heard or read, children too large to sleep in a stroller will not relax and revive unless you get them back to your hotel.

Thousands of rooms are available near Disneyland, many of them very affordable. With sufficient lead time you should have no difficulty finding accommodations that fulfill your requirements.

Be in Touch with Your Feelings   While we acknowledge that a Disneyland vacation seems like a major capital investment, remember that having fun is not necessarily the same as seeing everything. When you or your children start getting tired and irritable, call a time-out and regroup. Trust your instincts. What would really feel best right now? Another ride, a rest break with some ice cream, going back to the room for a nap? *The way to protect your investment is to stay happy and have a good time, whatever that takes.* You do not have to meet a quota for experiencing a certain number of attractions or watching parades or anything else. It's your vacation; you can do what you want.

Least Common Denominators   Remember the old saying about a chain being only as strong as its weakest link? The same logic applies to a family touring Disneyland. Somebody is going to run out of steam first, and when they do the whole family will be affected. Sometimes a cold soda and a rest break will get the flagging member back into gear. Sometimes, however, as Marshall Dillon would say, "You just need to get out of Dodge." Pushing the tired or discontented beyond their capacity is like driving on a flat tire: it may get you a few more miles down the road, but you will further damage your car in the process. Accept that energy levels vary among individuals, and be prepared to respond to small children or other members of your group who poop out. *Hint:* "After we've driven 600 miles to take you to Disneyland, you're going to ruin everything!" is not an appropriate response.

Setting Limits and Making Plans   The best way to avoid arguments and disappointment is to develop a game plan before you go. Establish some general guidelines for the day, and get everybody committed in advance. Be sure to include:

1. Wake-up time and breakfast plans.
2. What time you need to depart for the park.
3. What you need to take with you.
4. A policy for splitting the group up or for staying together.
5. A plan for what to do if the group gets separated or someone is lost.
6. How long you intend to tour in the morning and what you want to see, including fallback plans in the event an attraction is closed or too crowded.
7. A policy on what you can afford for snacks and refreshments.
8. A target time for returning to the hotel to rest.
9. What time you will return to the park, and how late you will stay.
10. Plans for dinner.
11. Advance agreement concerning bedtimes.
12. A policy for shopping and buying souvenirs, including who pays: Mom and Dad, or the kids.

Be Flexible   Having a game plan does not mean giving up spontaneity or sticking rigidly to an itinerary. Once again, listen to your intuition. Alter the plan if the situation warrants. Any day at Disneyland includes some surprises, so be prepared to roll with the punches.

About the *Unofficial Guide* Touring Plans   Parents who embark on one of our touring plans are often frustrated by the various interruptions and delays occasioned by their small children. In case you haven't given the subject much thought, here is what to expect:

1. Many small children will stop dead in their tracks whenever they see a Disney character. Our advice: live with it. An attempt to haul your children away before they have satisfied their curiosity is likely to precipitate anything from whining to a full-scale revolt.

2. The touring plans call for visiting attractions in a specified sequence, often skipping certain attractions along the way. Children do not like skipping *anything!* If they see something that attracts them they want to experience it *now.* Some children can be persuaded to skip attractions if parents explain things in advance. Other kids severely flip out at the threat of skipping something, particularly something in Fantasyland. A mom from Charleston, South Carolina, had this to say:

   Following the Touring Plans turned out to be a train wreck. The main problem with the plan is that it starts in Fantasyland. When we were on Dumbo, my five-year-old saw eight dozen other things in Fantasyland she wanted to see. The long and the short is that after Dumbo, there was no getting her out of there.

   Also on the subject of the touring plans, a Burlington, Vermont, mother of two made this observation:

   I found out that my kids were very curious about the castle because we had read Sleeping Beauty at home. Whenever I wanted to leave Fantasyland, I would just say "Let's go to the castle and see if Sleeping Beauty is there." Once we got as far as the front door to the castle it was no problem going out to the [central] hub and then to another land.

3. Children seem to have a genetic instinct when it comes to finding rest rooms. We have seen perfectly functional adults equipped with all manner of maps search interminably for a rest room. Small children, on the other hand, including those who cannot read, will head for the nearest rest room with the certainty of a homing pigeon. While you may skip certain attractions, you can be sure that your children will ferret out (and want to use) every rest room in the theme park.

Overheating, Sunburn, and Dehydration The most common problems for smaller children at Disneyland are overheating, sunburn, and dehydration. A small bottle of sunscreen carried in a pocket or fanny pack will help you take precautions against overexposure to the sun. Be sure to put some on children in strollers, even if the stroller has a canopy. Some of the worst cases of sunburn we have seen were on the exposed foreheads and feet of toddlers and infants in strollers. To avoid overheating, rest at regular intervals in the shade or in an air-conditioned restaurant or show.

Do not count on keeping small children properly hydrated with soft drinks and water fountain stops. Long lines often make buying refreshments problematic, and water fountains are not always handy. What's more, excited children may not realize or inform you that they're thirsty or overheated. We recommend renting a stroller for children age six years old and under and carrying plastic water bottles with you. If you forget to bring your own water containers, plastic squeeze bottles with caps are sold at the Emporium on Main Street for about $4.

Blisters   Sore feet and blisters are common for visitors of all ages, so wear comfortable, well-broken-in shoes and two pairs of thin socks (preferable to one pair of thick socks). If you or your children are unusually susceptible to blisters, carry some precut "Moleskin" bandages; they offer the best possible protection, stick great, and won't sweat off. When you feel a hot spot, stop, air out your foot, and place a Moleskin over the area before a blister forms. Moleskin is available by name at all drugstores. Sometimes small children won't tell their parents about a developing blister until it's too late. We recommend inspecting the feet of preschoolers two or more times a day.

First Aid   Registered nurses are on duty at all times in the First Aid Center, located two doors down from the Plaza Inn at the central hub end of Main Street. If you or your children have a medical problem, do not hesitate to use the First Aid Center. It's warmer and friendlier than most doctor's offices, and it's accustomed to treating everything from paper cuts to allergic reactions.

Children on Medication   For various reasons, some parents of children on medication for hyperactivity elect to discontinue or decrease the child's normal dosage at the close of the school year. Be forewarned that Disneyland might stimulate such a child to the point of system overload. Consult your physician before altering your child's medication regimen.

Sunglasses   If you want your smaller children to wear sunglasses, it's a good idea to affix a strap or string to the frames so the glasses will stay on during rides and can hang from the child's neck while indoors.

Things You Forgot or Things You Ran Out Of   Rain gear, diapers, diaper pins, formula, film, aspirin, topical sunburn treatments, and other sundries are available for sale at Disneyland. For some reason, rain gear is a bargain, but most other items are pretty high. Ask for goods you do not see displayed; some are stored behind the counter.

Strollers   They are available for a modest rental fee just inside the main entrance and to the right. The rental covers the entire day. If you rent a stroller and later decide to go back to your hotel for lunch, a swim, or a nap, turn in your stroller but hang on to your rental receipt. When you return to the park later in the day, present your receipt. You will be issued another stroller without an additional charge.

Strollers at Disneyland are large, sturdy models with sun canopies and cargo baskets. We have seen families load as many as three children on one of these strollers at the same time. The rental procedure is fast and efficient. Likewise, returning the stroller is a breeze. Even in the evening when several hundred strollers are turned in following the laser and fireworks show, there is no wait or hassle.

For infants and toddlers the strollers are a must, but we have observed many sharp parents renting strollers for somewhat older children (up to age five or six years). The stroller prevents parents from having to carry children when they run out of steam and provides an easy, convenient way to carry water, snacks, diaper bags, etc.

When you enter a show or board a ride, you will have to park your stroller, usually in an open, unprotected area. If it rains before you return, you will need a cloth, towel, or spare diaper to dry off the stroller.

Stroller Wars   Sometimes strollers disappear while you are enjoying a ride or a show. Do not be alarmed. You won't have to buy the missing stroller, and you will be issued a new stroller for your continued use. At Disneyland, replacement centers are located at the Star Trader in Tomorrowland, the Gag Factory in Mickey's Toontown, Pooh Corner in Critter Country, and Westward Ho in Frontierland. Lost strollers can also be replaced at the main rental facility near the park entrance.

While replacing a ripped-off stroller is no big deal, it is an inconvenience. One family complained that their stroller had been taken six times in one day. Even with free replacements, larceny on this scale represents a lot of wasted time. Through our own experiments, and suggestions from readers, we have developed several techniques for hanging on to your rented stroller:

1. Write your name in Magic Marker on a 6-by-9-inch card, put the card in a transparent freezer bag, and secure the bag to the handle of the stroller with masking or duct tape.

2. Affix something personal (but expendable) to the handle of the stroller. Evidently most strollers are pirated by mistake (since they all look the same) or because it's easier to swipe someone else's stroller (when yours

disappears) than to troop off to the replacement center. Since most stroller theft is a function of confusion, laziness, or revenge, the average pram pincher will balk at hauling off a stroller bearing another person's property. After trying several items, we concluded that a bright, inexpensive scarf or bandanna tied to the handle works well, and a sock partially stuffed with rags or paper works even better (the weirder and more personal the object, the greater the deterrent). Best of all is a dead mackerel dangling from the handle, though in truth, the kids who ride in the stroller prefer the other methods. Bound and determined not to have her stroller ripped off, an Ann Arbor, Michigan, mother describes her stroller security plan as follows:

> We used a variation on your stroller identification theme. We tied a clear plastic bag with a diaper in it on the stroller. Jon even poured a little root beer on the diaper for effect. Needless to say, no one took our stroller and it was easy to identify.

We receive quite a few letters from readers debating the pros and cons of bringing your own stroller versus renting one of Disney's. A mother from Falls Church, Virginia, with two small children opted for her own pram, commenting:

> I was glad I took my own stroller, because the rented strollers aren't appropriate for infants (we had a five-year-old and a five-month-old in tow). No one said anything about me using a bike lock to secure our brand-new Aprica stroller. However, an attendant came over and told us not to lock it anywhere, because it's a fire hazard! (Outside?) When I politely asked the attendant if she wanted to be responsible for my $300 stroller, she told me to go ahead and lock it but not tell anyone! I observed the attendants constantly moving the strollers. This seems very confusing—no wonder people think their strollers are getting ripped off!

As the reader mentioned, Disney cast members often rearrange strollers parked outside an attraction. Sometimes this is done simply to "tidy up." At other times the strollers are moved to make additional room along a walkway. In any event, do not assume that your stroller is stolen because it is missing from the exact place you left it. Check around. Chances are it will be "neatly arranged" just a few feet away.

Baby-Sitting Childcare services are unavailable in Disneyland and the Disneyland Hotel. An independent organization called the Fullerton Childcare Agency, however, provides in-room sitting for infants and children. If you pay the tab, Fullerton Childcare sitters will even take your kids to Disneyland.

All sitters are experienced and licensed to drive, and the Fullerton Child-care Agency is fully insured against theft. The basic rate for in-room sitting for one or two children is $36 for the first four hours, with a four-hour minimum, and $7 each hour thereafter. The charge for each additional child is $1 per hour. Combined families are charged $2 per hour for each additional child from the nonbooking family. There is no transportation fee, but the client is expected to pay for parking when applicable. All fees and charges must be paid in cash at the end of the assignment. To reserve a sitter, one or two days' advance notice is requested. You can reach Fullerton Childcare Agency by calling (714) 528-1640.

Caring for Infants and Toddlers   Disneyland has special centralized facilities for the care of infants and toddlers. Everything necessary for changing diapers, preparing formulas, warming bottles and food, etc., is available in ample quantity. A broad selection of baby supplies is for sale, and there are even rockers and special chairs for nursing mothers. Dads in charge of little ones are welcome at the Baby Center and can avail themselves of most services offered. In addition, babies can be changed without inconvenience in most of the larger rest rooms. The Baby Center is located across from the Plaza Inn at the central hub end of Main Street.

DISNEY, KIDS, AND SCARY STUFF

Disneyland is a family theme park. Yet some of the Disney adventure rides can be intimidating to small children. On certain rides, such as Splash Mountain and the roller-coaster rides (Space Mountain, Matterhorn Bobsleds, and Big Thunder Mountain Railroad), the ride itself may be frightening. On other rides, such as the Haunted Mansion and Snow White's Scary Adventures, it is the special effects. We recommend a little parent-child dialogue coupled with a "testing the water" approach. A child who is frightened by Pinocchio's Daring Journey should not have to sit through the Haunted Mansion. Likewise, if Big Thunder Mountain Railroad is too much, don't try Space Mountain or the Matterhorn Bobsleds.

Disney rides and shows are adventures. They focus on the substance and themes of all adventure, and indeed of life itself: good and evil, quest, death, beauty and the grotesque, fellowship and enmity. As you sample the variety of attractions at Disneyland, you transcend the mundane spinning and bouncing of midway rides to a more thought-provoking and emotionally powerful entertainment experience. Though the endings are all happy, the impact of the adventures, with Disney's gift for special effects, is often intimidating and occasionally frightening to small children.

There are rides with menacing witches, rides with burning towns, and rides with ghouls popping out of their graves, all done tongue-in-cheek and with a sense of humor, provided you are old enough to understand the joke. And bones, lots of bones: human bones, cattle bones, dinosaur bones, and whole skeletons are everywhere you look. There have to be more bones at Disneyland than at the Smithsonian Institute and UCLA Medical School combined. There is a stack of skulls at the headhunter's camp on the Jungle Cruise; a veritable platoon of skeletons sailing ghost ships in Pirates of the Caribbean; a haunting assemblage of skulls and

skeletons in the Haunted Mansion; and more skulls, skeletons, and bones punctuating Snow White's Scary Adventures, Peter Pan's Flight, and Big Thunder Mountain Railroad, to name a few.

One reader wrote us the following after taking his preschool children on Star Tours:

> *We took a four-year-old and a five-year-old and they had the shit scared out of them at Star Tours. We did this first thing in the morning and it took hours of Tom Sawyer Island and It's a Small World to get back to normal.*
>
> *Our kids were the youngest by far in Star Tours. I assume that either other adults had more sense or were not such avid readers of your book.*
>
> *Preschoolers should start with Dumbo and work up to the Jungle Cruise in the late morning, after being revved up and before getting hungry, thirsty, or tired. Pirates of the Caribbean is out for preschoolers. You get the idea.*

The reaction of young children to the inevitable system overload of Disneyland should be anticipated. Be sensitive, alert, and prepared for almost anything, even behavior that is out of character for your child at home. Most small children take Disney's variety of macabre trappings in stride, and others are quickly comforted by an arm around the shoulder or a little squeeze of the hand. For parents who have observed a tendency in their kids to become upset, we recommend taking it slow and easy by sampling more benign adventures like the Jungle Cruise, gauging reactions, and discussing with children how they felt about the things they saw.

Sometimes small children will rise above their anxiety in an effort to please their parents or siblings. This behavior, however, does not necessarily indicate a mastery of fear, much less enjoyment. If children come off a ride in ostensibly good shape, we recommend asking if they would like to go on the ride again (not necessarily right now, but sometime). The response to this question will usually give you a clue as to how much they actually enjoyed the experience. There is a lot of difference between having a good time and mustering the courage to get through something.

Evaluating a child's capacity to handle the visual and tactile effects of Disneyland requires patience, understanding, and experimentation. Each of us, after all, has our own demons. If a child balks at or is frightened by a ride, respond constructively. Let your children know that lots of people, adults as well as children, are scared by what they see and feel. Help them understand that it is okay with you if they get frightened and that their fear does not lessen your love or respect. Take pains not to compound the discomfort by making a child feel inadequate; try not to undermine self-esteem, impugn courage, or subject a child to ridicule. Most of all, do not induce guilt, as if your child's trepidation is ruining the family's fun. When older siblings are present, it is sometimes necessary to restrain their taunting and teasing.

A visit to Disneyland is more than an outing or an adventure for a small child. It is a testing experience, a sort of controlled rite of passage. If you help your little one work through the challenges, the time can be immeasurably rewarding and a bonding experience for both of you.

The Fright Factor

While each youngster is different, there are essentially six attraction elements that alone or combined can punch a child's buttons:

1. The Name of the Attraction   Small children will naturally be apprehensive about something called the "Haunted Mansion" or "Snow White's Scary Adventures."

2. The Visual Impact of the Attraction from Outside   Splash Mountain and Big Thunder Mountain Railroad look scary enough to give even adults second thoughts. To many small children these rides are visually terrifying.

3. The Visual Impact of the Indoor Queuing Area   Pirates of the Caribbean with its dark bayou scene and the Haunted Mansion with its "stretch rooms" are capable of frightening small children before they even board the ride.

4. The Intensity of the Attraction   Some attractions are so intense as to be overwhelming; they inundate the senses with sights, sounds, movement, and even smell. *Honey, I Shrunk the Audience,* for instance, combines loud music, laser effects, lights, and 3D cinematography to create a total sensory experience. For some preschoolers, this is two or three senses too many.

5. The Visual Impact of the Attraction Itself   As previously discussed, the sights in various attractions range from falling boulders to lurking buzzards, from grazing dinosaurs to attacking hippos. What one child calmly absorbs may scare the owl poop out of another child the same age.

6. Dark   Many Disneyland attractions are "dark" rides, i.e., they operate indoors in a dark environment. For some children, this fact alone is sufficient to trigger significant apprehension. A child who is frightened on one dark ride, for example Snow White's Scary Adventures, may be unwilling to try other indoor rides.

7. The Ride Itself; the Tactile Experience   Some Disney rides are downright wild—wild enough to induce motion sickness, wrench backs, and generally discombobulate patrons of any age.

A Bit of Preparation

We receive many tips from parents relating how they prepared their small children for their Disneyland experience. A common strategy is to acquaint children with the characters and the stories behind the attractions by reading Disney books and watching Disney videos at home. A more direct approach is to rent Disneyland travel videos that actually show the various attractions. Concerning the latter, a father from Arlington, Virginia, reported:

> *My kids both loved the Haunted Mansion, with appropriate preparation. We rented a tape before going so they could see it, and then I told them it was all "Mickey Mouse Magic" and that Mickey was just "joking you," to put it in their terms, and that there weren't any real ghosts, and that Mickey wouldn't let anyone actually get hurt.*

A mother from Gloucester, Massachusetts, handled her son's preparation a bit more extemporaneously:

> *The 3½-year-old liked It's a Small World, [but] was afraid of the Haunted Mansion. We just pulled his hat over his face and quietly talked to him while we enjoyed [the ride].*

ATTRACTIONS THAT EAT ADULTS

You may spend so much energy worrying about Junior's welfare that you forget to take care of yourself. If the ride component of the attraction (i.e., the actual motion and movement of the conveyance itself) is potentially disturbing, persons of any age may be adversely affected. There are several attractions that are likely to cause motion sickness or other problems for older children and adults.

Attractions That Eat Adults	
Tomorrowland	Star Tours
	Space Mountain
	Rocket Rods
Fantasyland	Mad Tea Party
	Matterhorn Bobsleds
Frontierland	Big Thunder Mountain Railroad
Adventureland	Indiana Jones Adventure
Critter Country	Splash Mountain

Small Child Fright Potential Chart

As a quick reference, we have provided a "Fright Potential Chart" to warn you which attractions to be wary of and why. Remember that the chart represents a generalization and that all kids are different. The chart relates specifically to kids three to seven years of age. On average, as you would expect, children at the younger end of the age range are more likely to be frightened than children in their sixth or seventh year.

Main Street, U.S.A.

Disneyland Railroad: Tunnel with dinosaur display frightens some small children.

The Walt Disney Story, featuring "Great Moments with Mr. Lincoln": Not frightening in any respect.

Main Street Cinema: Not frightening in any respect.

Main Street Vehicles: Not frightening in any respect.

Adventureland

Swiss Family Treehouse: Not frightening in any respect.

Jungle Cruise: Moderately intense, with some macabre sights; a good test attraction for little ones.

Enchanted Tiki Room: A small thunderstorm momentarily surprises very young children.

Indiana Jones Adventure: Visually intimidating with intense effects and a wild jerky ride. Switching-off option provided (see page 87).

New Orleans Square

Pirates of the Caribbean: Slightly intimidating queuing area; an intense boat ride with gruesome (though humorously presented) sights and two short, unexpected slides down flumes.

Haunted Mansion: Name of attraction raises anxiety, as do sights and sounds of waiting area. An intense attraction with humorously presented macabre sights. The ride itself is gentle.

Critter Country

Splash Mountain: Visually intimidating from the outside. Moderately intense visual effects. The ride itself is somewhat hair-raising for all ages, culminating in a 52-foot plunge down a steep chute. Switching-off option provided (see page 87).

Country Bear Playhouse: Not frightening in any respect.

Davy Crockett's Explorer Canoes: Not frightening in any respect.

Frontierland

Big Thunder Mountain Railroad: Visually intimidating from the outside with moderately intense visual effects. The roller coaster is wild enough to frighten many adults, particularly seniors. Switching-off option provided (see page 87).

Tom Sawyer Island: Some very small children are intimidated by dark, walk-through tunnels that can be easily avoided.

Frontierland Shootin' Exposition: Not frightening in any respect.

Golden Horseshoe Jamboree: Not frightening in any respect.

Mike Fink Keelboats: Not frightening in any respect.

Mark Twain Riverboat: Not frightening in any respect.

Sailing Ship Columbia: Not frightening in any respect.

Fantasyland

Mad Tea Party: Midway-type ride can induce motion sickness in all ages.

Mr. Toad's Wild Ride: Name of ride intimidates some. Moderately intense spook-house genre attraction with jerky ride. Only frightens a small percentage of preschoolers.

Snow White's Scary Adventures: Moderately intense spook-house genre attraction with some grim characters. Absolutely terrifying to many preschoolers.

Dumbo, the Flying Elephant: A tame midway ride; a great favorite of most small children.

King Arthur Carrousel: Not frightening in any respect.

It's a Small World: Not frightening in any respect.

Peter Pan's Flight: Not frightening in any respect.

Alice in Wonderland: Pretty benign, but frightens a small percentage of preschoolers.

Pinocchio's Daring Journey: Less frightening than Alice in Wonderland, but scares a few very young preschoolers.

Matterhorn Bobsleds: The ride itself is wilder than Big Thunder Mountain Railroad, but not as wild as Space Mountain. Switching off is an option (see page 87).

Casey Jr. Circus Train: Not frightening in any respect.

Storybook Land Canal Boats: Not frightening in any respect.

Mickey's Toontown

Mickey's House: Not frightening in any respect.

Minnie's House: Not frightening in any respect.

Roger Rabbit's Car Toon Spin: Intense special effects, coupled with a dark environment and wild ride; frightens many preschoolers.

Gadget's Go-Coaster: Tame as far as roller coasters go, but frightens some small children.

Chip 'n' Dale's Treehouse and Acorn Ball Crawl: Not frightening in
any respect.
Miss Daisy, Donald Duck's Boat: Not frightening in any respect.
Goofy's Bounce House: Not frightening in any respect.
Jolly Trolley: Not frightening in any respect.

Tomorrowland

Star Tours: Extremely intense visually for all ages; the ride itself is
one of the wildest in Disney's repertoire. Switching-off option
provided (see page 87).
Honey, I Shrunk the Audience: Extremely intense visual effects and
the loud volume scare many preschoolers.
Submarine Voyage: May frighten a very small percentage of
preschoolers. Less intense than Jungle Cruise.
Space Mountain: Very intense roller coaster in the dark;
Disneyland's wildest ride and a scary roller coaster by anyone's
standards. Switching-off option provided (see page 87).
AstroOrbiter: Waiting area is visually intimidating to preschoolers.
The ride is a lot higher, but just a bit wilder, than Dumbo.
Tomorrowland Autopia: The noise in the waiting area slightly
intimidates preschoolers; otherwise, not frightening.
Disneyland Monorail: Not frightening in any respect.
Rocket Rods: The speed combined with intense effects frightens many
young children. Switching-off option provided (see page 87).

Waiting Line Strategies for Adults with Small Children

Children hold up better through the day if you minimize the time they
have to spend in lines. Arriving early and using the touring plans in this
guide will reduce waiting time immensely. There are, however, additional
measures you can employ to reduce stress on little ones.

1. Line Games It is a smart parent who anticipates how restless children
get waiting in line and how a little structured activity can relieve the stress
and boredom. In the morning kids handle the inactivity of waiting in line
by discussing what they want to see and do during the course of the day.

Later, however, as events wear on, they need a little help. Watching for, and counting, Disney characters is a good diversion. Simple guessing games like "20 Questions" also work well. Lines for rides move so continuously that games requiring pen and paper are cumbersome and impractical. Waiting in the holding area of a theater attraction, however, is a different story. Here tic-tac-toe, hangman, drawing, and coloring can really make the time go by.

2. Last-Minute Entry   If a ride or show can accommodate an unusually large number of people at one time, it is often unnecessary to stand in line. The Mark Twain Riverboat in Frontierland is a good example. The boat holds about 450 people, usually more than are waiting in line to ride. Instead of standing uncomfortably in a crowd with dozens of other guests, grab a snack and sit in the shade until the boat arrives and loading is well under way. After the line has all but disappeared, go ahead and board.

With large-capacity theaters like *Honey, I Shrunk the Audience* in Tomorrowland, ask the entrance greeter how long it will be until guests are admitted to the theater for the next show. If the answer is 15 minutes or more, use the time for a rest room break or to get a snack; you can return to the attraction just a few minutes before the show starts. You will not be permitted to carry any food or drink into the attraction, so make sure you have time to finish your snack before entering.

The following are attractions you can usually enter at the last minute:

Main Street	*The Walt Disney Story*
Frontierland	Mark Twain Riverboat
	Sailing Ship *Columbia*
Critter Country	*Country Bear Playhouse*
Tomorrowland	*Honey, I Shrunk the Audience*

3. The Hail-Mary Pass   Certain waiting lines are configured in such a way that you and your smaller children can pass under the rail to join your partner just before boarding or entry. This technique allows the kids and one adult to rest, snack, cool off, or tinkle, while another adult or older sibling does the waiting. Other guests are understanding when it comes to using this strategy to keep small children content. You are likely to meet hostile opposition, however, if you try to pass older children or more than one adult under the rail. Attractions where it is usually possible to complete a Hail-Mary Pass include:

Adventureland	Swiss Family Treehouse
	Jungle Cruise
Fantasyland	Mad Tea Party
	Mr. Toad's Wild Ride
	Snow White's Scary Adventures

Fantasyland (cont.)	Dumbo, the Flying Elephant
	King Arthur Carrousel
	Peter Pan's Flight
	Casey Jr. Circus Train
	Storybook Land Canal Boats
Tomorrowland	Tomorrowland Autopia

4. Switching Off (also known as The Baby Swap)   Several attractions have minimum height and/or age requirements, usually 3' 4" tall to ride with an adult, or seven years of age *and* 3' 4" tall to ride alone. Some couples with children too small or too young forgo these attractions, while others split up and takes turns riding separately. Missing out on some of Disney's best rides is an unnecessary sacrifice, and waiting in line twice for the same ride is a tremendous waste of time.

A better way to approach the problem is to take advantage of an option known as "switching off" or "The Baby Swap." To switch off there must be at least two adults. Everybody waits in line together, both adults and children. When you reach a Disney attendant (known as a "greeter"), say you want to switch off. The greeter will allow everyone, including the small children, to enter the attraction. When you reach the loading area, one adult will ride while the other stays with the kids. The riding adult disembarks and takes responsibility for the children while the other adult rides. A third adult in the party can ride twice, once with each of the switching-off adults, so they do not have to experience the attraction alone. There are seven attractions where switching off is routinely practiced:

Tomorrowland	Star Tours
	Space Mountain
	Rocket Rods
Adventureland	Indiana Jones Adventure
Fantasyland	Matterhorn Bobsleds
Critter Country	Splash Mountain
Frontierland	Big Thunder Mountain Railroad

An Ada, Michigan, mother who discovered that the procedure for switching off varies from attraction to attraction offered this suggestion:

> *Parents need to tell the very first attendant they come to that they would like to switch-off. Each attraction has a different procedure for this. Tell every other attendant too, because they forget quickly.*

5. How to Ride Twice in a Row without Waiting   Many small children like to ride a favorite attraction two or more times in succession. Riding the second time often gives the child a feeling of mastery and accomplishment. Unfortunately, even in the early morning, repeat rides can be time-consuming. If you ride Dumbo as soon as Disneyland opens, for instance, you will only have a one or two-minute wait for your first ride. When you come back for your second ride, your wait will be about 12 minutes. If you want to ride a third time, count on a 20-minute or longer wait.

The best way for getting your child on the ride twice (or more) without blowing your whole morning is by using the "Chuck Bubba Relay" (named in honor of a reader from Kentucky):

a. Mom and little Bubba enter the waiting line.
b. Dad lets a certain number of people go in front of him (32 in the case of Dumbo) and then gets in line.
c. As soon as the ride stops, Mom exits with little Bubba and passes him to Dad to ride the second time.
d. If everybody is really getting into this, Mom can hop in line again, no less than 32 people behind Dad.

The Chuck Bubba Relay will not work on every ride because of differences in the way the waiting areas are configured (i.e., it is impossible in some cases to exit the ride and make the pass). For those rides where the Chuck Bubba Relay does work, however, here are the number of people to count off:

Mad Tea Party	53 people
Mr. Toad's Wild Ride	32 people
Snow White's Scary Adventures	30 people
Dumbo, the Flying Elephant	32 people
Alice in Wonderland	38 people (tough, but possible)
Casey Jr. Circus Train	34 people, if 2 trains are operating
King Arthur Carrousel	70 people
Peter Pan's Flight	25 people
Davy Crockett's Explorer Canoes	94 people, if 6 canoes are operating

If you are the second adult in line, you will reach a point in the waiting area that is obviously the easiest place to make the hand-off. Sometimes this point is where those exiting the ride pass closest to those waiting to board. In any event, you will know it when you see it. Once there, if the first parent has not arrived with little Bubba, just let those behind you slip past until Bubba shows up.

6. Last-Minute Cold Feet   If your small child gets cold feet at the last minute after waiting for a ride (where there is no age or height requirement), you can usually arrange with the loading attendant for a switch-off.

Switching Off

This situation arises frequently at Pirates of the Caribbean—small children lose their courage en route to the loading area.

There is no law that says you have to ride. If you get to the boarding area and someone is unhappy, just tell a Disney attendant you have changed your mind, and one will show you the way out.

7. Elevator Shoes for the Short and Brave   If you have a child who is crazy to go on the rides with height requirements, but who is just a little too short, slip heel lifts into his Nikes before he gets to the measuring point. Be sure to leave the heel lifts in because he may get measured again at the boarding area.

8. Throw Yourself on the Grenade, Mildred!   For by-the-book, do-the-right-thing parents determined to sacrifice themselves on behalf of their children, we provide a One-Day Touring Plan called the "Dumbo-or-Die-in-a-Day Touring Plan, for Parents with Small Children." This touring plan, detailed on pages 190–193, will ensure that you run yourself ragged. Designed to help you forfeit everything of personal interest for the sake of your children's pleasure, the plan is guaranteed to send you home battered and exhausted with extraordinary stories of devotion and heroic perseverance. By the way, the plan really works. Anyone under eight years old will love it.

9. Catch-22 at the Tomorrowland Autopia   Though the Autopia is a great treat for small children, they are required to be 4' 4" tall in order to drive. Since very few children age six and under top this height, the ride is essentially withheld from the very age group that would most enjoy it. To resolve this catch-22, go on the ride with your small child. The attendants will assume that you will drive. After getting into the car, however, shift your child over behind the steering wheel. From your position you will still be able to control the foot pedals. To your child it will feel like driving. Because the car travels on a self-guiding track, there is no way your child can make a mistake while steering.

10. Submarine Voyage   This attraction is a lot better at night, but don't expect short lines unless you ride during the evening parades, riverfront shows, or fireworks.

Lost Children

Lost children normally do not present much of a problem at Disneyland. All Disneyland employees are schooled in handling such situations should they arise. If you lose a child while touring, report the situation to a Disney employee; then check in at City Hall where lost children "logs" are maintained. In an emergency, an "alert" can be issued throughout the park through internal communications. If a Disney cast member (employee) encounters a lost child, the cast member will escort the child immediately to the Lost Children Office located by First Aid at the central hub end of Main Street.

It is amazingly easy to lose a child (or two) at Disneyland. We suggest that children under age eight be color-coded by dressing them in purple T-shirts or equally distinctive attire. It is also a good idea to sew a label into each child's shirt that states his or her name, your name, and the name of your hotel. The same thing can be accomplished less elegantly by writing the information on a strip of masking tape; hotel security professionals suggest that the information be printed in small letters, and that the tape be affixed to the outside of the child's shirt five inches or so below the armpit.

How Kids Get Lost

Children get separated from their parents every day at Disneyland under circumstances that are remarkably similar (and predictable).

1. Preoccupied Solo Parent In this scenario the only adult in the party is preoccupied with something like buying refreshments, loading the camera, or using the rest room. Junior is there one second and gone the next.

2. The Hidden Exit Sometimes parents wait on the sidelines while allowing two or more young children to experience a ride together. As it usually happens, the parents expect the kids to exit the attraction in one place and, lo and behold, the young ones pop out somewhere else. The exits of some Disney attractions are considerably distant from the entrances. Make sure you know exactly where your children will emerge before letting them ride by themselves.

3. After the Show At the completion of many shows and rides, a Disney staffer will announce, "Check for personal belongings and take small children by the hand." When dozens, if not hundreds, of people leave an attraction at the same time it is easy for parents to temporarily lose contact with their children unless they have them directly in tow.

4. Rest Room Problems Mom tells six-year-old Tommy, "I'll be sitting on this bench when you come out of the rest room." Three situations: One, Tommy exits through a different door and becomes disoriented (Mom may not know there is another door). Two, Mom decides belatedly that she will also use the rest room, and Tommy emerges to find her absent. Three, Mom pokes around in a shop while keeping an eye on the bench, but misses Tommy when he comes out.

If you cannot be with your child in the rest room, make sure there is only one exit. Designate a meeting spot more distinctive than a bench, and be specific and thorough in your instructions: "I'll meet you by this flag-pole. If you get out first, stay right here." Have your child repeat the directions back to you.

5. Parades   There are many special parades and shows at the theme park during which the audience stands. Children, because they are small, tend to jockey around for a better view. By moving a little this way and a little that way, it is amazing how much distance kids can put between you and them before anyone notices.

6. Mass Movements   Another situation to guard against is when huge crowds disperse after *Fantasmic!*, fireworks, a parade, or at park closing. With 5,000 to 12,000 people suddenly moving at once, it is very easy to get separated from a small child or others in your party. Extra caution is recommended following the evening parades, fireworks, and *Fantasmic!* Families should develop specific plans for what to do and where to meet in the event they are separated.

7. Character Greetings   A fair amount of activity and confusion is commonplace when the Disney characters are on the scene. See the next section on meeting the Disney characters.

The Disney Characters

For many years the costumed, walking versions of Mickey, Minnie, Donald, Goofy, and others have been a colorful supporting cast at Disneyland and Walt Disney World. Known unpretentiously as the "Disney characters," these large and friendly figures help provide a link between Disney animated films and the Disney theme parks.

Audiences, it has been observed, cry during the sad parts of Disney animated films and cheer when the villain is vanquished. To the emotionally invested, the characters in these features are as real as next-door neighbors, never mind they are simply drawings on plastic. In recent years, the theme park personifications of Disney characters have likewise become real to us. For thousands of visitors, it is not just some person in a mouse costume they see, it is really Mickey. Similarly, running into Goofy or Snow White in Fantasyland is a memory to be treasured, an encounter with a real celebrity.

About 250 of the Disney animated film characters have been brought to life in costume. Of these, a relatively small number (about 35) are "greeters" (the Disney term for characters who mix with the patrons). The remaining characters are relegated exclusively to performing in shows or participating in parades. Some only appear once or twice a year, usually in Christmas parades or Disney anniversary celebrations.

"I'm sorry, mister. He thinks you're a Disney character."

Character Watching   Character watching has developed into a pastime. Where families were once content to stumble across a character occasionally, they now relentlessly pursue them armed with autograph books and cameras. For those who pay attention, some characters are much more frequently encountered than others. Mickey, Minnie, and Goofy, for example, are seemingly everywhere, while Winnie the Pooh comes out only on rare occasions. Other characters can be seen regularly, but limit themselves to a specific location.

The fact that some characters are seldom seen has turned character watching into character collecting. Mickey Mouse may be the best known and most loved character, but from a collector's perspective he is also the most common. To get an autograph from Mickey is no big deal, but Daisy Duck's signature is a real coup. Commercially tapping into the character-collecting movement, Disney sells autograph books throughout Disneyland.

Preparing Your Children to Meet the Characters   Since most small children are not expecting Minnie Mouse to be the size of a forklift, it's best to discuss the characters with your kids before you go. Almost all of the characters are quite large, and several, like Brer Bear, are huge! All of them can be extremely intimidating to a preschooler.

On first encounter, it is important not to thrust your child on the character. Allow the little one to come to terms with this big thing from whatever distance the child feels safe. If two adults are present, one should stay close to the youngster while the other approaches the character and demonstrates that the character is safe and friendly. Some kids warm to the characters immediately, while some never do. Most take a little time, and often require several different encounters.

There are two kinds of characters: those whose costume includes a face-covering headpiece (animal characters plus some human characters like Captain Hook), and "face characters," who are actors who resemble the cartoon characters to such an extent that no mask or headpiece is necessary. Face characters include Mary Poppins, Ariel, Jasmine, Aladdin, Cinderella, Belle, Snow White, and Prince Charming, to name a few.

Only the face characters are allowed to speak. Headpiece characters do not talk or make noises of any kind. Because the cast members could not possibly imitate the distinctive cinema voice of the character, the Disney folks have determined it is more effective to keep them silent. Lack of speech notwithstanding, the headpiece characters are extremely warm and responsive and communicate very effectively with gestures. As with the characters' size, children need to be forewarned that the characters do not talk.

Parents need to understand that some of the character costumes are very cumbersome and that cast members often suffer from very poor visibility. You have to look close, but the eye holes are frequently in the mouth of the costume or even down on the neck. What this means in practical terms is that the characters are sort of clumsy and have a limited field of vision. Children who approach the character from the back or the side may not be noticed, even if the child is touching the character. It is perfectly possible in this situation for the character to accidentally step on the child or knock him or her down. The best way for a child to approach a character is from the front, and occasionally not even this works. For example, the various duck characters (Donald, Daisy, Uncle Scrooge, etc.), have to peer around their bills. If it appears that the character is ignoring your child, pick your child up and hold her in front of the character until the character responds.

It is okay to touch, pat, or hug the character if your child is so inclined. Understanding the unpredictability of children, the characters will keep their feet very still, particularly refraining from moving backwards or to the side. Most of the characters will sign autographs or pose for pictures. Once again, be sure to approach from the front so that the character will understand your intentions. If your child collects autographs, it is a good idea to carry a big, fat pen about the size of a magic marker. The costumes make it exceedingly difficult for the characters to wield a smaller pen, so the bigger the better.

The Big Hurt   Many children expect to bump into Mickey the minute they enter the park and are disappointed when he is not around. If your children are unable to settle down and enjoy things until they see Mickey, simply ask a Disney cast member where to find him. If the cast member does not know Mickey's whereabouts, he or she can find out for you in short order.

"Then Some Confusion Happened"   Be forewarned that character encounters give rise to a situation during which small children sometimes get lost. There is usually a lot of activity around a character, with both adults and children touching the character or posing for pictures. In the most common scenario, the parents stay in the crowd while their child marches up to get acquainted. With the excitement of the encounter, all the milling people, and the character moving around, a child may get turned around and head off in the wrong direction. In the words of a Salt

Lake City mom: "Milo was shaking hands with Dopey one minute, then some confusion happened and he [Milo] was gone." Families with several small children, and parents who are busy fooling around with cameras, can lose track of a youngster in a heartbeat. Our recommendation for parents of preschoolers is to stay with the kids when they meet the characters, stepping back only long enough to take a picture, if necessary.

Meeting Characters   You can *see* the Disney characters in live shows and in parades. For times, consult your daily entertainment schedule. If you have the time and money, you can share a meal with the characters (more about this later). But if you want to *meet* the characters, get autographs, and take photos, it's helpful to know where the characters hang out.

Responding to guest requests, Disneyland has added a lot of new information about characters on its handout park map. On the reverse side of the map, a listing specifies where and when certain characters will be available, and also provides information on character dining. On the map of the park itself, yellow stars are used to denote locations where characters can be found.

The last few years have seen a number of Disney initiatives aimed at satisfying guests' inexhaustible desire to meet the characters. In essence, Disney relegated four of the "fab five" (Mickey, Minnie, Pluto, and Donald) to all-day tours of duty in Mickey's Toontown. The fifth "fab," Goofy, works a similar schedule most days in Frontierland. Likewise, Pooh and Tigger can usually be found in Critter Country, Beauty and the Beast in Fantasyland, and Aladdin and Jasmine in Adventureland. Characters less in demand roam the lands consistent with their image (Brer Bear and Brer Fox in Critter Country, for example).

While making the characters routinely available has taken the guesswork out of finding them, it has likewise robbed character encounters of much of their surprise spontaneity. Instead of chancing on a character as you turn a corner, it is much more common now to wait in a queue in order to meet the character. Speaking of which, be aware that lines for face characters move m-u-c-h more slowly than do lines for nonspeaking characters. As you might surmise, because face characters are allowed to talk, they do, often engaging children in lengthy conversations, much to the consternation of the families stuck in the queue.

If you believe there are already quite enough lines in Disneyland, and furthermore, if you prefer to bump into your characters on the run, here's where the bears and chipmunks roam. There will almost always be a character in Town Square on Main Street and often at the central hub. Characters make appearances in all the "lands," but are particularly thick in Fantasyland and Mickey's Toontown. Snow White, Cinderella, and Princess Aurora hang out in the courtyard of the castle; Brer Fox and Brer Bear cruise Critter Country; and Pocahontas meets and greets in Frontierland. Characters not specifically mentioned continue to turn up randomly throughout the park.

Characters are also featured in the afternoon and evening parades, Frontierland waterfront shows, *Fantasmic!,* and shows on the Fantasyland Theatre stage. Characters also play a major role in shows at the Tomorrowland Terrace stage. Performance times for all of the shows and parades are listed in the Disneyland daily entertainment schedule. After the shows, characters will sometimes stick around to greet the audience.

Mickey Mouse is available to meet guests and pose for photos all day long in his dressing room at Mickey's Movie Barn in Mickey's Toontown. To reach the Movie Barn, proceed through the front door of Mickey's House and follow the crowd. If the line extends back to the entrance of Mickey's House, it will take you about 25–30 minutes to actually reach Mickey. When you finally get to his dressing room, one or two families at a time are admitted for a short, personal audience with Mickey.

"Casting? This is George at the character breakfast. There's been a mistake. We were supposed to get the Assorted Character Package with 1 Mickey, 1 Goofy, 1 Donald, 1 Pluto . . ."

Many children are so excited about meeting Mickey that they cannot relax to enjoy the other attractions. If Mickey looms large in your child's day, board the Disneyland Railroad at the Main Street Station as soon as you arrive at the park, and proceed directly to Mickey's Toontown (half a circuit). If you visit Mickey before 10 a.m., your wait will be short.

Minnie receives guests at her house most of the day as well, and Donald and Pluto are available for photos and autographs in the gazebo situated in front of the Toontown Town Hall. There is, of course, a separate line for each character. Also, be aware that the characters bug out for parades and certain other special performances. Check the daily entertainment schedule on the handout park map for performance times and plan your Toontown visit accordingly.

Character Dining   Guests traveling on certain Disneyland packages purchased through the Walt Disney Travel Company, the Magic Kingdom Club, or from independent tour operators can participate in a program called Magic Morning. Magic Morning allows guests into Disneyland 60–90 minutes before the park's opening; they can take a circuit trip on the Disneyland Railroad, enjoy certain attractions, and dine at a character breakfast. While the early bird breakfast permits eligible guests to have breakfast and meet some characters, the real selling point is being admitted to the park early. Packages that include Magic Morning are available for the Disneyland Hotel as well as for several less expensive lodging properties in the Disneyland area.

Those who wish to dine with the characters on days when the park opens early can go to a character breakfast at the Tomorrow Terrace (at the central hub end of Main Street and to the right). Served daily from 9 to 10:45 a.m., menu items range from $2 to 9. Seating is on a first-come, first-served basis. While many different characters attend, Mickey and Minnie are almost never among them.

Finally, there are excellent breakfast, lunch, and dinner character buffets at Goofy's Kitchen at the Disneyland Hotel. Chip 'n' Dale host breakfast and lunch, and Cinderella takes over at dinner. However, characters change every few months, so call ahead if you are interested. Breakfast is served daily from 7 to 11:30 a.m.; lunch is served Saturday and Sunday only from noon to 2:30 p.m.; dinner is served daily from 5 to 9 p.m. Generally the food is good. Children have their own child-sized serving line featuring their favorite foods. At dinner, for example, the children's serving line includes some combination of hot dogs, spaghetti, macaroni and cheese, minihamburgers, pizza, chicken nuggets, and fried fish. The adult line is separate and offers more sophisticated fare. Adult prices are about $15 for breakfast and lunch, and $18 for dinner. Children ages 4–12 eat for about $9 at all three meals, while children ages 3 and under are charged $3.

Part Four

Disneyland
in Detail

Arriving and Getting Oriented

If you drive, you will probably be directed to the new parking lot on the northwest corner of Katella Avenue and West Street. Parking costs $7 and the lot is large. Be sure to make a note of your section, row, and space. A tram will transport you to either the park entrance or to a tram loading/ unloading area connected to the entrance by a pedestrian corridor. Stroller and wheelchair rentals are to the right just beyond the turnstile. As you enter Main Street, City Hall is to your left, serving as the center for general information, lost and found, and entertainment information.

If you haven't been given a freebie Disneyland park map by now, City Hall is the place to pick one up. The map contains the daily entertainment schedule for live shows, parades, and other events; tells you where to find

Not to Be Missed at Disneyland	
Adventureland	Jungle Cruise
	Indiana Jones Adventure
Critter Country	Splash Mountain
New Orleans Square	Haunted Mansion
	Pirates of the Caribbean
Tomorrowland	Space Mountain
	Honey, I Shrunk the Audience
	Star Tours
Frontierland	Big Thunder Mountain Railroad
Live Entertainment	*Fantasmic!*

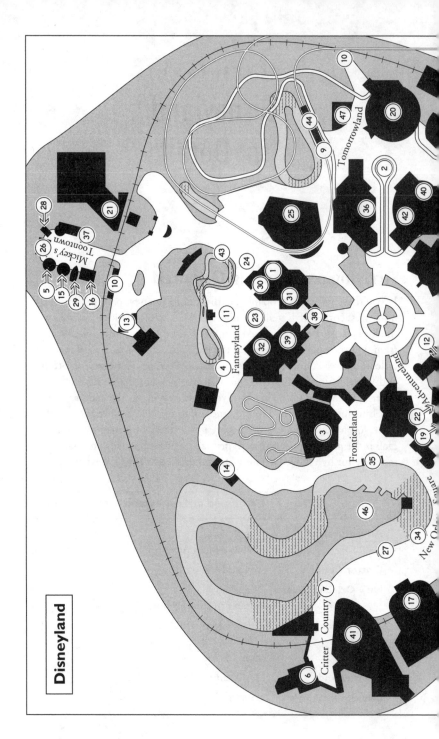

Disneyland

Mickey's Toontown

Fantasyland

Tomorrowland

Adventureland

Frontierland

New Orleans Square

Critter Country

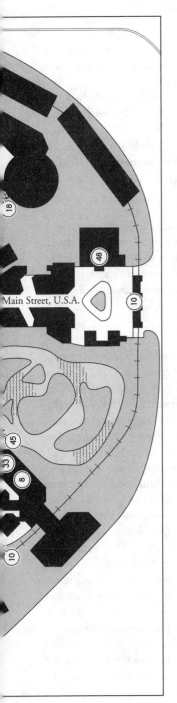

Main Street, U.S.A.

the characters; offers tips for good photos; lists all the attractions, shops, and eating places; and provides helpful information about first aid, baby care, assistance for the disabled, and more.

Notice on your map that Main Street ends at a central hub from which branch the entrances to four other sections of Disneyland: Adventureland, Frontierland, Fantasyland, and Tomorrowland. Two other "lands," New Orleans Square and Critter Country, can be reached through Adventureland and Frontierland. The newest land, Mickey's Toontown, is located on the far side of the railroad tracks from It's a Small World in Fantasyland. Sleeping Beauty Castle serves as the entrance to Fantasyland and is a focal landmark and the visual center of the park. The castle is a great place to meet if your group decides to split up for any reason during the day, and it can serve as an emergency meeting place if you are accidentally separated. Keep in mind, however, that the castle covers a lot of territory, so be specific about *where* to meet at the castle. Also be forewarned that parades and live shows sometimes make it difficult to access the entrance of the castle fronting the central hub.

STARTING THE TOUR

Everyone will soon find his or her own favorite and not-so-favorite attractions in Disneyland. Be open-minded and adventuresome. Don't dismiss a particular ride or show as not being for you until *after* you have tried it. Our personal experience as well as our research indicates that each visitor is different in terms of which Disney offerings he or she most enjoys. So don't miss seeing an attraction because a friend from home didn't like it; that attraction may turn out to be your favorite.

We do recommend that you take advantage of what Disney does best— the fantasy adventures like the Indiana Jones Adventure and the Haunted Mansion, and the AudioAnimatronic (talking robots, so to speak) attractions such as the Pirates of the Caribbean. Unless you have almost unlimited time, don't burn a lot of daylight browsing through the shops. Except for some special Disney souvenirs, you can find much of the same merchandise elsewhere. Try to minimize the time you spend on midway-type rides; you've probably got an amusement park, carnival, or state fair closer to your hometown. Don't, however, mistake rides like Space Mountain and the Big Thunder Mountain Railroad for amusement park rides. They may be of the roller-coaster genre, but they represent pure Disney genius. Similarly, do not devote a lot of time to waiting in lines for meals. Eat a good early breakfast before you come, snack on vendor-sold foods during the touring day, or follow the suggestions for meals incorporated into the various touring plans presented.

Main Street, U.S.A.

This section of Disneyland is where you'll begin and end your visit. We have already mentioned that assistance and information are available at City Hall. The Disneyland Railroad stops at the Main Street Station, and you can board here for a grand circle tour of the park, or you can get off the train in New Orleans Square, Mickey's Toontown/Fantasyland, or Tomorrowland.

Main Street is an idealized version of a turn-of-the-century American small-town street. Many visitors are surprised to discover that all the buildings are real, not elaborate props. Attention to detail here is exceptional—interiors, furnishings, and fixtures conform to the period. As with any real Main Street, the Disney version is essentially a collection of shops and eating places, with a city hall, a fire station, and an old-time cinema. A mixed-media attraction combines a presentation on the life of Walt Disney *(The Walt Disney Story)* with a patriotic remembrance of Abraham Lincoln. Horse-drawn trolleys, fire engines, and horseless carriages give rides along Main Street and transport visitors to the central hub (properly known as the Central Plaza).

Main Street Services

Most of the park's service facilities are centered in the Main Street section, including the following:

Wheelchair and Stroller Rental	To the right of the main entrance before you pass under the Railroad Station
Banking Services/Currency Exchange	To the right of *The Walt Disney Story* at the Railroad Station end of Main Street
Storage Lockers	Down Main Street one block (as you walk toward the castle) and to the right
Lost & Found	Down Main Street one block (as you walk toward the castle) and to the right
Live Entertainment & Parade Information	City Hall Building at the Railroad Station end of Main Street

Main Street Services (continued)	
Lost Adults & Messages	City Hall Building
Lost Children	At the central hub end of Main Street near the First Aid Center
Disneyland & Local Attraction Information	City Hall Building
First Aid	First Aid Center two doors from Plaza Inn at the central hub end of Main Street
Baby Center/Baby Care Needs	Across from the Plaza Inn

Disneyland Railroad

Type of Attraction: Scenic railroad ride around the perimeter of Disneyland; also transportation to New Orleans Square, Mickey's Toontown/Fantasyland, and Tomorrowland

Scope & Scale: Major attraction

When to Go: After 11 a.m. or when you need transportation

Special Comments: The Main Street and Mickey's Toontown/Fantasyland Stations are usually the least congested boarding points.

Author's Rating: ★★★ (Critical ratings are based on a scale of zero to five stars. Five stars is the best possible rating.)

Overall Appeal by Age Group:

Pre-school	Grade School	Teens	Young Adults	Over 30	Senior Citizens
★★★★	★★★	★★	★★★½	★★★½	★★★½

Duration of Ride: About 20 minutes for a complete circuit
Average Wait in Line per 100 People ahead of You: 8 minutes
Assumes: 3 trains operating
Loading Speed: Fast

Description and Comments   A transportation ride that blends an eclectic variety of sights and experiences with an energy-saving way of getting around the park. In addition to providing a glimpse of all the lands except Adventureland, the train passes through the Grand Canyon Diorama, a three-dimensional replication of the canyon, complete with wildlife, as it appears from the southern rim. Another sight on the train circuit is Primeval World, a depiction of a prehistoric peat bog and rain forest populated by AudioAnimatronic (robotic) dinosaurs. Opened in 1966, Primeval World was a precursor to a similar presentation in the Universe of Energy pavilion at Epcot.

Touring Tips Save the train ride until after you have seen the featured attractions, or use it when you need transportation. If you have small children who are hell-bent to see Mickey first thing in the morning, you might consider taking the train to Mickey's Toontown (a half-circuit) and visiting Mickey in his dressing room as soon as you enter the park. Many families find that this tactic puts the kids in a more receptive frame of mind for the other attractions. On busy days lines form at the New Orleans Square and Tomorrowland stations, but rarely at the Main Street or Mickey's Toontown/Fantasyland stations.

The Walt Disney Story, featuring "Great Moments with Mr. Lincoln"

Type of Attraction: Nostalgic movie documenting the Disney success story followed by an AudioAnimatronic patriotic presentation

Scope & Scale: Minor attraction

When to Go: During the hot, crowded period of the day

Author's Rating: Both presentations are very moving; ★★★

Overall Appeal by Age Group:

Pre-school	Grade School	Teens	Young Adults	Over 30	Senior Citizens
★	★★	★★	★★★½	★★★★	★★★★

Duration of Presentation: Disney Story: 7 minutes

Duration of Presentation: "Great Moments": 13 minutes

Preshow Entertainment: Disney exhibits

Probable Waiting Time: Usually no wait

Description and Comments A warm and well-produced remembrance of the man who started it all. Well worth seeing; especially touching for those old enough to remember Walt Disney himself. The attraction consists of a museum of Disney memorabilia, including a re-creation of Walt's office and a seven-minute film about Walt Disney. Especially interesting are displays illustrating the construction and evolution of Disneyland. Following the conclusion of the film about Walt Disney, guests are admitted to a large theater where "Great Moments with Mr. Lincoln" is presented. A patriotic performance, "Great Moments" features an extremely lifelike and sophisticated AudioAnimatronic Lincoln delivering some well-considered thoughts concerning the past and the future of the United States.

Touring Tips   You usually do not have to wait long for this show, so see it during the busy times of day when lines are long elsewhere or as you are leaving the park.

Main Street Cinema

Type of Attraction: Old-time movies and vintage Disney cartoons
Scope & Scale: Diversion
When to Go: Whenever you want
Author's Rating: Wonderful selection of hilarious flicks; ★★
Overall Appeal by Age Group:

Pre-school	Grade School	Teens	Young Adults	Over 30	Senior Citizens
★★½	★★½	★★½	★★★½	★★★½	★★★½

Duration of Presentation: Runs continuously
Preshow Entertainment: None
Probable Waiting Time: No waiting

Description and Comments   Excellent old-time movies including some vintage Disney cartoons. Since the movies are silent, six can be shown simultaneously. No seats, viewers stand.

Touring Tips   Good place to get out of the sun or rain or to kill time while others in your group shop on Main Street. Fun, but not something you can't afford to miss.

Transportation Rides

Description and Comments   Trolleys, buses, etc., that add color to Main Street.

Touring Tips   Will save you a walk to the central hub. Not worth waiting in line for.

MAIN STREET EATERIES AND SHOPS

Description and Comments   Snacks, food, and specialty/souvenir shopping in a nostalgic, happy setting.

Incidentally, the Emporium on Main Street and the Star Trader in Tomorrowland are the two best places for finding Disney trademark souvenirs.

Touring Tips The shops are fun but the merchandise can be had elsewhere (except for certain Disney trademark souvenirs). If seeing the park attractions is your objective, save the Main Street eateries and shops until the end of the day. If shopping is your objective, you will find the shops most crowded during the noon hour and near closing time. Remember, Main Street usually opens a half-hour earlier and closes a half-hour to an hour later than the rest of Disneyland.

Adventureland

Adventureland is the first "land" to the left of Main Street and embodies a safari/African motif. Since the opening of the Indiana Jones Adventure, the narrow thoroughfares of Adventureland have been mobbed, making pedestrian traffic difficult.

Enchanted Tiki Room

Type of Attraction: AudioAnimatronic Pacific Island musical show
Scope & Scale: Minor attraction
When to Go: Before 11 a.m. and after 6 p.m.
Author's Rating: Very, very unusual; ★★★
Overall Appeal by Age Group:

Pre-school	Grade School	Teens	Young Adults	Over 30	Senior Citizens
★★½	★★★	★★	★★★	★★★	★★★

Duration of Presentation: 14½ minutes
Preshow Entertainment: Talking totem poles
Probable Waiting Time: 11 minutes

Description and Comments An unusual sit-down theater performance in which more than 200 birds, flowers, and Tiki-god statues sing and whistle through a musical program.

Touring Tips One of the more bizarre of the Disneyland entertainments and sometimes very crowded. We like it in the early evening, when we can especially appreciate sitting for a bit in an air-conditioned theater.

A reader from Cookeville, Tennessee, took exception to the rating for preschoolers and wrote:

I know that visitor reactions vary widely, but the [Enchanted Tiki Room] was our toddler's favorite attraction. We nearly omitted it because of the rating for preschoolers.

Indiana Jones Adventure

Type of Ride: Motion simulator dark ride

Scope & Scale: Super headliner

When to Go: Before 9:30 a.m. or in the hour before closing

Special Comments: Children must be 46 inches tall to ride. (See "Switching Off" on page 87.)

Author's Rating: Not to be missed; ★★★★½

Overall Appeal by Age Group:

Pre-school	Grade School	Teens	Young Adults	Over 30	Senior Citizens
★★★½	★★★★★	★★★★★	★★★★★	★★★★½	★★★★

Duration of Ride: 3 minutes and 20 seconds

Average Wait in Line per 100 People ahead of You: 3 minutes

Assumes: Full-capacity operation with 18-second dispatch interval

Loading Speed: Fast

Description and Comments   The first new ride in Adventureland for many years, Indiana Jones Adventure is a combination track ride and motion simulator. Guests ride a military troop transport vehicle. In addition to moving along on the path, the vehicle also bucks and pitches (the simulator part) in sync with the visuals and special effects encountered. Though the plot is complicated and not altogether clear, the bottom line is that if you look into the Forbidden Eye, you're in big trouble. The Forbidden Eye, of course, stands out like Rush Limbaugh in drag, and *everybody* stares at it. The rest of the ride consists of a mad race to escape the temple as it collapses around you. In the process you encounter snakes, spiders, lava pits, rats, swinging bridges, and the house-size, granite bowling ball that everyone remembers from *Raiders of the Lost Ark.*

The Indiana Jones ride is a Disney masterpiece, nonstop action from beginning to end with brilliant visual effects. Elaborate even by Disney standards, the attraction provides a level of detail and variety of action that makes use of the entire Imagineering arsenal of high-tech gimmickry. Combining a setting as rich as Pirates of the Caribbean with a ride that rivals Star Tours, Indiana Jones is a powerhouse.

Sophisticated in its electronic and computer applications, Indiana Jones purports to offer a different experience on each ride. According to the designers, there are veritable menus of special effects that the computer can mix and match. In practice, however, we could not see much difference from ride to ride. There are, no doubt, subtle variations, but the ride is so

wild and frenetic that it's hard to apprehend subtlety. Between explosions and falling rocks your poor, fried brain simply does not register nuance. If you ride twice and your date says, "The rat on the beam winked at me that time," it's probably a good idea to get away from Disneyland for a while.

The adventure begins in the queue, which during our latest visit extended out the entrance of the attraction, over the bridge leading to Adventureland, around the central hub, and clear into Tomorrowland! When you ultimately work your way into the attraction area, you find your-self at the site of an archaeology expedition with the Temple of Doom entrance beckoning only 50 feet away. After crossing a wood bridge, you finally step into the temple. The good news is that you are out of the California sun. The bad news is that you have just entered Indiana Jones's indoor queuing area, a system of tunnels and passageways that extends to within 50 yards of the Santa Monica pier.

Fortunately, the queuing area is interesting. You wind through caves, down the interior corridors of the temple, and into subterranean rotundas where the archaeologists have been hard at work. Along the way there are various surprises, as well as a succession of homilies etched in an "ancient" language on the temple walls. During our first visit we decoded the messages with feverish intensity, hoping to find one that translated to "rest rooms." Trust us on this one: do *not* chug down Diet Cokes before you get into line for this attraction.

If you are dazed from spending what seems like half of your life in this line and are not up to deciphering the Disney hieroglyphics, not to worry. You will eventually stumble into a chamber where a short movie will explain the plot. From there it's back into the maze and finally on to the loading area. The ride itself is memorable. If you ride with a full bladder, it's absolutely unforgettable.

Touring Tips   Indiana Jones is mobbed from opening until closing. If you are eligible for early entry, arrive at the park 90 minutes before official opening time (when the park opens to the general public) and ride Indiana Jones first thing, followed by Space Mountain, Rocket Rods, Star Tours, and Splash Mountain. Occasionally, Indiana Jones is not open for the entire early entry period, but begins operating a half-hour before the official opening time. If you are not eligible for early entry, try to visit Disneyland on a day when early entry is not in effect. Arrive with your admission pass in hand 40 minutes before the official opening time. When you're admitted to the park, head straight for Indiana Jones.

During the first hour or so the park is open, Indiana Jones cast members often employ a line management technique known as "stacking." Simply stated, they allow the line for Indiana Jones to form outside of the attraction, leaving the cavernous inside queuing area virtually empty. Guests, of course, assume that the attraction is packed to the gills and that the outside line is overflow. Naturally, this discourages guests from getting in line. The reality is that the wait is not nearly as bad as it looks, and that it is probably as short as it will be all day. If you arrive in the park early and the Indiana Jones line appears huge, have the rest of your party get in line while you enter Indiana Jones *through the attraction exit* and check out the inside queue. If it is empty or sparsely populated, stacking is being practiced. Join your party in line and enjoy the attraction: your wait will be comparatively short. If the inside queue is bumper to bumper, try Indiana Jones later as suggested below. Stacking is also sometimes practiced during the hour just before the park closes.

There are two other things you should know. First, Indiana Jones, because it is new and high-tech, breaks down a lot. The Disney people will announce that the ride is broken but usually will not estimate how long repairs will take. From our experience, most glitches are resolved in 15–30 minutes, and probably the best advice is to stick it out. The second important note is that Disney has not quite figured out how to manage the huge line for Indiana Jones. In practical terms this means that the end of the line could be anywhere. Speaking from experience, we have queued up for Indiana Jones in Tomorrowland, in the central hub, and in Frontierland, as well as in Adventureland. If you are one of the first to enter the park and are waiting at the end of Main Street for the rest of Disneyland to open, ask a Disney cast member where the line for Indiana Jones will form. It's quite discouraging to hotfoot over to the entrance to the attraction and learn that the end of the line is somewhere in Frontierland.

If you miss Indiana Jones in the early morning, try again during a parade or *Fantasmic!*, or during the hour before the park closes. Regarding the latter, the Disney folks will usually admit to the attraction anyone in line at closing time. During our first visit to Indiana Jones, Disneyland closed at 7 p.m. We hopped in the line for Indiana Jones at 6:45 p.m. and actually got on the ride at 7:30 p.m.

Though the Indiana Jones ride is wild and jerky, it is primarily distinguished by its visual impact and realistic special effects. Thus, we encourage the over-50 crowd to give it a chance: we think you'll like it. As for children, most find the ride extremely intense and action-packed but not particularly frightening. We encountered very few children who met the 46-inch minimum height requirement who were in any way intimidated.

We should note that Indiana Jones siphons guests away from other major attractions. Since the opening of Indiana Jones, morning crowds at

Space Mountain, Splash Mountain, Matterhorn Bobsleds, the Haunted Mansion, Pirates of the Caribbean, and to a lesser extent, Star Tours, have diminished somewhat.

Jungle Cruise

Type of Ride: A Disney outdoor boat ride adventure

Scope & Scale: Major attraction

When to Go: Before 10:30 a.m. or after 6 p.m.

Author's Rating: A Disney standard; ★★★

Overall Appeal by Age Group:

Pre-school	Grade School	Teens	Young Adults	Over 30	Senior Citizens
★★★★	★★★★	★★★	★★★	★★★½	★★★½

Duration of Ride: 7½ minutes

Average Wait in Line per 100 People ahead of You: 3½ minutes

Assumes: 10 boats operating

Loading Speed: Moderate to slow

Description and Comments   A boat ride through jungle waterways. Passengers encounter elephants, lions, hostile natives, and a menacing hippo. A long-enduring Disney favorite with the boatman's spiel adding measurably to the fun. The ride was shortened by a minute and a half in 1995 when Indiana Jones (next door) commandeered part of the Jungle Cruise's acreage. On the bright side, the Jungle Cruise was spruced up with a nifty new entrance building and queuing area.

As more technologically advanced attractions have been added to the park over the years, the Jungle Cruise has, by comparison, lost some of its luster. Though still a good attraction, it offers few thrills and no surprises for Disneyland veterans, many of whom can rattle off the ride's narration right along with the guide. For park first-timers, however, the Jungle Cruise continues to delight.

Touring Tips   This ride loads slowly and long lines form as the park fills. To compound problems, guests exiting Indiana Jones tend to head for the Jungle Cruise. Go early, or during a parade or a performance of *Fantasmic!* Be forewarned that the Jungle Cruise has an especially deceptive line: just when you think you are about to board, you are shunted into yet another queuing maze (none of which are visible outside the ride). Regardless how short the line *looks* when you approach the Jungle Cruise, inquire about the length of the wait: at least you will know what you are getting into.

The 357th Stroller Squadron; the Mowin' Mamas.

Swiss Family Treehouse

Type of Attraction: Walk-through treehouse exhibit

Scope & Scale: Minor attraction

When to Go: Before 11 a.m. and after 5 p.m.

Special Comments: Requires climbing a lot of stairs

Author's Rating: A very creative exhibit; ★★★

Overall Appeal by Age Group:

Pre-school	Grade School	Teens	Young Adults	Over 30	Senior Citizens
★★★★	★★★★	★★★	★★★	★★★	★★★

Duration of Tour: 4–8 minutes

Average Wait in Line per 100 People ahead of You: 7 minutes

Assumes: Normal staffing

Loading Speed: Does not apply

Description and Comments   A fantastic replication of the shipwrecked family's home will fire the imagination of the inventive and the adventurous.

Touring Tips   A self-guided, walk-through tour that involves a lot of climbing up and down stairs but no ropes or ladders or anything fancy. People stopping during the walk-through to look extra long or to rest sometimes create bottlenecks that slow crowd flow. We recommend visiting this attraction in the late afternoon or early evening if you are on a one-day tour schedule.

ADVENTURELAND EATERIES

Description and Comments   With only one counter-service restaurant (Bengal Barbeque), a fruit stand, and a juice bar, pickings are a little slim in Adventureland. Bengal Barbeque offers marinated beef, chicken, bacon and asparagus, and veggie skewers ranging in price from $4–6. Though the skewers are tasty, the portions are small and not a good value for the money. If you find yourself hungry in Adventureland, you will find a much better selection of food in nearby New Orleans Square, Frontierland, or Main Street.

ADVENTURELAND SHOPS

The shops in Adventureland are set up like an African bazaar and feature safari clothing, tribal crafts, and Disney stuff. If you are on a tight schedule, skip the shops or try them on your second day.

New Orleans Square

Accessible via Adventureland and Frontierland, New Orleans Square is one of three lands that do not emanate from the central hub. The architecture and setting are Caribbean colonial, like New Orleans itself, with exceptional attention to detail.

Pirates of the Caribbean

Type of Ride: A Disney indoor adventure boat ride

Scope & Scale: Major attraction

When to Go: Before 11:30 a.m. or after 4:30 p.m.

Special Comments: Frightens some small children

Author's Rating: Our pick as one of Disneyland's very best; ★★★★

Overall Appeal by Age Group:

Pre-school	Grade School	Teens	Young Adults	Over 30	Senior Citizens
★★★	★★★★½	★★★★	★★★★	★★★★½	★★★★½

Duration of Ride: Approximately 14 minutes

Average Wait in Line per 100 People ahead of You: 3 minutes

Assumes: 42 boats operating

Loading Speed: Fast

Description and Comments   Another boat ride, this time indoors, through a series of sets depicting a pirate raid on an island settlement, from the bombardment of the fortress to the debauchery that follows the victory. Pirates of the Caribbean was the target in 1997 of a much-publicized political correctness controversy relating to the objectification of women and the "boys will be boys" way in which the pirates' debauchery was depicted. Ultimately, Disney was pressured into revamping the attraction (though not much).

Touring Tips   Another "not to be missed" attraction. Undoubtedly one of the most elaborate and imaginative attractions in Disneyland. Though engineered to move large crowds, this ride sometimes gets overwhelmingly busy in the early and midafternoon. Try to ride before noon or while a parade or *Fantasmic!* is in progress.

Disneyland Railroad

Description and Comments   The Disneyland Railroad stops in New Orleans Square on its circle tour around the park. See the description of the Disneyland Railroad under Main Street, U.S.A. for additional details regarding the sights en route.

"It's my husband. He refuses to get up early when he's on vacation."

Touring Tips   A pleasant and feet-saving way to commute to Mickey's Toontown/Fantasyland, Tomorrowland, or Main Street. Be advised, however, that the New Orleans Square Station is usually the most congested.

Haunted Mansion

Type of Ride: Indoor haunted-house ride
Scope & Scale: Major attraction
When to Go: Before 11:30 a.m. or after 6:30 p.m.
Special Comments: Frightens some very small children
Author's Rating: Some of Disneyland's best special effects; ★★★★
Overall Appeal by Age Group:

Pre-school	Grade School	Teens	Young Adults	Over 30	Senior Citizens
Varies	★★★★½	★★★★	★★★★	★★★★	★★★★

Duration of Ride: 5½-minute ride plus a 2-minute preshow
Average Wait in Line per 100 People ahead of You: 2½ minutes
Assumes: Both stretch rooms operating
Loading Speed: Fast

Description and Comments   A fun attraction more than a scary one. An ingenious preshow serves as a vehicle to deliver guests to the ride's boarding area, where they then board "Doom Buggies" for a ride through the mansion's parlor, dining room, library, halls, and attic before descending to an uncommonly active graveyard. Disney employs almost every special effect in its repertoire in the Haunted Mansion, making it one of the most inventive and different of all Disney attractions. In their souvenir guide the Disney people say, "Come face to face with 999 happy ghosts, ghouls, and goblins in a 'frightfully funny' adventure." That pretty well sums it up. Be warned that some youngsters build a lot of anxiety concerning what they think they will see. The actual attraction scares almost nobody.

Touring Tips   This attraction would be more at home in Fantasyland, but no matter, it's Disney at its best; another "not to be missed" feature. Because the Haunted Mansion is in an especially high-traffic corridor (between Pirates of the Caribbean and Splash Mountain), it stays busy all day. Try to see the Haunted Mansion before 11:30 a.m., after 6:30 p.m., or while a parade is in progress. In the evening, crowds for *Fantasmic!* gather in front of the Haunted Mansion, making it very difficult to access.

The Disney Gallery

Description and Comments Located up a set of stairs on the second floor of the building that houses Pirates of the Caribbean, this attraction consists of a collection of paintings, drawings, and models documenting the development and evolution of Disneyland. Included in the collection are design renderings of present and future attractions, as well as sketches for attractions proposed but never constructed. Exhibits showcasing art from Disney animated films and from other Disney theme parks are featured on a temporary basis.

Touring Tips Most folks are not aware of the gallery's existence, so it is rarely crowded. See it at your convenience. The gallery has an elevator, so it's wheelchair accessible.

NEW ORLEANS SQUARE EATERIES AND SHOPS

Description and Comments Shops and restaurants in New Orleans Square impart a special realism to the setting. The Blue Bayou, the only full-service restaurant in the park, is to the left of the Pirates of the Caribbean exit. With its waterside, bayou-at-dusk setting, the Blue Bayou offers an exotic, romantic atmosphere equaled by few restaurants anywhere. The menu was overhauled in 1997 and now features some Creole and Cajun selections. There's no need for long-time Blue Bayou patrons to panic, however: the Monte Cristo sandwiches have been retained. Reservations are generally required and should be made at the door of the restaurant as soon as possible after you enter the park.

Ethnic menu diversification has also improved selections at the French Market counter-service restaurant. Jambalaya and Cajun chicken breast sandwiches have been added to a line-up that includes angel hair pasta, French dip sandwiches, fried chicken, and beef stew. Prices run in the $8–10 range, with children's fried chicken or fettuccine meals available for about $4. More limited fare is available at the Royal Street Veranda, which serves clam chowder in a bread bowl for $5.

Possibly, the most overlooked counter-service restaurant in the park is La Petite Patisserie. Consisting of only two modest serving windows midblock on Royal Street, La Petite Patisserie serves good ham and turkey sandwiches to the few guests who stumble upon it.

Touring Tips Skip the restaurants and shops if you have only one or two days to visit. If you have some extra time, however, treat yourself to a meal at the Blue Bayou Restaurant. The food is a cut above the usual Disney fare and the atmosphere will knock you out. Make reservations at the door of the restaurant while your party waits in line for nearby Indiana Jones.

Critter Country

Critter Country, situated at the end of a cul-de-sac and accessible via New Orleans Square, sports a pioneer appearance not unlike that of Frontierland.

Country Bear Playhouse

Type of Attraction: AudioAnimatronic country hoedown stage show
Scope & Scale: Major attraction
When to Go: After 11 a.m. and before 5 p.m.
Author's Rating: Dated, but still a Disney classic; ★★★
Overall Appeal by Age Group:

Pre-school	Grade School	Teens	Young Adults	Over 30	Senior Citizens
★★★	★★★★	★★★	★★★½	★★★½	★★★½

Duration of Presentation: 15 minutes
Preshow Entertainment: None
Probable Waiting Time: 5–10 minutes

Description and Comments A cast of charming AudioAnimatronic (robotic) bears sing and stomp their way through a Western-style hoedown. One of Disneyland's most humorous and upbeat shows. Our only complaint is that no new renditions of the show have been produced for several years.

Touring Tips Though extremely popular, the playhouse is one of the most efficient crowd movers in the park. Try the playhouse between 11 a.m. and 5 p.m.

Splash Mountain

Type of Ride: Water-flume adventure boat ride
Scope & Scale: Headliner
When to Go: Before 9:45 a.m.
Special Comments: Children must be 3' 4" tall to ride; those under 7 years of age must ride with an adult. (See "Switching Off" on page 87.)
Author's Rating: A wet winner, not to be missed; ★★★★½
Overall Appeal by Age Group:

Pre-school	Grade School	Teens	Young Adults	Over 30	Senior Citizens
†	★★★★★	★★★★★	★★★★★	★★★★½	★★★★½

† Many preschoolers are too short to meet the height requirement, and others are intimidated from watching the ride while standing in line. Of

those preschoolers who actually ride, most give the attraction high marks;
★★★★ to ★★★★★.

Duration of Ride: About 10 minutes
Average Wait in Line per 100 People ahead of You: 3½ minutes
Assumes: Operation at full capacity
Loading Speed: Moderate

Description and Comments   Splash Mountain is an amusement park flume
ride Disney-style, bigger than life and more imaginative than anyone
thought possible. The ride combines steep chutes with a variety of Disney's
best special effects. Covering more than half a mile, the ride splashes
through swamps, caves, and backwood bayous before climaxing in a 52-foot
plunge and Brer Rabbit's triumphant return home. The entire ride is populated by more than 100 AudioAnimatronic characters, including Brer Rabbit, Brer Bear, and Brer Fox, all regaling riders with songs, including "Zip-
A-Dee-Doo-Dah."

Touring Tips   This ride is the most popular ride in Disneyland for patrons
of all ages; happy, exciting, and adventuresome all at once. Though eclipsed
somewhat by the newer Indiana Jones attraction, crowds nevertheless build
quickly during the morning at Splash Mountain and waits of more than
two hours are not uncommon once Disneyland fills up on a busy day. To
avoid the crowds, arrive at the park before opening time and get in line at
Splash Mountain no later than 45 minutes after Disneyland opens. Long
lines persist throughout the day until only a few minutes before closing.

There are four ways to experience Splash Mountain without a long wait.
The first is to be on hand when the park opens and to sprint over and get
in line before anyone else. The second way is to allow the initial mob of
Splash cadets to be processed through, and to arrive at Splash Mountain
about 20–40 minutes after the park opens or after riding Indiana Jones. A

third strategy is to get in line for Splash Mountain during a parade and/or a performance of *Fantasmic!* Be advised, however, that huge crowds gathering along the New Orleans Square and Frontierland waterfronts for *Fantasmic!* make getting to Splash Mountain very difficult (if not impossible) just before, during, and just after performances. Fourth, try Splash Mountain during the hour before closing, but first confirm with a Disney greeter that you will be able to ride if you get in line. We have received letters from readers complaining that the ride stopped operating at the published closing time, stranding several dozen people who had waited 20 minutes in line based on the assumption they would get to ride.

Early morning traffic to Splash Mountain decreased somewhat after the new Tomorrowland became fully operational in the late spring of 1998. If you are among the first to enter the park and want to experience all the "biggies," ride Indiana Jones first, followed by Space Mountain, Rocket Rods, Star Tours, and Splash Mountain.

It is almost a certainty that you will get wet, and possibly drenched, riding Splash Mountain. If you visit on a cool day, you may want to carry a plastic garbage bag. By tearing holes in the bottom and sides, you can fashion a sack dress of sorts to keep you dry. Be sure to tuck the bag under your bottom. The logboats have bench seats, which riders straddle. When water comes in over the bow, it tends to run down the length of the seat, soaking the crotches of everyone on board. By the way, it doesn't matter whether you ride in front or back. You will get wet regardless. If you have a camera, either leave it with a nonriding member of your party or wrap it in a plastic bag.

One final word: This is not just a fancy flume ride; it is a full-blown Disney adventure. The scariest part, by far, is the big drop into the pool (visible from the sidewalk in front of Splash Mountain), and even this plunge looks worse than it really is.

Flash Mountain

Type of Attraction: Water-flume adventure strip show

Scope & Scale: Eye-popper

When to Go: Spring break, weekend nights

Special Comments: A liberating experience

Author's Rating: Author is too near-sighted to rate accurately

Duration of Presentation: About 2 seconds

Description and Comments It was reported by the Associated Press that certain female Splash Mountain riders are behaving in a most un-Disneylike manner by "flinging their blouses open" as they plummet down the climactic plunge at the end of the ride (fully visible, we might add, to dozens of guests waiting in line in front of the attraction). Indeed, automatic cameras shooting souvenir photographs of participants have documented an astounding array of feminine anatomy in free-fall. The practice is apparently too spontaneous for Disneyland, which reports that it "has no plans at this time to change the theme of the attraction." Plus, ever mindful of guest safety, management has concerns about "undue congestion" in front of the ride and the "possibility of guests catching cold."

Touring Tips Spectators should stand during spring break or weekend nights on the walkway directly in front of Splash Mountain. Be sure to bring a sign denouncing such unchaste exhibitionist behavior, or depending on your point of view, a camera with a telescopic lens. If you are a participant, you will have approximately two minutes following the big plunge to get yourself back together before you arrive at the unloading area.

Davy Crockett's Explorer Canoes

Type of Ride: Scenic canoe ride
Scope & Scale: Minor attraction
When to Go: Before 11 a.m.
Special Comments: Skip if the lines are long; closes at dusk
Author's Rating: Most fun way to see Rivers of America; ★★★
Overall Appeal by Age Group:

Pre-school	Grade School	Teens	Young Adults	Over 30	Senior Citizens
★★★★	★★★★	★★★	★★★	★★★	★★★

Duration of Ride: 8–10 minutes depending on how fast you paddle
Average Wait in Line per 100 People ahead of You: 12½ minutes
Assumes: 6 canoes operating
Loading Speed: Slow

Description and Comments Paddle-powered (your paddle) ride around Tom Sawyer Island and Fort Wilderness. Runs the same route with the same sights as the Steamboat, the Sailing Ship, and the Mike Fink Keelboats. The canoes operate only on busier days and close at dusk. The sights are fun and the ride is a little different in that the patrons paddle the canoe. We think this is the most fun of any of the various river trips. Long lines from about 11 a.m. on reflect the popularity of this attraction.

Touring Tips The canoes represent one of four ways to see the same waterways. Since the canoes and keelboats are slower in loading, we usually opt for the larger Steamboat or Sailing Ship. If you are not up for a boat ride, a different view of the same sights can be had by hoofing around Tom Sawyer Island and Fort Wilderness. Try to ride before 11 a.m. or just before dusk. The canoes operate on selected days and seasonal periods only. If the canoes are a big deal to you, call ahead to make sure they are operating.

CRITTER COUNTRY EATERIES AND SHOPS

Description and Comments   Critter Country restaurants and shops offer the standard array of souvenirs and fast food. Brer Bar, a burger and hot dog joint in the farthest recess of the Critter Country cul-de-sac, is often over-looked by the crowds at mealtime. The main counter-service venue in Critter Country is the Hungry Bear Restaurant, which serves burgers, grilled chicken breasts, fried chicken tenders, and Caesar salads. Portions are large. Expect to pay $5–9 for a sandwich, fries, and drink. Children's meals featuring chicken tender strips are available for about $4. In keeping with the park's ongoing evaluation of menus, expect to see some new selections in Critter Country.

Touring Tips   Even with the tremendous popularity of Splash Mountain, the restaurants in Critter Country remain good bets for avoiding the lunch and dinner rush. The Hungry Bear Restaurant, in addition, offers a spacious open deck with a great view of the New Orleans Square and Frontierland river activity.

Frontierland

Frontierland adjoins New Orleans Square as you move clockwise around the park. The focus here is on the Old West, with log stockades and pioneer trappings.

Big Thunder Mountain Railroad

Type of Ride: Tame roller coaster with exciting special effects
Scope & Scale: Headliner
When to Go: Before 11:30 a.m. and after 6:30 p.m.
Special Comments: Children must be 3' 4" tall to ride (see "Switching Off" on page 87); those under age 7 must ride with an adult
Author's Rating: Great effects, though a relatively tame ride; ★★★★
Overall Appeal by Age Group:

Pre-school	Grade School	Teens	Young Adults	Over 30	Senior Citizens
★★★	★★★★	★★★★	★★★★	★★★★	★★★

Duration of Ride: 3⅓ minutes

Average Wait in Line per 100 People ahead of You: 3 minutes

Assumes: 5 trains operating

Loading Speed: Moderate to fast

Description and Comments   A roller-coaster ride through and around a Disney "mountain." The time is Gold Rush days, and the idea is that you are on a runaway mine train. Along with the usual thrills of a roller-coaster ride (about a five on a "scary scale" of ten), the ride showcases some first-rate examples of Disney creativity: lifelike scenes depicting a mining town, falling rocks, and an earthquake, all humorously animated.

Touring Tips   A superb Disney experience, but not too wild a roller coaster. The emphasis here is much more on the sights than on the thrill of the ride itself. Regardless, it's a "not to be missed" attraction.

As an example of how differently guests experience Disney attractions, consider this letter we received from a lady in Brookline, Massachusetts:

> *Being in the senior citizens' category and having limited time, my friend and I confined our activities to those attractions rated as four or five stars for seniors.*
>
> *Because of your recommendation and because you listed it as "not to be missed," we waited for one hour to board the Big Thunder Mountain Railroad, which you rated a "5" on a scary scale of "10." After living through 3½ minutes of pure terror, I will rate that attraction a "15" on a scary scale of "10." We were so busy holding on and screaming and even praying for our safety that we did not see any falling rocks, a mining town, or an earthquake. In our opinion the Big Thunder Mountain Railroad should not be recommended for seniors or preschool children.*

Raft to and from Tom Sawyer Island

Type of Ride: Transportation ride to Tom Sawyer Island
Scope & Scale: Minor attraction
Special Comments: Same information applies to return trip
Duration of Ride: A little over a minute one way
Average Wait in Line per 100 People ahead of You: 4½ minutes
Assumes: 3 rafts operating
Loading Speed: Moderate

Tom Sawyer Island and Fort Wilderness

Type of Attraction: Walk-through exhibit and rustic playground
Scope & Scale: Minor attraction
When to Go: Midmorning through late afternoon
Special Comments: Closes at dusk; muddy following a hard rain
Author's Rating: The place for rambunctious kids; ★★★
Overall Appeal by Age Group:

Pre-school	Grade School	Teens	Young Adults	Over 30	Senior Citizens
★★★★★	★★★★★	★★★½	★★★	★★★	★★★

Description and Comments   Tom Sawyer Island manages to impart something of a sense of isolation from the rest of the park. It has hills to climb, a cave and a treehouse to explore, tipsy bridges to cross, and paths to follow. It's a delight for adults but a godsend for children who have been in tow all day. They love the freedom of the exploration and the excitement of firing air guns from the walls of Fort Wilderness. Be advised that due to the scuffling of millions of tiny feet, there is not a blade of grass left intact on the entire island. Thus, after a good rain Tom Sawyer Island is miraculously transformed into Disney's Muddy Wallow. Parents should feel free within reasonable limits to allow their children to explore unfettered. In addition to the fact that the island is designed for rowdy kids, there are a goodly number of Disney security people (dressed as cavalry soldiers) to referee the transient cowboys and Indians.

As an aside, a mother of four from Duncan, South Carolina, found Tom Sawyer Island as much a refuge as an attraction, writing:

> I do have one tip for parents. In the afternoon when the crowds were at their peak, the weather was hottest and the kids started lagging behind, our organization began to suffer. We then retreated over to

*Tom Sawyer Island which proved to be a true haven. My husband
and I found a secluded bench and re-grouped while sipping iced tea
and eating delicious soft ice cream. Meanwhile, the kids were able
to run freely in the shade. Afterwards we were ready to tackle the
park again refreshed and with direction once more. Admittedly, I
got this tip from another guidebook.*

Touring Tips Tom Sawyer Island is not one of Disneyland's more cele-
brated attractions, but it's certainly one of the most well done. Attention to
detail is excellent and kids particularly revel in its adventuresome frontier
atmosphere. We think it's a must for families with children ages 5–15. If
your party is adult, visit the island on your second day, or stop by on your
first day if you have seen the attractions you most wanted to see. We like
Tom Sawyer Island from about noon until the island closes at dusk. Access
is by raft from Frontierland, and you may have to stand in line to board
both coming and going. Two or three rafts operate simultaneously, however,
and the round trip is usually pretty time-efficient. Tom Sawyer Island takes
about 35 minutes or so to see, but many children could spend a whole day.

Golden Horseshoe Stage

Type of Attraction: Western dance-hall stage show
Scope & Scale: Minor attraction
When to Go: Per your reservation
Special Comments: Food is available
Author's Rating: Delightfully zany show; ★★★½
Overall Appeal by Age Group:

Pre-school	Grade School	Teens	Young Adults	Over 30	Senior Citizens
★★★	★★★½	★★★½	★★★½	★★★★	★★★★

Description and Comments A PG-rated version of a Wild West dance-hall
show. Formats and presentations vary, but all shows feature live music and
corny humor, and some also include dancing. A limited menu of burgers,
hot dogs, chili, and desserts is available for those desiring to combine the
show with lunch. At less busy times of the year, no reservations are required
for some shows (usually the first show of the day and sometimes one or two
late afternoon shows).

Touring Tips Though the show is entertaining, it takes a big bite out of
your touring day. Reservations for *Golden Horseshoe* performances must be
made at the door of the saloon during the first hour the park is open. This

Doris explains the importance of knowing what you are getting in line for.

usually entails some standing in line. You are requested to return a half-hour before your seating time, and then must wait an additional half-hour once seated for the show to begin. The show itself lasts about 35 minutes. Thus, all told, you will have about two hours of your day tied up for a 35-minute show.

Disneyland has experimented for three years with both the show content and the reservations policy. Reservations and food service were dispensed with for a time and then reinstated. Our advice is to check the daily entertainment schedule on the day of your visit to ascertain the current status of this show.

Frontierland Shootin' Exposition

Type of Attraction: Electronic shooting gallery
Scope & Scale: Diversion
When to Go: Whenever convenient
Special Comments: Not included in your admission; costs extra
Author's Rating: A very nifty shooting gallery; ★★
Overall Appeal by Age Group:

Pre-school	Grade School	Teens	Young Adults	Over 30	Senior Citizens
★★★½	★★★½	★★★½	★★★	★★★	★★★

Description and Comments A very elaborate shooting gallery which costs 50¢ to play. One of the few attractions in Disneyland not included in the admission pass.

Touring Tips Good fun for them what likes to shoot, but definitely not a place to blow time if you are on a tight schedule. Try it on your second day if time allows.

Mike Fink Keelboats

Type of Ride: Scenic boat ride
Scope & Scale: Minor attraction
When to Go: Before 11 a.m.
Special Comments: Don't ride if the lines are long; closes at dusk
Author's Rating: ★★½
Overall Appeal by Age Group:

Pre-school	Grade School	Teens	Young Adults	Over 30	Senior Citizens
★★★	★★★	★★★	★★★	★★★	★★★

Duration of Ride: 10½ minutes
Average Wait in Line per 100 People ahead of You: 19 minutes
Assumes: 2 boats operating
Loading Speed: Slow

Description and Comments　Small river keelboats that circle Tom Sawyer Island and Fort Wilderness, taking the same route as the Explorer Canoes, the Mark Twain Riverboat, and the Sailing Ship *Columbia*. The top deck and the lower bow seats of the keelboat afford the best view but are exposed to the elements.

Touring Tips　Keelboats and the canoes load slowly, so we usually prefer the larger craft. The other way to see much of the area covered by the respective boat tours is to explore Tom Sawyer Island and Fort Wilderness on foot.

Mark Twain Riverboat

Type of Ride: Scenic boat ride
Scope & Scale: Minor attraction
When to Go: Between 11 a.m. and 5 p.m.
Special Comments: Suspends operation at dusk
Author's Rating: Provides an excellent vantage point; ★★★
Overall Appeal by Age Group:

Pre-school	Grade School	Teens	Young Adults	Over 30	Senior Citizens
★★★	★★★	★★½	★★★	★★★	★★★

Duration of Ride: About 14 minutes
Average Wait to Board: 10 minutes
Assumes: Normal operations
Loading Method: En masse

Description and Comments　Large-capacity, paddle-wheel riverboat that navigates the waters around Tom Sawyer Island and Fort Wilderness. A beautiful craft, the Riverboat provides a lofty perch from which to see Frontierland and New Orleans Square.

Touring Tips　One of four boat rides that survey the same real estate. Since the Explorer Canoes and the Mike Fink Keelboats are slower in loading, we think the Riverboat (along with the Sailing Ship *Columbia*, which is also large and loads at the same landing) makes more efficient use of touring time. If you are not in the mood for a boat ride, many of the same sights can be seen by hiking around Tom Sawyer Island and Fort Wilderness.

Sailing Ship *Columbia*

Type of Ride: Scenic boat ride
Scope & Scale: Minor attraction

Problem 406: Too Short to Ride

When to Go: Between 11 a.m. and 5 p.m.

Special Comments: Suspends operation at dusk

Author's Rating: A stunning piece of workmanship; ★★★½

Overall Appeal by Age Group:

Pre-school	Grade School	Teens	Young Adults	Over 30	Senior Citizens
★★★★	★★★½	★★★	★★★½	★★★	★★★

Duration of Ride: About 14 minutes

Average Wait to Board: 10 minutes

Assumes: Normal operations

Loading Method: En masse

Description and Comments   The *Columbia* is a stunning replica of a three-masted eighteenth-century merchant ship. Both above and below decks are open to visitors with below decks outfitted to depict the life and work environment of the ship's crew in 1787. The *Columbia* operates only on busier days and runs the same route as the canoes, keelboats, and the Mark Twain Riverboat. As with the other river craft, the *Columbia* suspends operations at dusk.

An Oregon reader, who liked the *Columbia* but had some problems with its officers, wrote:

> *It is truly a beautiful ship and would have been a pleasant ride but for the incessant jabbering of the "captain." A little humorous banter is always appreciated, but we were ready to strangle this guy. We went below deck for awhile to get away from him, and would recommend to others to do this, even with a more restrained captain, as it is a little museum complete with outfitted bunks and other sailing paraphernalia.*

Touring Tips   The *Columbia,* along with the Mark Twain Riverboat, provides a short-wait, high-carrying-capacity alternative for cruising the Rivers of America. We found the *Columbia* beautiful in her craftsmanship and by far the most aesthetically pleasing and historically interesting of any of the four choices of boat rides on the Rivers of America.

If you have time to be choosy, ride aboard the *Columbia*. After boarding, while waiting for the cruise to begin, tour below deck. Once the ride begins, come topside and stroll the deck, taking in the beauty and complexity of the rigging.

The *Columbia* does not usually require a long wait, making it a good bet during the crowded afternoon hours.

FRONTIERLAND EATERIES AND SHOPS

Description and Comments   More specialty and souvenir shopping. Festival of Food, behind Big Thunder Mountain, features barbecue and other grilled specialties, serving up one of the most satisfying meals in the park. We also like Casa Mexicana (tacos, enchiladas, burritos, taco salads) and the River Belle Terrace (roast chicken, pasta, salad); both are cafeteria-style restaurants that usually are not too crowded. With prices ranging $8–14 per person for a meal and a drink, all three eateries are somewhat more expensive than Disney's fast-food burgers and hot dogs. Children's meals, running about $4, are available at all three restaurants. Casa Mexicana is open every day, whereas Festival of Food and the River Belle Terrace are sometimes closed on less busy days.

Touring Tips   If you have two days to spend in the park, make mealtime reservations for a show at the *Golden Horseshoe* and enjoy lunch while you are waiting for the show. Though selections at the *Golden Horseshoe* have changed several times lately, burgers, hot dogs, chili, and fries were featured the last time we looked. Don't waste time browsing in shops unless you have a very relaxed schedule or came specifically to shop.

Fantasyland

Truly an enchanting place, spread gracefully like a miniature alpine village beneath the towers of Sleeping Beauty Castle, Fantasyland is the heart of the park.

Disneyland Railroad

Description and Comments   The Disneyland Railroad stops in Fantasyland/Mickey's Toontown on its circuit around the park. The station is located to the left of It's a Small World, next to the Fantasyland Theatre. From this usually uncrowded boarding point, transportation is available to Tomorrowland, Main Street, and New Orleans Square.

It's a Small World

Type of Ride: World brotherhood–themed indoor boat ride
Scope & Scale: Major attraction
When to Go: Anytime except after a parade
Author's Rating: A pleasant change of pace; ★★★
Overall Appeal by Age Group:

Pre-school	Grade School	Teens	Young Adults	Over 30	Senior Citizens
★★★★	★★★½	★★½	★★★	★★★	★★★½

Duration of Ride: 11–14 minutes

Average Wait in Line per 100 People ahead of You: 2½ minutes

Assumes: Busy conditions with 56 boats operating

Loading Speed: Fast

Description and Comments   A happy, upbeat attraction with a world brotherhood theme and a catchy tune that will roll around in your head for weeks. Small boats convey visitors on a tour around the world, with singing and dancing dolls showcasing the dress and culture of each nation. Almost everyone enjoys It's a Small World, but it stands, along with the *Enchanted Tiki Room,* as an attraction that some could take or leave while others consider it one of the real masterpieces of Disneyland. In any event, a woman from Holbrook, New York, wrote with this devilish suggestion for improvement:

> *Small World would be much better if each person got 3–4 softballs on the way in!*

Touring Tips   Though an older Disney attraction, It's a Small World is a fast-loading ride that's usually a good bet during the busier times of the day. The boats are moved along by water pressure, which increases as boats are added. Thus, the more boats in service when you ride (up to a maximum total of 60), the shorter the duration of the ride (and wait).

Peter Pan's Flight

Type of Ride: Indoor fantasy adventure ride
Scope & Scale: Minor attraction
When to Go: Before 10 a.m. and after 6 p.m.
Author's Rating: Happy and mellow; ★★★★
Overall Appeal by Age Group:

Pre-school	Grade School	Teens	Young Adults	Over 30	Senior Citizens
★★★★	★★★★	★★★½	★★★★	★★★★	★★★★

Duration of Ride: Just over 2 minutes
Average Wait in Line per 100 People ahead of You: 11 minutes
Assumes: 13 ships operating
Loading Speed: Slow

Description and Comments   Though not considered to be one of the major attractions, Peter Pan's Flight is superbly designed and absolutely delightful, with a happy theme, a reunion with some unforgettable Disney characters, beautiful effects, and charming music.

Touring Tips   Though not a major feature of Disneyland, we nevertheless classify it as the best attraction in Fantasyland. Try to ride before 10 a.m. or after 6 p.m., during the afternoon or evening parade(s), or during a performance of *Fantasmic!*

King Arthur Carrousel

Type of Ride: Merry-go-round
Scope & Scale: Minor attraction
When to Go: Before 11:30 a.m. or after 5 p.m.
Special Comments: Adults enjoy the beauty and nostalgia of this ride
Author's Rating: A showpiece carousel; ★★★
Overall Appeal by Age Group:

Pre-school	Grade School	Teens	Young Adults	Over 30	Senior Citizens
★★★★	★★½	★	★★½	★★★	★★★

Duration of Ride: A little over 2 minutes
Average Wait in Line per 100 People ahead of You: 8 minutes

Assumes: Normal staffing
Loading Speed: Slow

Description and Comments   A merry-go-round to be sure, but certainly one of the most elaborate and beautiful you will ever see, especially when lighted at night.

Touring Tips   Unless there are small children in your party, we suggest you appreciate this ride from the sidelines. If your children insist on riding, try to get them on before 11:30 a.m. or after 5 p.m. While nice to look at, the carousel loads and unloads very slowly.

Mr. Toad's Wild Ride

Type of Ride: Track ride in the dark
Scope & Scale: Minor attraction
When to Go: Before 11 a.m.
Author's Rating: Past its prime; ★★½
Overall Appeal by Age Group:

Pre-school	Grade School	Teens	Young Adults	Over 30	Senior Citizens
★★★½	★★★½	★★★½	★★★	★★★	★★★

Duration of Ride: Almost 2 minutes
Average Wait in Line per 100 People ahead of You: 9 minutes
Assumes: 12 cars operating
Loading Speed: Slow

Description and Comments   This is perhaps the ride that profited most by the 1983 Fantasyland renovation. Still, it is basically a twisting, curving ride in the dark past two-dimensional sets and props. There are a couple of clever effects, but basically it's at the technological basement of the Disney attraction mix.

Touring Tips   Not a great but certainly a popular attraction. Lines build early in the day and never let up. Catch Mr. Toad before 11 a.m.

Snow White's Scary Adventures

Type of Ride: Track ride in the dark
Scope & Scale: Minor attraction
When to Go: Before 11 a.m. and after 5 p.m.
Special Comments: Quite intimidating for preschoolers
Author's Rating: Worth seeing if the wait is not long; ★★★

Overall Appeal by Age Group:

Pre-school	Grade School	Teens	Young Adults	Over 30	Senior Citizens
★★★	★★★	★★½	★★★	★★★	★★★

Duration of Ride: Almost 2 minutes

Average Wait in Line per 100 People ahead of You: 9 minutes

Assumes: 10 cars operating

Loading Speed: Slow

Description and Comments Here you ride in a mining car in the dark through a series of sets drawn from *Snow White and the Seven Dwarfs.* The attraction has a Perils-of-Pauline flavor and features Snow White (whom you never see), as she narrowly escapes harm at the hands of the wicked witch. The action and effects are a cut above Mr. Toad's Wild Ride but not as good as Peter Pan's Flight.

Touring Tips Enjoyable but not particularly compelling. Experience it if the lines are not too long or on a second-day visit. Ride before 11 a.m. or after 5 p.m. if possible. Also, don't take the "scary" part too seriously. The witch looks mean, but most kids take her in stride. Or maybe not. A mother from Knoxville, Tennessee, commented:

> *The outside looks cute and fluffy, but inside, the evil witch just keeps coming at you. My five-year-old, who rode Space Mountain three times [and took other scary rides] right in stride, was near panic when our car stopped unexpectedly twice during Snow White. [After Snow White] my six-year-old niece spent a lot of time asking "if a witch will jump out at you" before other rides. So I suggest that you explain a little more what this ride is about. It's tough on preschoolers who are expecting forest animals and dwarfs.*

In point of fact, we receive more mail from parents about this ride than about all other Disneyland attractions combined. The bottom line is that it really punches the buttons of the six-and-under crowd. Many kids, once frightened by Snow White's Scary Adventures, balk at trying any other attractions that go into the dark, regardless how benign.

Alice in Wonderland

Type of Ride: Track ride in the dark

Scope & Scale: Minor attraction

When to Go: Before 11 a.m. or after 5 p.m.

Special Comments: Do not confuse with Mad Tea Party ride

Author's Rating: Good characterization and story line; ★★★

Overall Appeal by Age Group:

Pre-school	Grade School	Teens	Young Adults	Over 30	Senior Citizens
★★★½	★★★½	★★★	★★★	★★★	★★★

Duration of Ride: Almost 4 minutes

Average Wait in Line per 100 People ahead of You: 12 minutes

Assumes: 16 cars operating

Loading Speed: Slow

Description and Comments   An attraction that recalls the story of *Alice in Wonderland* with some nice surprises and colorful effects. Guests ride nifty caterpillar cars in this Disney spook-house adaptation.

Touring Tips   This is a very well done ride in the best Disney tradition, with familiar characters, good effects, and a theme you can follow. Unfortunately, it loads very slowly. Ride before 11 a.m. or after 5 p.m.

Pinocchio's Daring Journey

Type of Ride: Track ride in the dark

Scope & Scale: Minor attraction

When to Go: Before 11:30 a.m. and after 4:30 p.m.

Author's Rating: A big letdown; ★★

Overall Appeal by Age Group:

Pre-school	Grade School	Teens	Young Adults	Over 30	Senior Citizens
★★★	★★★	★★½	★★½	★★½	★★½

Duration of Ride: Almost 3 minutes

Average Wait in Line per 100 People ahead of You: 8 minutes

Assumes: 15 cars operating

Loading Speed: Slow

Description and Comments   Another twisting, curving track ride in the dark, this time tracing the adventures of Pinocchio as he tries to find his way home. The action is difficult to follow and lacks continuity. Although the sets are three-dimensional and more visually compelling than say, Mr. Toad, the story line is dull and fails to engage the guest. Definitely the least interesting of the Fantasyland dark rides.

Touring Tips   The word must be out on Pinocchio because the lines are seldom very long. Still, the time to avoid is between 11:30 a.m. and 4:30 p.m.

Sleeping Beauty

Type of Attraction: Walk-through diorama

Scope & Scale: Diversion

When to Go: Anytime

Author's Rating: Low-key and well done; ★★

Overall Appeal by Age Group:

Pre-school	Grade School	Teens	Young Adults	Over 30	Senior Citizens
★★★	★★★	★★	★★	★★	★★

Time Required: About 6 minutes

Average Wait in Line per 100 People ahead of You: 9 minutes

Description and Comments Located inside Sleeping Beauty Castle, this modest attraction consists of a series of dioramas depicting the story of the castle's namesake. Quiet, romantic, and virtually unheralded (the attraction was not listed even in the park's own guide for a couple of years), the Sleeping Beauty diorama is best seen during the hot, crowded part of the day.

Touring Tips This is a fun diversion when the lines are long elsewhere. Children get a big kick out of getting to walk around inside the castle. Be forewarned that the castle passageways are quite narrow and may provoke claustrophobia, particularly when the attraction is crowded.

Matterhorn Bobsleds

Type of Ride: Roller coaster

Scope & Scale: Major attraction

When to Go: During the first 90 minutes the park is open or during the hour before it closes

Special Comments: The only Disney (adult) roller coaster with no minimum height requirement for children

Author's Rating: Fun ride but not too scary; ★★★

WARNING!
For Bouffants, Rug Wearers, and Elvis Impersonators
This Ride Will Muss Your `Do

Overall Appeal by Age Group:

Pre-school	Grade School	Teens	Young Adults	Over 30	Senior Citizens
†	★★★★	★★★★	★★★★	★★★★	★★★

† Some preschoolers loved Matterhorn Bobsleds; others were frightened.

Duration of Ride: 2⅓ minutes

Average Wait in Line per 100 People ahead of You: 13 minutes

Assumes: Both tracks operating with 10 sleds per track with 23-second dispatch intervals

Loading Speed: Moderate

Description and Comments   The Matterhorn is the most distinctive landmark on the Disneyland scene, visible from almost anywhere in the park. Updated and renovated in 1995, the Matterhorn maintains its popularity and long lines year in and year out. The Matterhorn Bobsleds is a roller-coaster ride with an alpine motif. On the scary scale, the ride ranks about six on a scale of ten (a little less intimidating than Space Mountain). The special effects cannot compare to Space Mountain, but they do afford a few surprises.

Touring Tips   Lines for the Matterhorn form as soon as the gates open and persist throughout the day. Ride first thing in the morning or just before the park closes. If you are a roller-coaster person, ride Space Mountain and then hurry over and hop on the Matterhorn. If roller coasters are not the end-all for you, we recommend choosing one or the other of the roller coasters, or saving one for a second day.

The Matterhorn has two lines: one stretches from the boarding area nearest Fantasyland and around the base of the mountain to opposite the Alice in Wonderland ride; the other line extends from the boarding area on the Tomorrowland side of the mountain along the walkway opposite the Submarine Voyage.

One of the things we like about the Matterhorn is that the entire queuing area is visible. This makes the lines look more oppressive than they actually are (causing newly arrived guests to bypass the attraction), and also provides an opportunity to closely approximate the length of time you will have to wait. If the line extends toward Tomorrowland to a point across from the Kodak Photo Spot (overlooking the submarines), your wait to ride the Matterhorn Bobsleds will be about 16 minutes. Evaluating the line that extends toward Fantasyland, your wait from a spot opposite the mouth of the cave at Alice in Wonderland should be about 14 minutes. Because the queue winding toward Fantasyland is more narrow than the one extending toward Tomorrowland, it holds fewer guests (in spite of the fact that it looks longer). Thus, you will normally have a shorter wait in line on the Fantasy-land side than if you lined up opposite the submarines.

Because Disneyland parades pass along the Alice in Wonderland side of Matterhorn Mountain, that side of the Matterhorn attraction is closed during the parade. If you watch the parade from this area, you are in a great position to hop on the Matterhorn without a wait when the closed side reopens.

Casey Jr. Circus Train

Type of Ride: Miniature train ride
Scope & Scale: Minor attraction
When to Go: Before 11 a.m. and after 5 p.m.
Author's Rating: A quiet, scenic ride; ★★½
Overall Appeal by Age Group:

Pre-school	Grade School	Teens	Young Adults	Over 30	Senior Citizens
★★★★	★★★	★½	★★★	★★★	★★★

Duration of Ride: A little over 3 minutes
Average Wait in Line per 100 People ahead of You: 12 minutes
Assumes: 2 trains operating
Loading Speed: Slow

Description and Comments   A long-standing attraction and a pet project of Walt Disney, Casey Jr. circulates through a landscape of miniature towns, farms, and lakes. There are some stunning bonsai specimens visible from this ride, as well as some of the most manicured landscaping you are ever likely to see.

Touring Tips   This ride covers the same sights as the Storybook Land Canal Boats, but does it faster and with less of a wait. Accommodations for adults, however, are less than optimal on this ride, with some passengers having to squeeze into diminutive caged cars (after all, it is a circus train). If you do not have children in your party, you can enjoy the same sights more comfortably by riding the Storybook Land Canal Boats.

Storybook Land Canal Boats

Type of Ride: Scenic boat ride
Scope & Scale: Minor attraction
When to Go: Before 10:30 a.m. and after 5:30 p.m.
Author's Rating: Pretty, tranquil, and serene; ★★★

Overall Appeal by Age Group:

Pre-school	Grade School	Teens	Young Adults	Over 30	Senior Citizens
★★★	★★½	★★½	★★★½	★★★½	★★★½

Duration of Ride: 9½ minutes

Average Wait in Line per 100 People ahead of You: 16 minutes

Assumes: 7 boats operating

Loading Speed: Slow

Description and Comments Guide-operated boats wind along canals situated beneath the same miniature landscapes visible from the Casey Jr. Circus Train. This ride, offering stellar examples of bonsai cultivation, selective pruning, and miniaturization, is a must for landscape gardening enthusiasts. Updated in 1994, the landscapes now include scenes from more recent Disney features, in addition to those from such classics as *The Wind in the Willows* and *The Three Little Pigs*.

Touring Tips The boats are much more comfortable than the train; the view of the miniatures is better; and the pace is more leisurely. On the down side, the lines are long, and if not long, definitely slow-moving, and the ride itself takes a lot of time. Our recommendation is to ride Casey Jr. if you have children or are in a hurry. Take the boat if your party is all adults or your pace is more leisurely. If you ride the Canal Boats, try to get on before 10:30 a.m.

Dumbo, the Flying Elephant

Type of Ride: Disneyfied midway ride

Scope & Scale: Minor attraction

When to Go: Before 10 a.m. or during the late evening parades, fireworks, and *Fantasmic!* performances

Special Comments: Dumbo was renovated and upgraded in 1991

Author's Rating: An attractive children's ride; ★★★½

Overall Appeal by Age Group:

Pre-school	Grade School	Teens	Young Adults	Over 30	Senior Citizens
★★★★★	★★★½	★★	★½	★½	★½

Duration of Ride: 1⅔ minutes

Average Wait in Line per 100 People ahead of You: 12 minutes

Assumes: Normal staffing

Loading Speed: Slow

Description and Comments   A nice, tame, happy children's ride based on the lovable Disney flying elephant. An upgraded rendition of a ride that can be found at state fairs and amusement parks across the country. Shortcomings notwithstanding, Dumbo is the favorite Disneyland attraction of most preschoolers. A lot of readers take us to task for lumping Dumbo in with state fair midway rides. These comments from a reader in Armdale, Nova Scotia, are representative:

> *I think you have acquired a jaded attitude. I know [Dumbo] is not for everybody, but when we took our oldest child (then just four), the sign at the end of the line said there would be a 90-minute wait. He knew and he didn't care, and he and I stood in the hot afternoon sun for 90 blissful minutes waiting for his 90-second flight. Anything that a four-year-old would wait for that long and that patiently must be pretty special.*

Touring Tips   This is a slow-load ride that we recommend you bypass unless you are on a very relaxed touring schedule. If your kids are excited about Dumbo, try to get them on the ride before 10 a.m., during the parades and *Fantasmic!*, or just before the park closes.

Mad Tea Party

Type of Ride: Midway-type spinning ride

Scope & Scale: Minor attraction

When to Go: Before 11 a.m. and after 5 p.m.

Special Comments: You can make the teacups spin faster by turning the wheel in the center of the cup

Motion Sickness WARNING!

Author's Rating: Fun but not worth the wait; ★★

Overall Appeal by Age Group:

Pre-school	Grade School	Teens	Young Adults	Over 30	Senior Citizens
★★★½	★★★★	★★★★	★★★	★★	★★

Duration of Ride: 1½ minutes

Average Wait in Line per 100 People ahead of You: 8 minutes

Assumes: Normal staffing

Loading Speed: Slow

Description and Comments   Well done in the Disney style, but still just an amusement park ride. *Alice in Wonderland*'s Mad Hatter provides the theme and patrons whirl around feverishly in big teacups. A rendition of this ride, sans Disney characters, can be found at every local carnival and fair.

Touring Tips   This ride, aside from not being particularly unique, is notoriously slow loading. Skip it on a busy schedule if the kids will let you. Ride in the morning of your second day if your schedule is more relaxed. A warning for parents who have not given this ride much thought: teenagers like nothing better than to lure an adult onto the teacups and then turn the wheel in the middle (which makes the cup spin faster) until the adults are plastered against the side of the cup and are on the verge of throwing up. Unless your life's ambition is to be the test subject in a human centrifuge, do not even consider getting on this ride with anyone younger than 21 years of age.

Fantasyland Theatre

Description and Comments   Originally installed as a teen nightspot called Videopolis, this venue has been converted into a sophisticated amphitheater where concerts and elaborate stage shows are performed according to the daily entertainment schedule. Better productions that have played the Fantasyland Theatre stage include *Beauty & The Beast Live* and *The Spirit of Pocahontas,* both musical stage adaptations of the respective Disney animated features. If either of these presentations are being performed during your visit, we rank Fantasyland Theatre as "not to be missed."

Touring Tips   Some of the shows produced here are first-rate and definitely worth your time. On busy days, many guests arrive 45–60 minutes in advance to get good seats. Because the shows tend to be less than a half-hour in duration, however, it is no hardship to watch the show standing, and standing room is usually available up to five minutes before show time. In the summer, evening performances are more comfortable.

FANTASYLAND EATERIES AND SHOPS

Description and Comments   Fantasyland offers the most attractions of any of the lands and the fewest places to eat. With the exception of the Village Haus counter-service restaurant and Meeko's, most of the food service in Fantasyland is supplied by street vendors. Add the day-long congestion to the scenario and Fantasyland ties with Mickey's Toontown as the best place in the park not to eat. If you are hungry, it's much easier to troop over to Frontierland, New Orleans Square, or even back to Main Street than to grab a bite in Fantasyland. Plus, the Village Haus, the only full-scale eatery in Fantasyland, specializes in burgers, pizza, and the like—i.e., nothing distinctive, different, or worth the hassle.

Touring Tips Fast food is anything but in Fantasyland, and shopping is ho-hum. Don't waste time on the shops unless you have a relaxed schedule or unless shopping is a big priority.

Mickey's Toontown

Mickey's Toontown is situated across the Disneyland Railroad tracks from Fantasyland. Its entrance is a tunnel that opens into Fantasyland just to the left of It's a Small World. As its name suggests, Toontown is a fanciful representation of the wacky cartoon community where all of the Disney characters live. Mickey's Toontown was inspired by the Disney animated feature *Who Framed Roger Rabbit?*, in which humans were able to enter the world of cartoon characters.

Mickey's Toontown consists of a colorful collection of miniature buildings, all executed in exaggerated cartoon style with rounded edges and brilliant colors. Among the buildings are Mickey's and Minnie's houses, both open to inspection inside and out.

In addition to serving as a place where guests can be certain of finding Disney characters at any time during the day, this newest land also serves as an elaborate interactive playground where it's OK for the kids to run, climb, and let off steam.

Mickey's Toontown is rendered with masterful attention to artistic humor and detail. The colorful buildings each have a story to tell or a gag to visit upon an unsuspecting guest. There is an explosion at the Fireworks Factory every minute or so, always unannounced. Across the street, the sidewalk is littered with crates containing strange contents addressed to exotic destinations. If you pry open the top of one of the crates (easy to do), the crate will emit a noise consistent with its contents. A box of "train parts," for example, broadcasts the sound of a racing locomotive when you lift the top.

Everywhere in Mickey's Toontown are subtleties and absurdities to delight the imagination. Next to Goofy's Bounce House there is an impact crater, shaped like Goofy, marking the spot where he missed his swimming pool while high diving. A sign in front of the local garage declares, "If we can't fix it we won't."

While adults will enjoy the imaginative charm of Mickey's Toontown, it will quickly become apparent that not much is there for them to do. Most of the attractions in Mickey's Toontown are for kids, specifically smaller children. Attractions open to adults include a dark ride drawn from *Who Framed Roger Rabbit?* (sort of a high-tech rendition of Mr. Toad's Wild Ride), a diminutive roller coaster, and a trolley that is more decorative than functional. Everything else in Mickey's Toontown is for children.

In many ways, Mickey's Toontown is a designer playground, a fanciful cousin to Tom Sawyer Island in Frontierland. What distinguishes Mickey's Toontown is that the play areas are specially designed for smaller children, it's much cleaner than Tom Sawyer Island (i.e., no dirt), and finally, in the noblest Disney tradition, you must wait in line for virtually everything.

Also be forewarned that Mickey's Toontown is not very large, especially in comparison with neighboring Fantasyland. A tolerable crowd in most of the other lands will seem like Times Square on New Year's Eve in Mickey's Toontown. Couple this congestion with the unfortunate fact that none of the attractions in Mickey's Toontown are engineered to handle huge crowds, and you come face to face with possibly the most attractive traffic jam the Disney folks have ever created. Our advice is to see Mickey's Toontown earlier in the day, before 11 a.m., or in the evening while the parades and *Fantasmic!* are going on.

Mickey's House

Type of Attraction: Walk-through tour of Mickey's House and Movie Barn, ending with a personal visit with Mickey

Scope & Scale: Minor attraction and character-greeting opportunity

When to Go: Before 10:30 a.m. and after 5:30 p.m.

Author's Rating: Well done; ★★★

Overall Appeal by Age Group:

Pre-school	Grade School	Teens	Young Adults	Over 30	Senior Citizens
★★★★★	★★★★½	★★★½	★★★½	★★★½	★★★½

Duration of Attraction: 15–30 minutes (depending on the crowd)

Average Wait in Line per 100 People ahead of You: 20 minutes

Assumes: Normal staffing

Touring Speed: Slow

Description and Comments   Mickey's House is the starting point of a self-guided tour that winds through the famous mouse's house, into the backyard and past Pluto's doghouse, and then into Mickey's Movie Barn. This last hearkens back to the so-called "barn" studio where Walt Disney created a number of the earlier Mickey Mouse cartoons. Once in the Movie Barn, guests watch vintage Disney cartoons while awaiting admittance to Mickey's Dressing Room.

In small groups of one or two families, guests are ultimately conducted into the dressing room where Mickey awaits to pose for photos and sign autographs. The visit is not lengthy (two to four minutes), but there is adequate time for all of the children to hug, poke, and admire the star.

Touring Tips   The cynical observer will discern immediately that Mickey's House, backyard, Movie Barn, etc., are no more than a cleverly devised queuing area designed to deliver guests to Mickey's Dressing Room for the Mouse Encounter. For those with some vestige of child in their personalities, however, the preamble serves to heighten anticipation while providing the opportunity to get to know the corporate symbol on a more personal level. Mickey's House is well conceived and contains a lot of Disney memorabilia. You will notice that children touch everything as they proceed through the house, hoping to find some artifact that is not welded or riveted into the set (an especially tenacious child during one of our visits was actually able to rip a couple of books from a bookcase).

Meeting Mickey and touring his house is best done during the first two hours the park is open or, alternatively, in the evening during the parades and *Fantasmic!* performances. If meeting Mickey is at the top of your child's list, you might consider taking the Disneyland Railroad from Main Street to the Toontown/Fantasyland station as soon as you enter the park. Some children are so obsessed with seeing Mickey that they cannot enjoy anything else until they get Mickey in the rearview mirror.

Minnie's House

Type of Attraction: Walk-through exhibit
Scope & Scale: Minor attraction and character-greeting opportunity
When to Go: Before 11:30 a.m. and after 4:30 p.m.
Author's Rating: OK but not great; ★★½
Overall Appeal by Age Group:

Pre-school	Grade School	Teens	Young Adults	Over 30	Senior Citizens
★★★★	★★★½	★★½	★★½	★★½	★★½

Duration of Tour: About 10 minutes
Average Wait in Line per 100 People ahead of You: 12 minutes
Touring Speed: Slow

Description and Comments   Minnie's House consists of a self-guided tour through the various rooms and backyard of Mickey Mouse's main squeeze. Similar to Mickey's House, only predictably more feminine, Minnie's House likewise showcases some fun Disney memorabilia. Among the highlights of the short tour are the fanciful appliances in Minnie's kitchen. Like Mickey, Minnie is usually present to receive guests.

Touring Tips The main difference between Mickey's House and Minnie's House is that Minnie's House cannot accommodate as many guests. See Minnie early and before Mickey to avoid waiting outdoors in a long queue. Be advised that neither Mickey nor Minnie is available during parades.

Roger Rabbit's Car Toon Spin

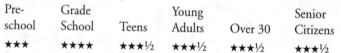

Motion
Sickness

WARNING!

Type of Ride: Track ride in the dark
Scope & Scale: Major attraction
When to Go: Before 10:30 a.m. and after 6:30 p.m.
Author's Rating: ★★★
Overall Appeal by Age Group:

Pre-school	Grade School	Teens	Young Adults	Over 30	Senior Citizens
★★★	★★★★	★★★½	★★★½	★★★½	★★★½

Duration of Ride: A little over 3 minutes
Average Wait in Line per 100 People ahead of You: 7 minutes
Assumes: Full capacity operation
Loading Speed: Moderate

Description and Comments A so-called dark ride where guests become part of a cartoon plot. The idea is that you are renting a cab for a tour of Toontown. As soon as your cab gets under way, however, weasels throw a slippery glop (known as "dip") on the road, sending the cab into a more or less uncontrollable spin. This spinning continues as the cab passes through a variety of sets populated by cartoon and AudioAnimatronic characters and punctuated by simulated explosions. As a child of the '60s put it, "It was like combining Mr. Toad's Wild Ride with the Mad Tea Party [spinning teacups] while tripping on LSD."

The main problem with the Car Toon Spin is that, because of the spinning, you are often pointed in the wrong direction to appreciate (or even see) many of the better visual effects. Furthermore, the story line is loose. The attraction lacks the continuity and humor of Splash Mountain or the suspense of the Haunted Mansion or Snow White's Scary Adventures.

A reader from Milford, Michigan, echoed our sentiments, lamenting:

> *The most disappointing ride to me was Roger Rabbit's Car Toon Spin. I stood 45 minutes for a fun house ride and the wheel was so difficult to operate that I spent most of my time trying to steer the bloody car and missed the point of the ride.*

Touring Tips The ride is popular both for its novelty and its newness, and it is one of the few Mickey's Toontown attractions that parents (with strong stomachs) can enjoy with their children. Because the ride stays fairly thronged with people all day long, the best time to ride is before 10:30 a.m., during parades and *Fantasmic!,* and in the hour before the park closes.

The spinning, incidentally, can be controlled by the guests. If you don't want to spin, you don't have to. If you do elect to spin, you still will not be able to approach the eye-popping speed attainable on the teacups at the Mad Tea Party. Sluggish spinning aside, our advice for those who are at all susceptible to motion sickness is not to get near this ride if you are touring with anyone under 21 years of age.

Gadget's Go-Coaster

Type of Ride: Small roller coaster

Scope & Scale: Minor attraction

When to Go: Before 10:30 a.m., during the parades and *Fantasmic!* in the evening, and just before the park closes

Author's Rating: Great for little ones but not worth the wait for adults; ★★

Overall Appeal by Age Group:

Pre-school	Grade School	Teens	Young Adults	Over 30	Senior Citizens
★★★★	★★★½	★★½	★★½	★★½	★★

Duration of Ride: About 50 seconds

Average Wait in Line per 100 People ahead of You: 10 minutes

Assumes: Normal staffing

Loading Speed: Slow

Description and Comments   Gadget's Go-Coaster is a very small roller coaster; the idea is that you are miniaturized and riding around in an acorn shell. The ride itself is pretty zippy, but it is over so quickly you hardly know you've been anywhere. In fact, of the 52 seconds the ride is in motion, 32 seconds are consumed in exiting the loading area, being ratcheted up the first hill, and braking into the off-loading area. The actual time you spend careening around the track is a whopping 20 seconds.

Touring Tips   Because the cars of this dinky roller coaster are too small for most adults, there is a fair amount of whiplashing for taller people. Add to that the small carrying capacity of the ride (the track is too short for more than one train to operate) and you have a real engineering brain fart. Unfortunately, the ride is visually appealing. All the kids want to ride, subjecting the whole family to incarceration in a line whose movement can only be discerned by time-lapse photography. Our recommendation to parties touring without children: skip Gadget's Go-Coaster. If there are children in your group, you've got a problem. Try to ride during the first hour the park is open, during the parades and *Fantasmic!*, or just before the park closes.

Chip 'n' Dale's Treehouse and Acorn Ball Crawl

Type of Ride: Imaginative children's play area

Scope & Scale: Diversion

When to Go: Before 10:30 a.m. and after 5:30 p.m.

Author's Rating: Good exercise for the small fry; ★★

Overall Appeal by Age Group:

Pre-school	Grade School	Teens	Young Adults	Over 30	Senior Citizens
★★★★	★★★½	NA	NA	NA	NA

Duration of Play: Varies

Average Wait in Line per 100 People ahead of You: 20 minutes for the Acorn Crawl

Description and Comments The play area consists of a treehouse with slides and a pit full of plastic acorns that kids can wallow around in.

Touring Tips Located in the most remote corner of Mickey's Toontown and obscured by the crowd waiting to ride the roller coaster next door, the Treehouse and Acorn Crawl are frequently overlooked. Of all the attractions in Mickey's Toontown, this is the easiest to get the kids into without much of a wait. Most any child that can fit is allowed to rummage around in the Treehouse, but only children older than three years and shorter than 48 inches may squirm among the plastic acorns. As an aside, avoid the acorn pit after a rain; it can be a little damp. The best time to experience the Treehouse and Acorn Crawl is before 11:30 a.m. and after 5:30 p.m.

Miss Daisy, Donald Duck's Boat

Type of Attraction: Creative play area with a boat theme

Scope & Scale: Diversion

When to Go: Before 10:30 a.m. and after 4:30 p.m.

Author's Rating: Great fun for children; ★★

Overall Appeal by Age Group:

Pre-school	Grade School	Teens	Young Adults	Over 30	Senior Citizens
★★★★	★★★½	NA	NA	NA	NA

Duration of Play: Varies

Average Wait in Line per 100 People ahead of You: Usually no waiting

Description and Comments   Another children's play area, this time with a tugboat theme. Children can climb nets, ring bells, survey Toontown from the captain's bridge, and scoot down slides. The idea is that Donald Duck (who, as everyone knows, lives in Duckburg) is visiting Toontown.

Touring Tips   Kids more or less wander on and off of the *Miss Daisy,* and usually there is not any sort of organized line or queuing area. Enjoy this play area at your leisure and stay as long as you like.

Goofy's Bounce House

Type of Attraction: A play area where children jump in an inflated enclosure

Scope & Scale: Diversion

When to Go: Before 10:30 a.m., during the evening parades and *Fantasmic!,* and during the two hours before the park closes

Author's Rating: A rambunctious child's dream; ★★½

Overall Appeal by Age Group:

Pre-school	Grade School	Teens	Young Adults	Over 30	Senior Citizens
★★★★	★★★★	NA	NA	NA	NA

Bouncing Time: 3 minutes

Average Wait in Line per 100 People ahead of You: 28 minutes

Assumes: 2 minutes between jumping sessions

Loading Speed: Slow

Description and Comments   Goofy's Bounce House is a house with a totally inflated interior. Up to 15 children are admitted at a time for 3 minutes of jumping, lunging, tumbling, and careening off the walls, floor, and furniture. A Disney cast member supervises the activity and endeavors to prevent mid-air collisions.

Touring Tips   One of Toontown's most popular attractions, the Bounce House is the exclusive domain of children over 3 years old and shorter than 52 inches. Children enter the house from the side and remove their shoes. Adults can observe the mayhem from windows at the front of the house. Goofy's Bounce House is another example of an appealing idea executed on a scale too small to handle the attraction's great popularity and demand. On a crowded day, a small child can grow beyond the height limit in the time it takes him to get to the front of the line. Experience this attraction before 10:30 a.m., during parades and *Fantasmic!,* or during the two hours before park closing.

Jolly Trolley

Type of Ride: A cartoonlike trolley that putters around Toontown

Scope & Scale: Diversion

When to Go: Before 11:30 a.m. and after 4:30 p.m.

Author's Rating: No big deal; ★

Overall Appeal by Age Group:

Pre-school	Grade School	Teens	Young Adults	Over 30	Senior Citizens
★★	★★	½	½	★½	★

Duration of Ride: Varies

Average Wait in Line per 100 People ahead of You: 25 minutes

Description and Comments   The Jolly Trolley is more of a visual decoration than a bona fide ride. The trolley bumps along a short circular route through Toontown that could be walked in three minutes. How long the trolley takes to make the complete circuit depends on how many pedestrians (usually plenty) are blocking the track.

Touring Tips   Though a good photo opportunity, the Jolly Trolley is otherwise expendable.

CHARACTER WATCHING

Description and Comments   If you want to see characters, Mickey's Toontown is the place to go. In addition to Mickey, who receives guests all day in his dressing room, and Minnie, who entertains in her house, you are also likely to see Donald and Pluto in front of Toontown Hall and bump into such august personages as Daisy, Roger Rabbit, and a host of others lurking around the streets. It would be a rare event to visit Toontown without bumping into a few characters. From time to time, horns sound and whistles blow atop the Toontown City Hall, followed by a fanfare rendition of the Mickey Mouse Club theme song. This indicates, as a mom from Texas explained to us, that "some characters are fixin' to come out." And there you have it.

TOONTOWN EATERIES AND SHOPS

Description and Comments   Food service in Mickey's Toontown is limited to drinks, snacks, hot dogs, and pizza. The Gag Factory, which sells Disney souvenirs, is one of the park's more entertaining shopping venues. Even if you do not buy anything, the place is fun to walk through.

Tomorrowland

Tomorrowland is a futuristic mix of rides and experiences that relates to technological development and what life will be like in the years to come.

An exhaustive renovation of Tomorrowland was begun in 1996 and completed in 1998. Before the renovation, Tomorrowland's 40-year-old buildings more resembled '70s motel architecture than anyone's vision of the future. Tomorrowland's renovated design is more enduring, reflecting a nostalgic vision of the future as imagined by dreamers and scientists in the 1920s and '30s. Frozen in time, Tomorrowland now conjures up visions of Buck Rogers, fanciful mechanical rockets, and metallic cities spread beneath towering obelisks. Disney refers to the "new" Tomorrowland as the "Future That Never Was." *Newsweek* dubs it "retro-future."

In the new Tomorrowland, *Honey, I Shrunk the Audience* replaced *Captain EO*. The large circular building that once housed America Sings contains Innoventions, a collection of hands-on exhibits featuring cutting-edge consumer products, including virtual reality games. The Rocket Jets ride, reincarnated as the AstroOrbiter, sports a campy Jules Verne look, but it still goes around in circles. Circle-Vision is now a loading and preshow area for Rocket Rods, a thrill ride that replaced the PeopleMover. Star Tours and the venerable Space Mountain have been retained, as have the Submarine Voyage and the Tomorrowland Autopia.

Star Tours

Type of Attraction: Space flight simulation ride

Scope & Scale: Headliner

When to Go: Before 10 a.m.

Special Comments: Frightens many small children; expectant mothers are also advised against riding.

Author's Rating: A blast; not to be missed; ★★★★½

Overall Appeal by Age Group:

Pre-school	Grade School	Teens	Young Adults	Over 30	Senior Citizens
★★★★	★★★★★	★★★★★	★★★★★	★★★★★	★★★★★

Duration of Ride: Approximately 7 minutes

Average Wait in Line per 100 People ahead of You: 6 minutes

Assumes: 4 simulators operating

Loading Speed: Moderate

Description and Comments This attraction is so amazing, so real, and so much fun that it just makes you grin and giggle. The attraction consists of a ride in a flight simulator modeled after those used for training pilots and astronauts. Guests, supposedly on a little vacation outing in space, are piloted by a droid (android, a.k.a. humanoid, a.k.a. robot) on his first flight with real passengers. Mayhem ensues almost immediately as scenery flashes by at supersonic speed and the simulator bucks and pitches. You could swear you are moving at light speed. After several minutes of this, the droid somehow gets the spacecraft landed and you discover you are about ten times happier than you were before you boarded.

Touring Tips This ride will be a Disneyland headliner for some time to come and can be counted on to draw large crowds throughout the day. If you enjoy the wilder rides, ride Indiana Jones as soon as the park opens, and follow that with Space Mountain, Rocket Rods, Star Tours, and Splash Mountain. Be aware that the crowds in Tomorrowland are larger on cold or rainy days when many guests skip Splash Mountain (a water-flume ride in Critter Country). Children must be at least 40 inches tall and 3 years of age to ride Star Tours.

Space Mountain

Type of Ride: Roller coaster in the dark

Scope & Scale: Headliner

When to Go: During the first hour the park is open, during the hour before closing, or between 6 and 7 p.m.

Special Comments: Children must be 3'4" tall to ride (see "Switching Off" on page 87); those under age 7 must ride with an adult

Author's Rating: Good roller coaster with excellent special effects; ★★★★

Overall Appeal by Age Group:

Pre-school	Grade School	Teens	Young Adults	Over 30	Senior Citizens
†	★★★★★	★★★★★	★★★★	★★★★	†

† Children must be 3'4" tall to ride. Some preschoolers loved Space Mountain, and others were frightened. The sample size of senior citizens who experienced this ride was too small to develop an accurate rating.

Duration of Ride: 2¾ minutes

Average Wait in Line per 100 People ahead of You: 3½ minutes

Assumes: 11 cars operating at 20-second dispatch intervals

Loading Speed: Moderate to fast

For those who think the graphic above is a joke, listen to a teen from Colchester, Connecticut, who wrote us about her bad hair day:

> *WARN Space Mountain riders to take off hair scrunchies. I lost my best one on it and couldn't get it back. This ride was fast, curvy, and very hairdo messing.*

Description and Comments   Space Mountain is a roller coaster in the dark. Totally enclosed in a mammoth futuristic structure, the attraction is a marvel of creativity and engineering. The theme of the ride is a space flight through the dark recesses of the galaxy. The effects are superb and the ride is one of the wildest in the Disney repertoire. As a roller coaster, Space Mountain is a little wilder than the Matterhorn Bobsleds, but it has much better special effects, including some sound and special effects system upgrades incorporated in 1997. Space Mountain is considerably more intense than the Big Thunder Mountain Railroad and much more interesting than the Matterhorn Bobsleds. If you are a Disneyland veteran, be forewarned that the entrance to Space Mountain has been reconfigured as part of the Tomorrowland renovation.

Touring Tips   Space Mountain is a "not to be missed" feature (if you can handle a fairly wild roller-coaster ride). People who are not timid about going on roller coasters will take Space Mountain in stride. What sets Space Mountain apart is that the cars plummet through the dark with only occasional lighting effects piercing the gloom.

We recommend riding Indiana Jones as soon as the park opens, followed in order by Space Mountain, Rocket Rods, Star Tours, and Splash Mountain. If you miss Space Mountain in the morning, try again during parades and *Fantasmic!,* or during the hour before the park closes. Except at opening, always ask the Disney staffer at the entrance how long the wait will be. After opening, any wait of less than 35 minutes is good.

Submarine Voyage

Type of Ride: Adventure/scenic boat ride
Scope & Scale: Major attraction
When to Go: Before 10 a.m. or during the hour before the park closes
Author's Rating: Interesting and fun; ★★★
Overall Appeal by Age Group:

Pre-school	Grade School	Teens	Young Adults	Over 30	Senior Citizens
★★★★	★★★★	★★★	★★★½	★★★½	★★★

Duration of Ride: Approximately 10 minutes
Average Wait in Line per 100 People ahead of You: 5 minutes
Assumes: 8 submarines operating
Loading Speed: Slow to moderate

Description and Comments This attraction is equipped with modern submarines, in contrast to the Captain Nemo models once used at Walt Disney World in Florida. The ride consists of a submarine voyage that encounters mermaids, sea serpents, a variety of marine life (robotic), sunken ships, giant squids, and other sights and adventures. An older ride, the Submarine Voyage struggles to maintain its image alongside such marvels as Indiana Jones and Splash Mountain.

Touring Tips This is a slow-loading, moderate-capacity ride. To avoid long lines, ride before 10 a.m., during parades and *Fantasmic!*, or right before the park closes.

Tomorrowland Autopia

Type of Ride: Drive-'em-yourself miniature cars
Scope & Scale: Minor attraction
When to Go: Before 10 a.m. and after 5 p.m.
Special Comments: Must be 4' 4" tall to drive
Author's Rating: Boring for adults (★); great for preschoolers
Overall Appeal by Age Group:

Pre-school	Grade School	Teens	Young Adults	Over 30	Senior Citizens
★★★½	★★★	★	½	½	½

Duration of Ride: Approximately 4½ minutes
Average Wait in Line per 100 People ahead of You: 6 minutes

Assumes: 35 cars operating on each track

Loading Speed: Slow

Description and Comments   An elaborate miniature freeway with gasoline-powered cars that will travel at speeds of up to seven miles an hour. The raceway design, with its sleek cars, auto race noises, and highway signs, is quite alluring. In fact, however, the cars poke along on a track that leaves the driver with little to do. Pretty ho-hum for most adults and teenagers. Of those children who would enjoy the ride, many are excluded by the requirement that drivers be 4'4" tall.

Touring Tips   This ride is appealing to the eye, but definitely expendable on a schedule for adults. Preschoolers, however, love it. If your preschooler is too short to drive, ride along and allow him or her to steer (the car runs on a guide rail) while you work the foot pedal.

A mom from North Billerica, Massachusetts, writes:

> *I was truly amazed by the number of adults in the line. Please emphasize to your readers that these cars travel on a guided path and are not a whole lot of fun. The only reason I could think of for adults to be in line was an insane desire to go on absolutely every ride. The other feature about the cars is that they tend to pile up at the end, so it takes almost as long to get off as it did to get on. Parents riding with their preschoolers should keep the car going as slow as it can without stalling. This prolongs the preschooler's joy and decreases the time you will have to wait at the end.*

AstroOrbiter

Type of Ride: Very mild midway-type thrill ride

Scope & Scale: Minor attraction

When to Go: Before 10 a.m. or during the hour before the park closes

Author's Rating: Not worth the wait; ★

Overall Appeal by Age Group:

Pre-school	Grade School	Teens	Young Adults	Over 30	Senior Citizens
★★★★	★★★½	★★★	★★	★	★

Motion Sickness
WARNING!

Duration of Ride: 1½ minutes

Average Wait in Line per 100 People ahead of You: 13 minutes

Assumes: Normal staffing

Loading Speed: Slow

Description and Comments Though the look is different and the attraction has been relocated at the central hub entrance to Tomorrowland, the new AstroOrbiter ride is essentially a makeover of the old Rocket Jets, i.e., a visually appealing midway-type ride involving small rockets that rotate on arms around a central axis. Be aware that the AstroOrbiter flies higher and faster than Dumbo and that it frightens some small children. The ride also apparently messes with certain adults, as a mother from Israel attests:

> *I think your assessment of the Rocket Jets [AstroOrbiter] as "very mild" is way off. I was able to sit through all the "Mountains" and the "Tours" . . . without my stomach reacting even a little, but after the Rocket Jets [AstroOrbiter] I thought I would be finished for the rest of the day. Very quickly I realized that my only chance for survival was to pick a point on the toe of my shoe and stare at it (and certainly not lift my eyes out of the "jet") until the ride was over. My four-year-old was my copilot, and she loved the ride (go figure) and she had us up high the whole time. It was a nightmare—people should be forewarned.*

Touring Tips AstroOrbiter is essentially the same ride as the old Rocket Jets: slow to load and expendable on any schedule. If you take a preschooler on this ride, place your child in the seat first and then sit down yourself.

Starcade

Description and Comments Starcade is nothing more or less than a large (200-plus games) electronic games arcade. The *pièce de résistance* is the SEGA R360, a jet combat simulator game—players actually roll upside down in the course of play. Though the game is expensive—$4 for about two minutes of play—many teens and young adults regard it as the highlight of their Disneyland day.

Touring Tips Enjoy your time in the area with a pocket full of quarters.

Disneyland Railroad

Description and Comments The Disneyland Railroad makes a regular stop at the Tomorrowland Railroad Station. For additional details about the railroad see Disneyland Railroad in the Main Street, U.S.A. write-up.

Touring Tips This station becomes fairly crowded on busy days. If you are interested primarily in getting there, it may be quicker to walk.

Innoventions

Type of Attraction: Multifaceted attraction featuring static and hands-on exhibits relating to products and technologies of the near future

Scope & Scale: Major diversion

When to Go: On your second day or after you have seen all the major attractions

Special Comments: Most exhibits demand time and participation to be rewarding; not much gained here by a quick walk-through

Author's Rating: Very commercial, but well presented; ★★★

Overall Appeal By Age Group:

Pre-school	Grade School	Teens	Young Adults	Over 30	Senior Citizens
★½	★★★	★★★★	★★★★	★★★	★★★

Description and Comments Innoventions is housed in the large circular building last occupied by the AudioAnimatronic musical *America Sings.* Modeled after a similar attraction at Epcot in Walt Disney World, Innoventions was part of the 1996–98 Tomorrowland renovation. The attraction consists of a huge, busy collection of industry-sponsored walk-through and hands-on exhibits. Dynamic, interactive, and forward looking, Innoventions most closely resembles a high-tech trade show. Featured products provide guests with a preview of consumer and industrial goods of the near future. Electronics, communications, and entertainment technologies, as you would expect, play a prominent role. Exhibits, many of which will change each year, demonstrate such products as virtual reality games, high-definition TV, voice-activated appliances, and various CD-ROM applications, among others. There are several major exhibit areas, each sponsored by a different manufacturer or research lab. The emphasis in the respective exhibits is on the effect of the product or technology on daily living.

Touring Tips Guests display a wide range of reactions to the many Innoventions exhibits. We can only suggest that you form your own opinion. In terms of touring strategy, we recommend you spend time at Innoventions on your second day. If you only have one day, visit sometime during the evening if you have the time and endurance. Be warned, however, that many Innoventions exhibits are technical in nature and may not be compatible with your mood or level of energy toward the end of a long day. Also be advised that you cannot get much of anything out of a quick walk-through of Innoventions; you have to invest a little time to understand what is going on. Finally, and predictably, teens and other electronic game buffs may well find Innoventions to be their favorite Disneyland attraction.

Honey, I Shrunk the Audience

Type of Attraction: 3D film with special effects

Scope & Scale: Headliner

When to Go: Before 11 a.m. or during the late afternoon and evening

Special Comments: Replaced *Captain EO* as part of the Tomorrowland renovation

Author's Rating: An absolute hoot! Not to be missed; ★★★★½

Overall Appeal by Age Group:

Pre-school	Grade School	Teens	Young Adults	Over 30	Senior Citizens
★★★½	★★★★½	★★★★½	★★★★	★★★★	★★★½

Duration of Presentation: Approximately 17 minutes

Preshow Entertainment: 8 minutes

Probable Waiting Time: 12 minutes (at suggested times)

Description and Comments   *Honey, I Shrunk the Audience* is a 3D offshoot of Disney's feature film, *Honey, I Shrunk the Kids.* Replacing the long-running *Captain EO* (starring Michael Jackson), *Honey, I Shrunk the Audience* features a similar array of special effects, including simulated explosions, smoke, fiber optics, lights, water spray, and even moving seats. Where *Captain EO* had a brotherly love message, *Honey, I Shrunk the Audience* is played strictly for laughs.

Touring Tips   The audio level is ear-splitting for productions in this theater. Small children are sometimes frightened by the sound volume, and many adults report that the loud soundtrack is distracting and even uncomfortable.

Honey, I Shrunk the Audience is an exceptionally popular attraction. Try to work the production into your touring schedule before 11 a.m. or in the late afternoon or evening. The theater is large, so don't be intimidated if the line is long. Finally, try to avoid seats in the first several rows. If you are too close to the screen, the 3D images do not focus properly.

Rocket Rods

Type of Attraction: High-speed track ride

Scope & Scale: Headliner

When to Go: Before 10 a.m.

Special Comments: May frighten small children; expectant mothers are also advised against riding.

Author's Rating: New, but not exceptional; ★★★

Overall Appeal by Age Group:

Pre-school	Grade School	Teens	Young Adults	Over 30	Senior Citizens
★★★	★★★½	★★★	★★★	★★★	★★½

Duration of Ride: A little more than 4 minutes

Average Wait in Line per 100 People ahead of You: 4 minutes

Assumes: Operation at full capacity

Loading Speed: Moderate to fast

Description and Comments Tomorrowland's newest thrill ride and the park's fastest ride, with speeds slightly exceeding that of Space Mountain, has had a tough time latching on to a name or an identity. Several names, including Rocket Sleds, Rockets Pods, and finally, Rocket Rods, were run up the flagpole. Rocket Rods takes the place of the old PeopleMover and covers pretty much the same route, only much faster.

Disneyland vets will remember that the PeopleMover provided a convoluted tour of Tomorrowland, popping in and out of buildings (including Space Mountain and Star Tours) that house the land's attractions, restaurants, and shops. Basically the new ride takes you on the same tour, but at warp speed, augmented by well-executed laser and strobe light effects that occur whenever the five-passenger vehicles pass through an enclosed area.

The entrance is in the old Circle-Vision building, opposite Star Tours, and a new 360° Circle-Vision film has been incorporated into the preshow experience.

Touring Tips Though billed as the headliner attraction of the renovated Tomorrowland, Rocket Rods does not have the cohesive theming or visual impact that makes Star Tours Tomorrowland's perennial favorite.

Though too early to tell, our speculation is that Rocket Rods will not permanently supplant Indiana Jones or Space Mountain in popularity. Our recommendation for now, however, is to see Rocket Rods before Indiana Jones and Space Mountain if, and only if, the wait is less than 20 minutes.

Disneyland Monorail System

Type of Ride: Transportation/scenic

Scope & Scale: Major attraction

When to Go: During the hot, crowded period of the day (11:30 a.m.–5 p.m.)

Special Comments: Take the Monorail to the Disneyland Hotel for lunch

Author's Rating: Nice relaxing ride with some interesting views of the park; ★★★

Overall Appeal by Age Group:

Pre-school	Grade School	Teens	Young Adults	Over 30	Senior Citizens
★★★	★★★	★★★	★★★	★★★	★★

Duration of Ride: 12–15 minutes round-trip

Average Wait in Line per 100 People ahead of You: 10 minutes

Assumes: Three Monorails operating

Loading Speed: Moderate to fast

Description and Comments   The Monorail is a futuristic transportation ride that affords the only practical opportunity for escaping the park during the crowded lunch period and early afternoon. Boarding at the Tomorrowland Monorail Station, you can commute to the Disneyland Hotel complex, where it's possible to have a nice lunch without fighting the crowds. For those not interested in lunch, the Monorail provides a tranquil trip to the hotel and back with a nice view of the parking lot and parts of Fantasyland and Tomorrowland.

Touring Tips   We recommend using the Monorail to commute to the Disneyland Hotel for a quiet relaxing lunch away from the crowds and the heat. Recommendations for restaurants at the Disneyland Hotel can be found in the section on dining. If you only wish to experience the ride, go whenever you wish; the waits to board are seldom long except in the two hours before closing.

TOMORROWLAND EATERIES

Description and Comments   A new buffeteria-style restaurant was recently opened in the old Mission to Mars building and serves old-world fare such as pizza, pasta, garlic bread, and salad. Tomorrowland Terrace will remain and will serve such foods of the future as hamburgers, fries, and chicken nuggets.

Live Entertainment and Special Events

Live entertainment in the form of bands, Disney character appearances, parades, singing and dancing, and ceremonies further enliven and add color to Disneyland on a daily basis. For specific information about what's happening on the day you visit, stop by City Hall as you enter the park and pick up the daily entertainment schedule. Be forewarned, however, that if you are on a tight schedule, it is impossible to both see the park's featured attractions and take in the numerous and varied live performances offered. In our One-Day Touring Plans we exclude the live performances in favor of seeing as much of the park as time permits. This is a considered tactical decision based on the fact that the parades and *Fantasmic!,* Disneyland's river spectacular, siphon crowds away from the more popular rides, thus shortening waiting lines.

The color and pageantry of live happenings around the park are an integral part of the Disneyland entertainment mix and a persuasive argument for second-day touring. Though live entertainment is varied, plentiful, and nearly continuous throughout the day, several productions are preeminent.

Fantasmic!

Description and Comments   *Fantasmic!* is a mixed-media show presented one or more times each evening the park is open late (10 p.m. or later). Staged at the end of Tom Sawyer Island opposite the Frontierland and New Orleans Square waterfronts, *Fantasmic!* is far and away the most extraordinary and ambitious outdoor spectacle ever attempted in any theme park. Starring Mickey Mouse in his role as the sorcerer's apprentice from *Fantasia,* the production uses lasers, images projected on a shroud of mist, fireworks, lighting effects, and music in combinations so stunning you can scarcely believe what you have seen.

The plot is simple: good vs. evil. The story gets lost in all the special effects at times, but no matter—it is the spectacle, not the story line, that is so overpowering. While *beautiful, stunning,* and *powerful* are words that immediately come to mind, they fail to convey the uniqueness of this presentation. It could be argued, with some validity, that *Fantasmic!* alone is worth the price of Disneyland admission. Needless to say, we rate *Fantasmic!* as "not to be missed."

Touring Tips   It is not easy to see *Fantasmic!* For the first show particularly, guests begin staking out prime viewing spots along the edge of the New Orleans Square and Frontierland waterfronts as much as four hours in advance. Similarly, good vantage points on raised walkways and terraces are also grabbed up early on. A mom from Lummi Island, Washington, dismantled her Disney stroller to make a nest: "We used the snap-off cover on the rental stroller to sit on during *Fantasmic!,* the ground was really cold." Along similar lines, a middle-aged New York man wrote, saying, "Your excellent guidebook also served as a seat cushion while waiting seated on the ground. Make future editions thicker for greater comfort."

The best seats in the house are at the water's edge. For adults, it is really not necessary to have an unobstructed view of the staging area, because most of the action is high above the crowd. Children standing in the closely packed crowd, however, are able to catch only bits and pieces of the presentation.

Probably the most painless strategy for seeing *Fantasmic!* is to attend the second or third show (on nights when the park is open until midnight). Usually the second performance follows the first performance by about an hour and a half. If you let the crowd for the first show clear out and then take up your position, you should be able to find a good vantage point. The evening parade, which winds through Fantasyland and down Main Street, often runs concurrently with *Fantasmic!* for the first and second shows of the evening, essentially splitting the crowd between the two events. At the second *Fantasmic!* and second parade, however, there are fewer people in the park and viewing conditions are less crowded. Though there is no parade to siphon guests away from *Fantasmic!* at the late (third) show, the number of people in the park has diminished to the point where competition for good vantage points is roughly the same as for the second performance.

Rain and wind conditions sometimes cause *Fantasmic!* to be canceled. Unfortunately, Disney officials usually do not make a final decision about whether to proceed or cancel until just before show time. We have seen guests wrapped in ponchos sit stoically in rain or drizzle for more than an hour with no assurance that their patience and sacrifice would be rewarded. Unless you can find a covered viewing spot, we do not recommend staking out vantage points on rainy or especially windy nights. On nights like these, pursue your own agenda until ten minutes or so before show time, and then head to the waterfront to see what happens.

For $35 you can view *Fantasmic!* from the balcony of the Disney Gallery (in New Orleans Square), easily the best vantage point available. Included in the price is a dessert buffet. Because the balcony can accommodate only 15 guests, each show sells out fast. If you want to be one of the balcony elite, rush to the Guest Relations window between the main entrance and the kennels first thing in the morning to sign up. The window opens at the same time as the park on Magic Mornings (early entry days) and 30 minutes before park opening on other days. Tickets sell out fast, so queue up at least a half-hour before the window opens.

Finally, make sure to hang on to children during *Fantasmic!* and to give them explicit instructions for regrouping in the event you are separated. Be especially vigilant when the crowd disperses after the show.

Parades

Description and Comments   All the Disney theme parks the world over are famous for their parades. On days when the park closes early there is an afternoon parade. On days when the park closes late (10 p.m. to 1 a.m.), there are always evening parades, and often an afternoon parade as well.

The parades are full-blown Disney productions with some combination of floats, huge inflated balloons of the characters, marching bands, old-time vehicles, dancers, and, of course, literally dozens of costumed Disney characters. Themes for the parades vary from time to time, and special holiday parades are always produced for Christmas and Easter.

Touring Tips   Parades usually begin in Fantasyland to the right of It's a Small World and proceed between the Matterhorn and Alice in Wonderland to the central hub. After taking a lap around the hub, the parade continues down Main Street, circles Town Square, and exits through a gate to the right of the Town Square Cafe. Sometimes the parades run the reverse route.

The parades always serve to diminish the lines for attractions. One of our favorite parade strategies is to watch a parade (that begins in Fantasyland) as it passes It's a Small World, and then hightail it over to Indiana Jones in Adventureland while the parade is still making its way around the central hub and down Main Street.

The Smith family from East Wimple stakes out their viewing spot for *Fantasmic!*

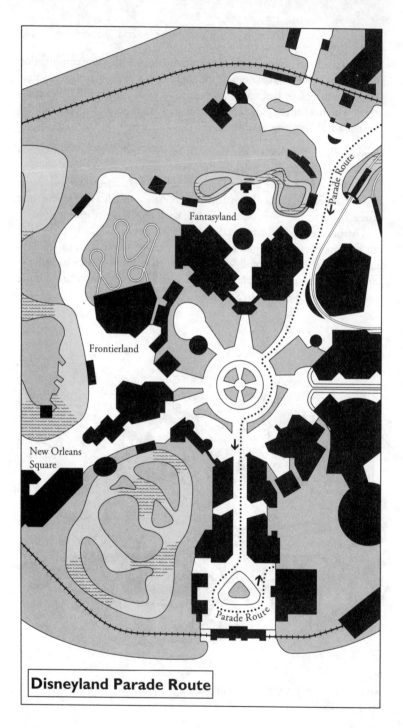

Fantasyland

Frontierland

New Orleans
Square

Parade Route

Parade Route

Disneyland Parade Route

Main Street is the most crowded area from which to watch a parade when it begins at Town Square. The opposite is true when the parade begins in Fantasyland. The upper platform of the Main Street train station affords the best viewing perspective along the route. The best time to get a position on the platform is when the parade begins in Fantasyland. When this happens, good spots on the platform are available right up to the time the parade begins. When you are at the end of the parade route, you can assume it will take the parade 15–18 minutes to get to you.

Keep an eye on your children during the parades and give them explicit instructions for regrouping in the event you are separated. Children constantly jockey for better viewing positions. A few wiggles this way and a few wiggles the other and presto, they are lost in the crowd. Finally, be especially vigilant when the crowd disperses after the parade. Thousands of people suddenly strike out in different directions, creating a perfect situation for losing a child or two.

Live Entertainment throughout the Park

Parades and *Fantasmic!* make up only a part of the daily live entertainment offerings at Disneyland. The following is an incomplete list of other performances and events that are scheduled with some regularity and that require no reservations.

Disneyland Band   Disneyland's all-purpose band entertains around the park.

Sax Quintet   A versatile quintet of saxes that plays on Main Street.

Big Thunder Breakdown Boys   Bluegrass music in Critter Country and Frontierland.

Royal Street Bachelors   A strolling Dixieland band often seen in New Orleans Square.

Mountain Climbers   Real climbers scale the Matterhorn in Fantasyland.

Disney Rock Groups   High-energy Disney rock groups perform daily in Tomorrowland according to the daily entertainment schedule.

Retreat Ceremony   Daily at around dusk in Town Square a small band and honor guard lower the flag and release a flock of white homing pigeons.

Fantasy in the Sky   A wonderful fireworks display that usually follows the early evening parade; watch from in front of Casey Jr. in Fantasyland.

Tomorrowland Terrace Stage   The stage at Tomorrowland Terrace is the site of daily concerts, usually featuring Disney rock groups.

Sword in the Stone Ceremony   An audience-participation ceremony based on the Disney animated feature of the same name. Merlin the Magician selects youngsters from among the guests to test their courage and strength by removing the sword Excalibur from the stone. Staged each day near King Arthur Carrousel according to the daily entertainment schedule.

Festival of Fools   An elaborate theater-in-the-round featuring live shows based on some recent Disney animated feature. The *Hunchback of Notre Dame* production was especially worthwhile. Festival of Fools is located behind Big Thunder Mountain on the path connecting Frontierland and Fantasyland. Performance times are per the daily entertainment schedule.

Bands about Disneyland   Various banjo, Dixieland, steel drum, marching, and fife and drum bands roam the park daily.

Disney Character Appearances   Disney characters appear at random throughout the park but are routinely present in Mickey's Toontown and Fantasyland, and on Main Street.

Disney Character Breakfasts and Dinners   Disney characters join guests for breakfast each morning until 10:45 a.m. at the Tomorrowland Terrace (to the right at the end of Main Street). Disney characters also join guests for breakfast and dinner at Goofy's Kitchen at the Disneyland Hotel.

Eating in Disneyland

The food at Disneyland has improved substantially over the past couple of years. True, the fare is still overpriced and there are plenty of culinary land mines to avoid, but on average things are looking up. In 1997 the park reassessed all of its full-service and counter-service menus. The upshot was the addition of a number of new selections, which, in addition to providing more choice and variety, lend authenticity and an ethnic touch to the various theme areas. It is fun, for example, to at last enjoy jambalaya in New Orleans Square. If, however, you prefer simpler, more traditional fare, don't worry: there is no chance that hamburgers or hot dogs will become endangered species at Disneyland.

A Word about Fast Food at Disneyland

To give you some sense of what fast food and snacks in the park will cost, we provide the following list:

Coffee: $1.50	Salads: $2–8
Bottled water: $2.50	Fries: $1.75

Potato chips: $1
Ice cream: $2–5
Sandwiches, burgers, hot dogs: $3–8
Sandwich combos: $6–9
Soft drinks, iced tea, lemonade: $2.10

Pizza: $3–7
Popcorn: $2
Churro: $2
Children's meals: $4

Healthy Food at Disneyland

One of the most commendable developments in food service at Disneyland has been the introduction of healthier foods and snacks. Diabetics, vegetarians, weight watchers, and guests on restricted diets should have no trouble finding something to eat. Ditto for anyone else who is simply seeking wholesome, nutritious food. Healthy food is available at all full-service restaurants, most fast-food counters, and even from vendors. Fresh fruit, for example, can now be purchased from Disneyland street vendors.

Alternatives and Suggestions for Eating at Disneyland

1. Eat a good breakfast before arriving at Disneyland. You do not want to waste touring time eating breakfast at the park. Besides, there are some truly outstanding breakfast specials at restaurants outside of Disneyland.

2. Having eaten a good breakfast, keep your tummy happy as you tour by purchasing snacks from the vendors stationed throughout the park. This is especially important if you have a tight schedule; you cannot afford to spend a lot of time waiting in line for food.

3. Disneyland's premier full-service restaurant is the Blue Bayou in New Orleans Square. The restaurant serves palatable, though rarely outstanding,

food in an extraordinary bayou setting that overlooks the Pirates of the Caribbean boat ride.

Reservations can be made at the door of the restaurant. All of the Disneyland restaurants are accustomed to dealing with small children, both well behaved and otherwise.

4. Disneyland restaurants are most crowded between 11:30 a.m. and 2:30 p.m. Restaurants with decent food that are sometimes overlooked include the Festival of Food and Casa Mexicana (both in Frontierland), and Brer Bar and the Hungry Bear Restaurant in Critter Country. Another good choice is the Plaza Inn on Main Street.

If you are on a tight schedule and the park closes early, stay until closing and eat dinner outside of Disneyland before returning to your hotel. If the park stays open late, eat an early dinner at about 4 or 4:30 p.m. in the Disneyland eatery of your choice. You should miss the last wave of lunch diners and sneak in just ahead of the dinner crowd. However, if you wish to wait and have a late dinner, you can eat without much hassle after 8:30 p.m., but you will miss the evening parades, fireworks, and other live entertainment.

5. If you are tired of fighting crowds and eating at odd times, try catching the Monorail at the Tomorrowland Monorail station and commuting to the Disneyland Hotel for lunch or dinner at one of its seven restaurants, or for a little relaxation and decompression at one of its four watering holes. The coming and going isn't nearly as time-consuming as it appears, and you will probably be able to get a better meal with faster service in a more relaxed atmosphere. The trip over and back takes very little time, and because most of the hotel guests have left for the park, the hotel restaurants are often slack, particularly at lunch.

Granville's Steak House at the Disneyland Hotel, though expensive, is the best Disney restaurant in or out of the park. You can make dinner reservations via phone at City Hall at the Town Square end of Main Street, or call (714) 956-6755. Your waiter will tout the porterhouse, but the filet mignon and the New York strip are better. The Shipyard Inn at the Disneyland Hotel is also pretty decent, but not in the same league as Granville's. More casual restaurants at the Disneyland Hotel are Stromboli's Ristorante, a pizza and pasta specialty eatery with a nice outdoor dining terrace, and the Neon Cactus Sports Bar and Grill.

For feedtrough dining at the Disneyland Hotel try Goofy's Kitchen, which serves breakfast and dinner character buffets (you eat *with* the characters). Goofy's offers an excellent spread for adults and a separate, kid-sized serving line for the little guys. The children's buffet features a veritable hit

parade of kids' favorites, including hot dogs, fried fish, spaghetti, and macaroni and cheese. For lighter fare or sandwiches, try Grandma Mazie's Picnic Basket or the Monorail Cafe, both located close to the Monorail platform.

If none of the restaurants at the Disneyland Hotel appeal to you, there's Yamabuki, a Japanese restaurant and sushi bar, and the P.C.H. Grill, serving steak, seafood, and pasta, at the Disneyland Pacific Hotel next door. If none of these suit you, or are too pricey, it is easy to take a taxi to a nearby non-Disney restaurant.

6. The stage side of the Tomorrowland Terrace serves cold deli sandwiches. It is possible to buy a cold lunch (except for the drinks) before 11 a.m. and then carry your food until you are ready to eat. We met a family that does this routinely, with Mom always remembering to bring several

small plastic bags for packing the food. Drinks can be purchased at the appropriate time from any convenient drink vendor.

7. Most fast-food eateries in Disneyland have more than one service window. Regardless of the time of day, check out the lines at all of the windows before queuing up. Sometimes a manned, but out-of-the-way window will have a much shorter line or no line at all. Be forewarned that most patrons in the food lines are buying for their whole family or group, and that the 10 people in line ahead of you will require the serving of 30 to 40 meals, not just 10.

8. Sometimes cafeteria-style restaurants will move you through faster than the fast-food eateries. Since at the cafeterias it is customary for each family member to go through the line and select his or her own meal, you can get a better idea of how many people must be served before you. Twenty-five people ahead of you in a cafeteria line will usually signify a shorter wait than ten ahead of you in a fast-food line.

9. For your general information, the Disney people have a park rule against bringing your own food and drink. We interviewed one woman who, ignoring the rule, brought a huge picnic lunch for her family of five, packed into a large diaper/baby paraphernalia bag. Upon entering the park she secured the bag in a locker at the Main Street guest locker facility and retrieved it later when the family was hungry. A San Diego family returned to their van in the parking lot for lunch. There they had a cooler, lawn chairs, and plenty of food, in the college football tailgating tradition.

Because dining in restaurants (particularly Disney restaurants), is so expensive, we get a lot of suggestions from readers on how to cut costs. Representative are these notes passed along by a mom from Bridgeton, Missouri:

We shopped [in advance], and arrived with our steel Coleman cooler well stocked with milk and sandwich fixings. I froze a block of ice in a milk bottle, and we replenished with ice from the resort ice machine daily. I also froze small packages of deli-type meats for later in the week. We ate cereal, milk and fruit each morning, with boxed juices. I also had a hot pot to boil water for instant coffee, oatmeal, and soup.

Each child had a belt bag of his own, which he filled from a special box of "goodies" each day. I made a great mystery of filling that box in the weeks before the trip. Some things were actual food, like packages of crackers and cheese, packets of peanuts and raisins. Some were worthless junk, like candy and gum. They grazed from their belt bags at will throughout the day, with no interference from mom and dad. Each also had a small, rectangular plastic water

*bottle that could hang in the belt. We filled these at water fountains
before getting into lines, and were the envy of many.*

*We left the park before noon, ate sandwiches, chips and soda in
the room, and napped. We purchased our evening meal in the park,
at a counter service eatery. We budgeted for both morning and
evening snacks from a vendor, but often did not need them. It made
the occasional treat all the more special.*

Incidentally, if you are looking for quiet, intimate dining, your chances
of finding it are directly proportional to your distance from Disneyland:
i.e., the farther the better. A honeymooner from Slidell, Louisiana, learned
this lesson the hard way, writing:

*We made dinner reservations at some of the nicer Disney
restaurants. When we made reservations we made sure they were
past the dinner hours and we tried to stress that we were on our
honeymoon. [At] every restaurant we went to, we were seated next
to large families. The kids were usually tired and cranky and, after
a long day in the park, were not excited about sitting through a
[lengthy] meal. It's very difficult to enjoy a romantic dinner when
there are small children crawling around under your table. We
looked around the restaurant and always noticed lots of non-
children couples. Our suggestion is this: seat couples without
children together and families with kids elsewhere. If Disney is such
a popular honeymoon destination, then some attempt should be
made to keep romantic restaurants romantic.*

Shopping in Disneyland

Shops in Disneyland add realism and atmosphere to the various theme settings and make available an extensive inventory of souvenirs, clothing, nov-
elties, decorator items, and more. Much of the merchandise displayed (with
the exception of Disney trademark souvenir items) is available back home
and elsewhere. In our opinion, shopping is not one of the main reasons for
visiting Disneyland. We recommend bypassing the shops on a one-day visit.
If you have two or more days to spend in Disneyland, browse the shops
during the early afternoon when many of the attractions are crowded.
Remember that Main Street—with its multitude of shops—opens earlier
and closes later than the rest of the park.

Our recommendations notwithstanding, we realize that for many guests
Disney souvenirs and memorabilia are irresistible. If you have decided that
you would look good in a Goofy hat with shoulder-length floppy ears, you

are in the right place. What's more, you have plenty of company. One of our readers writes:

> I've discovered that people have a compelling need to buy Disney
> stuff when they are at Disneyland. When you get home you wonder
> why you ever got a cashmere sweater with Mickey Mouse
> embroidered on the breast, or a tie with tiny Goofys all over it.
> Maybe it's something they put in the food.

If you buy something and don't want to drag it around, have the salesperson route your goods to Package Pick-Up. Allow a minimum of two hours from time of purchase for the transfer to be completed. Package Pick-Up is located at the News Stand, to the right of the main entrance as you leave the park. If you are a guest at the Disneyland Hotel, your purchases will be delivered on request directly to your room.

If you have a problem with your purchases, need to make a return, or simply forgot to pick up something for Uncle Ned, you can call Disneyland Exclusive Merchandise at (800) 760-3566, Monday–Saturday, 8 a.m. to 5 p.m. PST, and get it all worked out over the phone. Uncle Ned's gift plus anything else you buy will be shipped UPS standard delivery.

Part Five

Touring Plans

Touring Plans: What They Are and How They Work

When we interviewed Disneyland visitors who toured the park on a slow day, say in early December, they invariably waxed eloquent about the sheer delight of their experience. However, when we questioned visitors who toured on a moderate or busy day, they spent most of the interview telling us about the jostling crowds and how much time they stood in line. What a shame, they said, that you should devote so much time and energy to fighting the crowds in a place as special as Disneyland.

Given this complaint, we descended on Disneyland with a team of researchers to determine whether a touring plan could be devised that would move the visitor counter to the flow of the traffic and allow him to see virtually the whole park in one day with only minimal waits in line. On some of the busiest days of the year, our team monitored traffic flow into and through the park, noting how the park filled and how the patrons were distributed among the various lands. Likewise, we observed which rides and attractions were most popular and where bottlenecks were most likely to form.

After many long days of collecting data, we devised a number of preliminary touring plans, which we tested during Easter week, one of the busiest weeks of the entire year. Each day, individual members of our research team toured the park according to one of the preliminary plans, noting how long it took to walk from place to place and how long the wait in line was for each ride or show. Combining the knowledge gained through these trial runs, we devised a master plan, which we retested and fine-tuned. This plan, with very little variance from day to day, allowed us to experience most of the major attractions, except for Indiana Jones, and many of the lesser ones, in one day, with an average in-line wait at each ride/show of less than five minutes.

From this master plan we developed a number of alternative plans that take into account the varying tastes and personal requirements of different Disneyland patrons. We devised a plan, for instance, for adults touring without small children that takes advantage of their ability to move around the park quickly. Another plan was assembled for parents touring with children under the age of eight. Each plan operates with efficiency comparable to the master plan but addresses the special needs and preferences of its intended users.

Finally, after all of the plans were tested by our staff, we selected (using convenience sampling) a number of everyday Disneyland patrons to test the plans. The only prerequisite for membership in the test group (the visitors who tested the touring plans) was that the guest must have been visiting a Disney theme park (including Walt Disney World) for the first time. A second group of ordinary Disneyland patrons was chosen for a "control group"—first-time visitors who toured the park according to their own plans but who made notes of what they did and how much time they spent waiting in lines.

When the two groups were compared, the results were no less than amazing. On days when the park's attendance exceeded 50,000, visitors touring on their own (without the plan) *averaged* 2.6 hours' more waiting in line per day than the patrons touring according to our plan, and they experienced 33% fewer rides and attractions.

WILL THE PLANS CONTINUE TO WORK ONCE THE SECRET IS OUT?

Yes! First, all of the plans require that a patron be on hand when Disneyland opens. Many vacationers simply refuse to make this early rising sacrifice, but you can see more in the one hour just after the park opens than in several hours once the park begins to fill. Second, it is anticipated that less than 1% of any given day's attendance will have been exposed to the plans—not enough to bias the results. Last, most groups will deviate from the plans somewhat, skipping certain rides or shows as a matter of personal taste.

We have discovered that tour groups of up to 100 people are using our touring plans. A woman from Seattle writes:

> At Star Tours, a tour guide with your book was waiting at the exit waving a flag and screaming, "Hurry next door to ride Space Mountain. Don't go to the bathroom!" We practically had to dive for cover while several dozen high school kids went stampeding by.

Unless your party is as large as the tour group, this development should not cause you any undue stress. Because there are so many in the touring group, they move slowly and stop periodically to collect stragglers. In short, you should have no problem passing the group after the initial encounter.

VARIABLES THAT WILL AFFECT THE SUCCESS OF THE TOURING PLANS

How quickly you move from one ride to another; when and how many refreshment and rest room breaks you take; when, where, and how you eat meals; and your ability (or lack thereof) to find your way around will all impact the success of the plans. Additionally, smaller groups almost always move faster than larger groups, and an all-adult party will cover more ground than a family with young children. Switching off (see page 87), among other things, inhibits families with little ones from moving expeditiously. Plus, some children simply cannot conform to the "early to rise" conditions of the touring plans. A mom from Nutley, New Jersey, had this to say:

> *The touring plans all advise getting to parks at opening—we just couldn't burn the candle at both ends. Our kids (10, 7, & 4) would not go to sleep early and couldn't be up at dawn and still stay relatively sane. It worked well for us to let them sleep a little later, go out and bring breakfast back to the room while they slept, and still get a relatively early start by not spending time on eating breakfast out. We managed to avoid long lines with an occasional early morning, and hitting popular attractions during parades, mealtimes, and late evenings.*

And a family from Centerville, Ohio, volunteered this:

> *The toughest thing about your tour plans was getting the rest of the family to stay with them, at least to some degree. Getting them to pass by attractions in order to hit something across the park was no easy task (sometimes impossible).*

Finally, as a Connecticut woman alleges, the touring plans are incompatible with some readers' personalities (and bladders):

> *I want to know if next year when you write those "day" schedules if you could schedule bathroom breaks in there too. You expect us to be at a certain ride at a certain time with no stops in between. In one of the letters in your book a guy writes, "You expect everyone to be theme park commandos." When I read that I thought, there is a man who really knows what a problem the schedules are if you are a laid-back, slow-moving careful detail noticer. What were you thinking when you made these schedules?*

These difficulties notwithstanding, we recommend continuous, expeditious touring until around 11:30 a.m. After that hour, breaks and so on will not affect the plans significantly. If you are touring on a day with shorter hours (10 a.m.–6 p.m.) and the attendance is large, you may wish to avail yourself of one of the time-saving lunch options listed in the section "Eating in Disneyland."

Events beyond your control can sometimes have a profound effect on the touring plans. Chief among these are the manner and time it takes to bring a particular ride to full capacity. For example, Big Thunder Mountain Railroad, a roller coaster, has five trains. On a given morning it may begin operation with two of the five trains and then add the other three, if and when needed. If the line builds rapidly before the Disney operators decide to go to full capacity, you could have a long wait, even early in the morning.

What time you arrive for a Disney theater performance can also affect the touring plans. Usually, you need wait only until the end of the presentation then in progress. If a show at the *Country Bear Playhouse* is 15 minutes long and you arrive 1 minute after a show has begun, your wait for the next show will be 14 minutes. Conversely, if you happen to arrive just as the ongoing show is wrapping up, your wait will be only a minute or two. It's the luck of the draw.

GENERAL OVERVIEW

The Disneyland Touring Plans are step-by-step plans for seeing as much as possible with a minimum of time wasted standing in line. They are designed to assist you in avoiding crowds and bottlenecks on days of moderate to heavy attendance. On days of lighter attendance (see "Selecting the Time of Year for Your Visit," pages 19–21), the plans will still save you time but will not be as critical to successful touring.

CHOOSING THE RIGHT TOURING PLAN

Six different touring plans are presented:

- One-Day Touring Plan, for Adults
- Author's Select One-Day Touring Plan
- Dumbo-or-Die-in-a-Day Touring Plan, for Adults with Small Children
- Two-Day Touring Plan, for Adults with Small Children
- Two-Day Touring Plan A, for Daytime Touring or for When the Park Closes Early (before 8 p.m.)
- Two-Day Touring Plan B, for Morning and Evening Touring or for When the Park Is Open Late (after 8 p.m.)

If you have two days to spend at Disneyland, the two-day touring plans are by far the most relaxed and efficient. Two-Day Touring Plan A takes advantage of early morning touring opportunities when lines are short and the park has not yet filled with guests. This plan works well all year and is particularly recommended for days when Disneyland closes before 8 p.m. On the other hand, Two-Day Touring Plan B combines the efficiencies of early morning touring on the first day with the splendor of Disneyland at night on the second day. This plan is perfect for guests who wish to sample both the attractions and the special magic of Disneyland after dark, including parades and fireworks. The Two-Day Touring Plan, for Adults with Small Children, spreads the experience over two more relaxed days and incorporates more attractions that both children and parents will enjoy.

If you have only one day but wish to see as much as possible, use the One-Day Touring Plan, for Adults. This plan will pack as much into a single day as is humanly possible, but it is pretty exhausting. If you prefer a more relaxed visit, try the Author's Select One-Day Touring Plan. This plan features the best Disneyland has to offer (in the author's opinion), eliminating some of the less impressive attractions.

If you have small children, you may want to use the Dumbo-or-Die-in-a-Day Touring Plan, for Adults with Small Children. This plan includes most of the children's rides in Fantasyland and Mickey's Toontown, and omits roller-coaster rides and other attractions that small children cannot ride (because of Disney's age and height requirements), as well as rides and shows that are frightening for small children. Because this plan calls for adults to sacrifice many of the better Disney attractions, it is not recommended unless you are touring Disneyland primarily for the benefit of your children. In essence, you pretty much stand around, sweat, wipe noses, pay for stuff, and watch the children have fun. It's great.

An alternative (to the Dumbo Plan) would be to use the One-Day Touring Plan, for Adults, or the Author's Select One-Day Touring Plan, and take advantage of "switching off," a technique whereby children accompany adults to the loading area of rides with age and height requirements, but do not actually ride (see page 87). Switching off allows adults to enjoy the wilder rides while keeping the whole group together.

We are inundated with mail from readers requesting that we develop additional touring plans. Plans we have been asked to create include a plan for ninth and tenth graders, a plan for rainy days, a seniors' plan, a plan for folks who sleep late, a plan that omits rides that "bump, jerk, and clonk," a plan for gardening enthusiasts, and a plan for single women.

As it turns out, the plans can be adapted to accommodate most agendas. If you want to sleep in, skip one step in the plan of your choice for every 15 minutes after the park's opening that you arrive. If you arrive an hour after the park opens, for example, skip the first four steps and begin the touring with Step 5. You will forfeit the opportunity to experience some of the park's most popular rides without a long wait, but you will still have a

Max is annoyed because he can't find a Touring Plan for cross-dressing unicyclists.

plan to get you through the remainder of the day. If there are certain types of rides that you do not enjoy, bypass them when they are called for in the touring plans. The bottom line is that the touring plans are easily customized to meet your needs.

When following a touring plan, relax, be mellow, and expect some surprises and possible setbacks. A woman from Trappe, Pennsylvania, describes what can happen if you go overboard. Her experience took place at Walt Disney World in Florida, but it could happen just as easily at Disneyland.

You cannot emphasize enough the dangers of using your touring plans that were printed in the back of the book, especially if the person using them has a compulsive personality. I have a compulsive personality. I planned for this trip for two years, researched it by use of guidebooks, computer programs, video tapes, and information received from [Disney]. I had a two-page itinerary for our trip in addition to your touring plans of the theme parks. On night three of our trip, I ended up taking a non-scheduled trip to the emergency room. When the doctor asked what seemed to be the problem, I responded, "I don't know, but I can't stop shaking, and I can't stay here very long because I have to get up in a couple hours to go to [the theme park] according to my itinerary." Diagnosis: an anxiety attack caused by my excessive itinerary. He gave me a shot of something, and I slept through the first four attractions the next morning. This was our third trip to WDW (not including one trip to Disneyland); on all previous trips I used only the Steve Birnbaum book and I suffered no ill effects. I am not saying your book was not good. It was excellent! However, it should come with a warning label for people with compulsive personalities.

We once again emphasize that the touring plans presented in this book are intended to be flexible. The idea is that you adapt them to the personal preferences of your group. If you do not want to experience a ride that bumps and jerks, simply skip any such attractions when they come up in the touring plans. If you are a ninth grader and want to ride Space Mountain three times in a row, go ahead and ride. Will it decrease the effectiveness of the touring plan? Sure, but the plan was only created to help you have fun. Don't let the tail wag the dog: it's your day.

THE SINGLE-DAY TOURING CONUNDRUM

Touring Disneyland in a single day is complicated by the fact that Disneyland's premier attractions, Splash Mountain in Critter Country, Indiana Jones in Adventureland, and Star Tours, Space Mountain, and Rocket Rods in Tomorrowland, are almost at opposite ends of the park, making it virtually impossible to ride all five without encountering a long line at one attraction or another. If you ride Space Mountain, Star Tours, and Rocket Rods right after the park opens, you will ride without much, if any, wait. By the time you exit Tomorrowland and hustle over to Indiana Jones or Splash Mountain, those lines will have grown to frightening proportions. The same situation prevails if you ride Indiana Jones and Splash Mountain first: Indiana Jones and Splash Mountain—no problem; Star Tours, Space Mountain, and Rocket Rods—big lines. From ten minutes after opening until just before closing, you can expect long waits for these headliner attractions.

The only effective way to experience all five rides without significant waiting is to tour Disneyland on two days, and ride Space Mountain, Rocket Rods, and Star Tours first thing one morning and Splash Mountain and Indiana Jones first thing the other. If you have only one day and are basically unwilling to suffer a lengthy wait (45 minutes to 2 hours) for these rides, you can do one of two things. Your first option is to ride Indiana Jones and Splash Mountain when the park opens and the Tomorrowland

trio during an evening parade and/or *Fantasmic!* or just before the park closes. Many guests who attempt this strategy fail because they become too worn out to stay through the evening.

The second option, which we recommend in the one-day touring plans, requires a lot of hustle and still involves waits of 25–40 minutes. It is sort of a "bite the bullet" strategy, but all things considered, it probably works best. Make sure you arrive early and rush straight to Indiana Jones and ride. After Indiana Jones, proceed to Tomorrowland and ride Space Mountain, Rocket Rods, and Star Tours, in that order. Finally, head for Critter Country to ride Splash Mountain. If your group is small and you are fast, your wait should be less than 10 minutes, respectively, at Indiana Jones and Space

Mountain, about 20 minutes at Rocket Rods and Star Tours, and about 30 minutes at Splash Mountain. To summarize, the best way to experience all of Disneyland's wilder rides in one day, with the least amount of waiting, is to ride in the following sequence:

1. Indiana Jones
2. Space Mountain
3. Rocket Rods
4. Star Tours
5. Splash Mountain
6. Big Thunder Mountain
7. Matterhorn Bobsleds

If early admission (see below for a full explanation) is in effect, this sequence will only work for those who enter early. On non–early admission days, the sequence will work for anyone who is on hand when the park opens.

The main drawback to this sequence (other than running like a crazy person all over the park), is that you will zip through the elaborate Indiana Jones queuing area. We find the queuing area at Indiana Jones entertaining enough to almost qualify as an attraction in its own right. There is so much to see and experience that you really miss a lot if you sprint directly to the loading area without spending some time in the queue. All things considered, however, you're probably better off missing some of the Indiana Jones build-up than getting stuck in a two-hour line.

EARLY ADMISSION AND MAGIC MORNING

Early admission and Magic Morning are programs whereby guests visiting Disneyland on certain package vacations and/or with certain passports are admitted to the park 60–90 minutes early. During this time they can experience attractions that operate early for the guests' enjoyment. Attractions that open early vary from day to day, but often include all the attractions in Fantasyland and Tomorrowland, as well as the Indiana Jones ride in Adventureland. Guests who arrive early have a huge advantage over those who must wait at the turnstiles for the park to open. Specifically, they can ride attractions that are open early to their hearts' content and be ready to hustle over to Splash Mountain when the entire park opens for the general public. The head start puts them in a position to sail through the entire day without much waiting. A guest who arrives later is at a considerable disadvantage. When admitted, this guest will find many attractions already crowded and a large number of the early admission folks already heading to other attractions.

Early admission and Magic Morning days vary throughout the year. Some weeks early admission is in effect every other day; other weeks it's on just one or two days; and some weeks, regrettably, it's almost every day. Early admission and Magic Morning are valuable perks. Their availability should be a key consideration in buying a Disneyland package or admission pass. Definitely take advantage of early admission and Magic Morning if it is included in your package or type of pass. Also, remember this: it is impossible to arrive too early. If official opening time is 9 a.m., arrive at the turnstiles by 7:20 a.m. If the park opens to the public at 8 a.m., arrive by 6:20 a.m. Make sure you purchase your admission before the day you intend to visit the park.

If you are not visiting on a package, if your package does not offer early admission, or if you do not have a Flex Signature Passport or Passport Plus (see "Admission Options"), call (714) 999-4565 and determine which days early admission will be in effect. If you cannot get through on 999-4565, call (714) 778-6600, the number for the Disneyland Hotel. On the park info number, you will probably get a very long-winded recorded message and a menu of options. To shortcut directly to the early admission info, press 1, then 7 on your touchtone phone. Another recording will tell which days are scheduled for early admission. Avoid those days if possible. If you do not have early entry privileges and will be spending two days at Disneyland, use our Two-Day Touring Plan B and do your morning touring on a non–early admission day.

PARK OPENING PROCEDURES

Your progress and success during your first hour of touring will be affected by the particular opening procedure the Disney people use that day.

A. All guests are held at the turnstiles until the park opens (which may or may not be at the official opening time). On admittance, all lands are open. If this is the case on the day you visit, blow right past Main Street and head for the first attraction on whatever touring plan you are following.

B. Guests are admitted to Main Street a half-hour to an hour before the remaining lands open. Access to the other lands is blocked by a rope barrier at the central hub end of Main Street on these days. On admittance, move to the rope barrier and stake out a position as follows:

If you are going to Indiana Jones or Splash Mountain first, take up a position in front of the Plaza Pavilion restaurant at the central hub end of Main Street on the left. Wait next to the rope barrier blocking the walkway to Adventureland. When the rest of the park is opened (and the rope is dropped), proceed quickly to Adventureland for Indiana Jones, or Critter Country by way of Adventureland and New Orleans Square for Splash Mountain. Because the line for Indiana Jones disrupts pedestrian traffic throughout Adventureland, the Disney people sometimes form the queue for the attraction at the central hub or at the entrance to Frontierland. Before the rope drops, try to ascertain from a Disney cast member where the line will form. It's a real bummer to beat 10,000 people to the door of the attraction only to find that the line starts somewhere else.

If you are going to Space Mountain, Rocket Rods, or Star Tours first, wait on the right at the central hub end of Main Street. When the rope drops at opening time, bear right and zip into Tomorrowland.

If you are going to Fantasyland or Frontierland first, proceed to the end of Main Street and line up at the rope right of center.

If you are going to Mickey's Toontown first, ascend to the platform of the Main Street Station of the Disneyland Railroad and board the first train of the day. Ride half a circuit, disembarking at the Fantasyland/Toontown Station. The train pulls out of the Main Street Station at the same time the rope is dropped at the central hub end of Main Street.

If you are eligible for early admission (all Disneyland Hotel and Disney Pacific Hotel guests, visitors who have purchased certain Walt Disney Travel Company vacation packages, and Flex Signature Passport and Passport Plus holders) you will be provided with credentials that will allow you to board the Monorail or pass through the turnstiles when the park opens to early entrants. For package purchasers the credentials usually consist of a signed Flex Signature Passport and a guest I.D. card from your hotel. For guests of the Disneyland hotels, bring your park admission and your Disney Resort Guest I.D. to the Monorail station.

TOURING PLAN CLIP-OUT POCKET OUTLINES

For your convenience, we have prepared outline versions of all the touring plans presented in this guide. The Pocket Outline versions present the same touring itineraries as the detailed touring plans, but with vastly abbreviated directions. First, select the touring plan that is most appropriate for your party, and then familiarize yourself with the detailed version of the plan. Once you understand how the touring plan works, clip out the Pocket Outline version of your selected plan from the back of this guide and carry it with you as a quick reference when you visit the theme park.

The Touring Plans
PRELIMINARY INSTRUCTIONS FOR ALL TOURING PLANS
Before You Go

1. Buy your admission in advance (see "Admission Options" on pages 15–18).

2. Call (714) 999-4560 and determine which days early admission (a program whereby certain guests are allowed into the park 60–90 minutes early) will be in effect during your visit. If you are visiting Disneyland on a package or pass that includes early admission, take advantage of the early entry option. Otherwise, try to avoid early touring on early admission days.

3. Call (714) 999-4560 the day before you go for the official opening time.

4. Become familiar with the park opening procedures (described on page 182) and read over the touring plan of your choice so that you will have a basic understanding of what you are likely to encounter.

At Disneyland

On days of moderate to heavy attendance follow the touring plans exactly, deviating only when you do not wish to experience a listed show or ride. For instance, the touring plan may direct you to go next to Space Mountain, a roller-coaster ride. If you do not like roller coasters, simply skip that step and proceed to the next.

1. For morning touring, arrive at the park about 30–40 minutes before the official opening time. Purchase your admission if you have not done so previously. The ticket windows (as opposed to entrance gates) on the far left are usually less crowded.

2. During holiday periods and the summer, line up in front of Entrance Gate 11, 12, or 13, and wait to be admitted to the park. Entrance gates are numbered from left to right, so Gates 11, 12, and 13 will be toward the far right. Disney employees usually direct guests to lines in front of other gates, so do not be surprised if all the other lines are long and there is nobody waiting in front of Gate 11, 12, or 13. You will feel foolish standing there all by yourself, but have faith; these gates will open at the same time as all the other gates. During off-peak times of year, wait to be admitted in the shortest line you see, irrespective of gate number. Remember, entrance gates are different from ticket windows. Ticket windows sell admission passes. You enter the park at the entrance gates after you have purchased your admission.

3. If your gate is not attended, don't worry; sometimes the gate operators are not posted until just a minute before opening. The Disney people have installed a new system of automated turnstiles.

After inserting your admission pass into a slot, the system reads the pass. If your pass is valid it will be automatically returned, and you will be allowed to move through the turnstile.

4. When you are admitted to the park, move as fast as you can down Main Street to the central hub. Because Disneyland utilizes two basic opening procedures, you will probably encounter one of the following:

   a. The entire park will be open. If this is the case, proceed as quickly as possible to the first attraction listed on your touring plan.

   b. Only Main Street will be open. In this case, position yourself by the rope barrier at the central hub and be ready to hustle to the first ride listed on your touring plan when the remainder of the park is opened.

SPECIAL INSTRUCTIONS FOR GUESTS WITH EARLY ADMISSION PRIVILEGES

For Parties without Young Children

If you have early admission privileges, arrive an hour and 40 minutes before the official opening time. When admitted to the park, try to experience Indiana Jones, Star Tours, Space Mountain, Rocket Rods, Matterhorn Bobsleds, and Peter Pan's Flight, in that order. Break off touring a few minutes before the general public is admitted (usually 30 minutes before the official opening time). Position yourself to head to Splash Mountain, then to Big Thunder Mountain, and then to the Jungle Cruise. Following the Jungle Cruise, begin the touring plan of your choice, bypassing any attractions called for in the plan that you experienced during early admission.

For Parties with Young Children

Arrive an hour and 40 minutes before the official opening time. When admitted to the park, try to experience Dumbo, Peter Pan's Flight, Alice in Wonderland (all in Fantasyland), and then Submarine Voyage and the Tomorrowland Autopia (both in Tomorrowland), in that order. Break off touring a few minutes before the general public is admitted (usually 30 minutes before the official opening time). Position yourself to head to the Jungle Cruise in Adventureland. Following the Jungle Cruise, begin the touring plan of your choice, bypassing any attractions called for in the plan that you experienced during early admission.

ONE-DAY TOURING PLAN FOR ADULTS

For: Adults without small children.

Assumes: Willingness to experience all major rides (including roller coasters) and shows.

Be forewarned that this plan requires a lot of walking and some backtracking; this is necessary to avoid long waits in line. A little extra walking coupled with some hustle in the morning will save you two to three hours of standing in line. Also be aware that you might not complete the tour. How far you get will depend on the size of your group, how quickly you move from ride to ride, how many times you pause for rest or food, how quickly the park fills, and what time the park closes.

Note: The success of this touring plan hinges on your entering the park when it first opens. Do not use this plan when early admission is in effect (see explanation above) unless you have early entry privileges. If you are not eligible for early admission, use this plan on a day when early admission is not in effect. Call (714) 999-4560 to learn which days the early admission program will be operating during your visit.

1. Arrive 30–40 minutes before the official opening time and purchase your admission, if necessary.

2. Line up in front of Gate 11, 12, or 13 (during busy periods of the year) or in front of any entrance gate with a short line.

3. When you are admitted to the park, move posthaste to the far end of Main Street. If there is no rope barrier, continue quickly and without stopping to Adventureland and ride Indiana Jones. If there is a rope barrier, wait until the park opens and then race to Indiana Jones.

4. After Indiana Jones, backtrack to the central hub and cross to Tomorrowland as fast as your feet will carry you and ride Space Mountain.

5. Following Space Mountain, bear left and across the Tomorrowland plaza to Rocket Rods. Ride.

6. After exiting Rocket Rods, bear right to ride Star Tours. Expect to encounter a modest wait.

7. Return to Adventureland via the central hub, and from there pass through New Orleans Square to Critter Country. Ride Splash Mountain.

8. Across from the exit to Splash Mountain, take in a performance at the *Country Bear Playhouse*. If you are a Disneyland veteran and consider the *Playhouse* expendable, skip ahead to Step 9.

9. Backtrack to New Orleans Square and experience the Haunted Mansion.

10. Bear right on leaving the Haunted Mansion and ride Pirates of the Caribbean.

11. Return to the New Orleans Square/Frontierland waterfront. Keeping the waterfront on your left, proceed to Big Thunder Mountain.

12. While at the waterfront, take a ride on the Mark Twain Riverboat or the Sailing Ship *Columbia*.

13. This is a pretty good time to grab a bite if you are hungry. See the section "Eating in Disneyland" for suggestions.

14. Go to Fantasyland via the central hub and ride Peter Pan's Flight. If the wait seems prohibitive, try again during the afternoon parade.

15. Exit Peter Pan to the right and proceed to the Storybook Land Canal Boats. If the weather is nice and the line is not too long, go ahead and ride.

16. Exiting the Canal Boats, you will find yourself in an area where there are a lot of stage and parade presentations from 11:45 a.m. to 3:30 p.m. After checking the daily entertainment schedule, interrupt the touring plan if there is a live performance you would like to see.

17. Bear left around the Canal Boats to Mickey's Toontown. Ride Roger Rabbit's Car Toon Spin, if you are interested.

18. Departing Mickey's Toontown, cross under the railroad tracks and turn left. Ride It's a Small World.

19. Turn right, backtracking toward Mickey's Toontown and the railroad tracks. Ride the Disneyland Railroad all the way around the park once and then stay on for one additional stop. Disembark in Tomorrowland.

20. In Tomorrowland, see *Honey, I Shrunk the Audience*. If a show is not scheduled to begin within 15 minutes or so, check out Innoventions in the big round building next to Space Mountain.

21. The Matterhorn Bobsleds and the Submarine Voyage are close by if you consider them worth the wait. If not, try them again later during the evening parade or *Fantasmic!*

22. Leave Tomorrowland and return to Adventureland via the central hub. Experience the *Enchanted Tiki Room*.

23. Turn left upon exiting the *Enchanted Tiki Room* and explore the Swiss Family Treehouse.

24. Turning right from the Treehouse, go next door and take the Jungle Cruise.

25. Return to Fantasyland during the first showing of the evening parade. Ride Snow White's Scary Adventures, Pinocchio's Daring Journey, Alice in Wonderland and, if you missed it earlier, Peter Pan's Flight.

26. If you have some time left before closing, backtrack to pick up any attractions you may have missed or bypassed because the lines were too long. Check out any parades, fireworks, or live performances that interest you. Grab a bite to eat. Save Main Street until last, since it remains open after the rest of the park closes.

27. Continue to tour until everything closes except Main Street or you are ready to leave. Finish your day by browsing along Main Street and viewing *The Walt Disney Story,* featuring "Great Moments with Mr. Lincoln."

AUTHOR'S SELECT ONE-DAY TOURING PLAN

For: Adults touring without small children.
Assumes: Willingness to experience all major rides (including roller coasters) and shows.

This touring plan is selective and includes only those attractions that, in the authors' opinions, represent the best Disneyland has to offer.

Be forewarned that this plan requires a lot of walking and some backtracking; this is necessary to avoid long waits in line. A little extra walking coupled with some hustle in the morning will save you two to three hours of standing in line. Note also that you might not complete the tour. How far you get will depend on the size of your group, how quickly you move from ride to ride, how many times you pause for rest or food, how quickly the park fills, and what time the park closes. With a little zip and some luck, it is possible to complete the touring plan even on a busy day when the park closes early.

Note: The success of this touring plan hinges on your being among the first to enter the park when it opens. Do not use this plan when early admission (see explanation above) is in effect unless you have early admission privileges. If you are not eligible for early admission, use this plan on a day when early admission is not in effect. To learn which days the early admission program is operating during your visit, call (714) 999-4560.

1. Arrive 30–40 minutes before the official opening time and purchase your admission, if necessary.

2. Line up in front of Gate 11, 12, or 13 (during busy periods of the year) or in front of any entrance gate with a short line.

3. When you are admitted to the park, move posthaste to the far end of Main Street. If there is no rope barrier, continue quickly and without stopping to Adventureland and ride Indiana Jones. If there is a rope barrier, wait until the park opens and then race to Indiana Jones.

4. After Indiana Jones, backtrack to the central hub and cross to Tomorrowland as fast as your feet will carry you and ride Space Mountain.

5. Following Space Mountain, bear left and across the Tomorrowland plaza to Rocket Rods. Ride.

6. After exiting Rocket Rods, bear right to ride Star Tours. Expect to encounter a modest wait.

7. Return to Adventureland via the central hub, and from there pass through New Orleans Square to Critter Country. Ride Splash Mountain.

8. Across from the exit to Splash Mountain, take in a performance at the *Country Bear Playhouse*. If you are a Disneyland veteran and consider the *Playhouse* expendable, skip ahead to Step 9.

9. Backtrack to New Orleans Square and experience the Haunted Mansion.

10. Bear right on leaving the Haunted Mansion and ride Pirates of the Caribbean.

11. Return to New Orleans Square/Frontierland waterfront. Keeping the waterfront on your left, proceed to Big Thunder Mountain.

12. While at the waterfront, take a ride on the Mark Twain Riverboat or the Sailing Ship *Columbia*.

13. This is a pretty good time to grab a bite if you are hungry. See the section "Eating in Disneyland" for suggestions.

14. Go to Fantasyland via the central hub and ride Peter Pan's Flight. If the wait seems prohibitive, try again during the afternoon parade.

15. Exiting Peter Pan, you will be close to several stage show and parade venues. After checking the daily entertainment schedule, interrupt the touring plan if there is a live performance you would like to see.

16. Bear left around the Storybook Land Canal Boats to Mickey's Toontown. Ride Roger Rabbit's Car Toon Spin if the wait is not prohibitive. Be forewarned that most of the line is inside the building.

17. Departing Mickey's Toontown, cross under the railroad tracks and turn left. Ride It's a Small World.

18. Turn right, backtracking toward Mickey's Toontown and the railroad tracks. Ride the Disneyland Railroad all the way around the park once and then stay on for one additional stop. Disembark in Tomorrowland.

19. In Tomorrowland, see *Honey, I Shrunk the Audience.* If a show is not scheduled to begin within 15 minutes or so, check out Innoventions in the big round building next to Space Mountain.

20. Leave Tomorrowland and return to Adventureland via the central hub. Explore the Swiss Family Treehouse.

21. Turning right from the Treehouse, go next door and take the Jungle Cruise.

22. Return to Fantasyland during the first showing of the evening parade. Ride Snow White's Scary Adventures and, if you missed it earlier, Peter Pan's Flight.

23. If you have any time left before closing, backtrack to pick up any attractions you may have missed or bypassed because the lines were too long. Check out any parades, fireworks, or live performances that interest you. Grab a bite to eat. Save Main Street until last, since it remains open after the rest of the park closes.

24. Continue to tour until everything closes except Main Street or you are ready to go. Finish your day by browsing along Main Street and viewing *The Walt Disney Story,* featuring "Great Moments with Mr. Lincoln."

DUMBO-OR-DIE-IN-A-DAY TOURING PLAN, FOR ADULTS WITH SMALL CHILDREN

For: Parents with children under age seven who feel compelled to devote every waking moment to the pleasure and entertainment of their small children, and rich people who are paying someone else to take their children to the theme park.

Assumes: Periodic stops for rest, rest rooms, and refreshment.

The name of this touring plan notwithstanding, this itinerary is not a joke. Regardless of whether you are loving, guilty, masochistic, truly selfless, insane, or saintly, this touring plan will provide a small child with about as perfect a day as is possible at Disneyland.

This touring plan represents a concession to those adults who are determined, even if it kills them, to give their small children the ultimate Disneyland experience. The plan addresses the preferences, needs, and desires of small children to the virtual exclusion of those of adults or older siblings. If you left the kids with a sitter yesterday, or wouldn't let little Marvin eat barbecue for breakfast, this is the perfect plan for expiating your guilt. This is also a wonderful plan if you are paying a sitter, nanny, or chauffeur to take your children to Disneyland.

If this description has intimidated you somewhat or if you have concluded that your day at Disneyland is as important as your children's, use the One-Day Touring Plan, for Adults, making use of the "switching-off" option (see page 87) at those attractions that impose height or age restrictions.

Because the children's attractions in Disneyland are the most poorly engineered in terms of handling large crowds, the following touring plan is the least efficient of the six plans we present. It represents the best way, however, to experience most of the child-oriented attractions in one day if that is what you are determined to do. We do not make recommendations in this plan for meals. If you can, try to hustle along as quickly as is comfortable until about noon. After noon it won't make much difference if you stop to eat or take it a little easier.

Note: The success of this touring plan hinges on your being among the first to enter the park when it opens. Do not use this plan when early admission (see the preceding explanation) is in effect unless you have early admission privileges. If you are not eligible for early admission, use this plan on a day when early admission is not in effect. To learn which days the early admission program is operating during your visit, call (714) 999-4560.

1. Arrive 30–40 minutes before the official opening time and purchase your admission, if necessary.

2. Line up in front of Gate 11, 12, or 13 (during busy periods of the year) or in front of any entrance gate with a short line.

3. When you are admitted to the park, move quickly to the far end of Main Street. If there is no rope barrier, continue to Fantasyland via the castle without stopping.

4. In Fantasyland, ride Dumbo, the Flying Elephant.

5. In Fantasy-land, ride Peter Pan's Flight. Bear right on exiting; go past Mr. Toad's Wild Ride and around the corner to Alice in Wonderland.

6. Ride Alice in Wonderland.

7. Exit Alice in Wonderland to the left and ride the Mad Tea Party.

8. Next, head toward It's a Small World in the far corner of Fantasyland. Bypassing the ride for the moment, cross under the Disneyland Railroad tracks into Mickey's Toontown.

9. In Mickey's Toontown, try Roger Rabbit's Car Toon Spin if your children are plucky.

10. In Mickey's Toontown, ride Gadget's Go-Coaster.

11. While in Mickey's Toontown, let off some steam in Goofy's Bounce House.

12. Tour Mickey's House and visit Mickey in his dressing room.

13. After seeing Mickey, turn right to enjoy Chip 'n' Dale's Treehouse and Acorn Ball Crawl.

14. Following your dip in the nut pit, go to the far side of Mickey's House and tour Minnie's House.

15. Round out your visit to Mickey's Toontown with an inspection of the *Miss Daisy,* tied up next to Goofy's Bounce House.

16. Depart Toontown. Take the Disneyland Railroad from the Fantasyland/Toontown Station to New Orleans Square. Walk if you have a stroller that does not collapse.

17. In New Orleans Square, see Pirates of the Caribbean. If your children were frightened by Roger Rabbit's Car Toon Spin in Mickey's Toontown, skip ahead to Step 19.

18. Go left on leaving Pirates of the Caribbean to experience the Haunted Mansion. If your children were not frightened at Pirates of the Caribbean, they will do fine at the Haunted Mansion.

19. Turn left again and head for Critter Country. Take in a show at the *Country Bear Playhouse.*

20. Bear to the left after exiting the *Playhouse* and follow the waterfront to Frontierland. Take a raft to Tom Sawyer Island. Allow the kids plenty of time to explore.

21. After returning from the island, catch the Disneyland Railroad at the New Orleans Square Station and return to the Fantasyland/Toontown Station.

22. In Fantasyland, ride It's a Small World.

23. Cross the Small World Mall and ride the Casey Jr. Circus Train or the Storybook Land Canal Boats, whichever has the shortest wait.

24. In Fantasyland, ride King Arthur Carrousel.

25. In Fantasyland, also ride Pinocchio's Daring Journey if the wait does not exceed 15 minutes. Otherwise skip ahead to Step 26.

26. Exit Pinocchio to your left and head to Frontierland.

27. In Frontierland, ride the Mark Twain Riverboat or the Sailing Ship *Columbia,* whichever departs first.

28. Leave Frontierland and go to Adventureland. Explore the Swiss Family Treehouse if the wait is less than 15 minutes. Otherwise, skip ahead to Step 29.

29. In Adventureland, see the show at the *Enchanted Tiki Room.*

30. Leave Adventureland, cross the central hub, and enter Tomorrowland via the path that runs along the right side (as you face it from the central hub) of the Matterhorn.

31. In Tomorrowland, take the Disneyland Monorail for a round-trip ride.

32. After the Monorail, walk across the plaza, keeping the Astro-Orbiter (formerly the Rocket Jets) on your left. Proceed to *Honey, I Shrunk the Audience.* Be aware that the 3D effects and the high volume level frighten some preschoolers. If your kids have been a little sensitive during the day, skip ahead to Step 33.

33. While in Tomorrowland, ride the Tomorrowland Autopia.

34. This concludes the touring plan. Use any time remaining to revisit favorite attractions, see attractions that were not included in the touring plan, or visit attractions you skipped because the lines were too long. Also, consult your daily entertainment schedule for parades, Fantasyland Theatre productions, or other live entertainment that might interest you. As you drag your battered and exhausted family out of the park at the end of the day, bear in mind that it was you who decided to cram all this stuff into one day. We just tried to help you get organized.

TWO-DAY TOURING PLAN FOR ADULTS WITH SMALL CHILDREN

For: Parents with children under age seven who wish to spread their Disneyland visit over two days.

Assumes: Frequent stops for rest, rest rooms, and refreshment.

This touring plan represents a compromise between the observed tastes of adults and the observed tastes of younger children. Included in this touring plan are many of the midway-type rides that your children may have the opportunity to experience (although in less exotic surroundings) at local fairs and amusement parks. These rides at Disneyland often require long waits in line and consume valuable touring time that could be better spent experiencing the many rides and shows found only at a Disney theme park, and which best demonstrate the Disney genius. This touring plan is heavily weighted toward the tastes of younger children. If you want to balance it a bit, try working out a compromise with your kids to forgo some of the carnival-type rides (Mad Tea Party, Dumbo, King Arthur Carrousel, Gadget's Go-Coaster) or such rides as the Tomorrowland Autopia.

Another alternative is to use one of the other two-day touring plans and take advantage of "switching off" (see page 87). This technique allows small children to be admitted to rides such as Indiana Jones, Space Mountain, Rocket Rods, Big Thunder Mountain Railroad, and Splash Mountain. The children wait in the loading area as their parents ride one at a time; the nonriding parent waits with the children.

Timing: The following Two-Day Touring Plan takes advantage of early morning touring. On each day you should complete the structured part of the plan by 3 p.m. or so. We highly recommend returning to your hotel by midafternoon for a nap and an early dinner. If the park is open in the evening, come back to the park by 7:30 or 8 p.m. for the evening parade, fireworks, and *Fantasmic!*

Day One

Note: Day One of this touring plan will not be adversely affected if you tour on an early admission day. On Day Two, however, avoid early admission unless you have early entry privileges. If necessary, switch days so that you will not be following the Day Two itinerary on a day when early admission is in effect.

1. Arrive 30–40 minutes before the official opening time and purchase your admission, if necessary.

2. Line up in front of Gate 11, 12, or 13 (during busy periods of the year) or in front of any entrance gate with a short line.

3. When you are admitted to the park, move quickly to the far end of Main Street. If there is no rope barrier, continue without stopping to Adventureland and the Jungle Cruise.

4. Ride the Jungle Cruise.

5. Exit the Jungle Cruise to the left. Leave Adventureland, passing through New Orleans Square on the way to Critter Country. Ride Splash Mountain, taking advantage of the "switching-off" option if your children are too young or too short to ride.

6. Return to New Orleans Square and experience the Haunted Mansion. If your children were frightened by the Jungle Cruise or seem intimidated by the prospect of the Haunted Mansion, skip ahead to Step 8.

7. After the Haunted Mansion, turn right and try Pirates of the Caribbean.

8. Exit Pirates to the left (back toward the Haunted Mansion) and go to the Frontierland/New Orleans Square Station. Take the Disneyland Railroad one stop to the Fantasyland/Toontown Station. Be aware that only collapsible strollers are allowed on the train. If you have a Disney rental stroller, walk to Mickey's Toontown.

Note: Because the needs of small children are so varied, we have not built specific instructions for eating into the touring plan. Simply stop for refreshments or a meal when you feel the urge. For best results, however, try to keep moving in the morning. In the afternoon, eat, rest often, and adjust the pace to your liking.

9. Cross under the Disneyland Railroad tracks into Mickey's Toontown.

10. In Mickey's Toontown, try Roger Rabbit's Car Toon Spin if your children are plucky and you have a strong stomach.

11. In Mickey's Toontown, ride Gadget's Go-Coaster.

12. While in Mickey's Toontown, let off some steam in Goofy's Bounce House.

13. Tour Mickey's House and visit Mickey in his dressing room.

14. After seeing Mickey, turn right to enjoy Chip 'n' Dale's Treehouse and Acorn Ball Crawl.

15. After a few laps among the nuts, go to the far side of Mickey's House and tour Minnie's House.

16. Round out your visit to Mickey's Toontown with an inspection of the *Miss Daisy,* tied up next to Goofy's Bounce House.

17. Depart Mickey's Toontown the same way you entered, bearing left after you pass under the railroad tracks. Proceed to It's a Small World and ride.

18. Next, return to the Fantasyland/Toontown Station. Take the Disneyland Railroad all the way around the park (back to Toontown). Stay on for one more stop and then disembark in Tomorrowland. If you have a stroller that cannot go on the train, make a complete circuit on the train without the stroller and then walk from Toontown to Tomorrowland.

19. Proceed to *Honey, I Shrunk the Audience,* across the plaza to the left of AstroOrbiter (formerly the Rocket Jets). Enjoy a performance of *Honey, I Shrunk the Audience.*

20. After the performance, exit right and check out Innoventions.

21. This concludes the touring plan for Day One. Use any time remaining to revisit favorite attractions, see attractions that were not included in the touring plan, or visit attractions you skipped because the lines were too long. Also, consult your daily entertainment schedule for parades, Fantasyland Theatre productions, or other live entertainment that might interest you. If the park is open in the evening, consider going back to your hotel for a nap and dinner and returning after 7 p.m. for a parade and *Fantasmic!*

Day Two

Note: Day One of this touring plan will not be adversely affected if you tour on an early admission day. Day Two, however, will be severely impacted. If necessary, switch days so that you will not be following Day Two of the itinerary on a day when early admission is in effect.

1. Arrive 30–40 minutes before the official opening time and purchase your admission, if necessary.

2. Line up in front of Gate 11, 12, or 13 (during busy periods of the year) or in front of any entrance gate with a short line.

3. When admitted to the park, move quickly to the far end of Main Street. If there is no rope barrier, continue on to Tomorrowland and ride Star Tours.

4. Turn left on exiting Star Tours and proceed to the central hub. From there, enter Fantasyland through the castle.

5. In Fantasyland, ride Dumbo, the Flying Elephant.

6. Backtracking toward the castle, ride Peter Pan's Flight.

7. Exiting Peter Pan to the right, ride Mr. Toad's Wild Ride.

8. Exit Mr. Toad to the right and bear right around the corner to Alice in Wonderland. Ride.

9. After Alice in Wonderland, try the Mad Tea Party next door.

10. Next, ride the Storybook Land Canal Boats, across the walk from the Mad Tea Party.

11. Bear right after the Canal Boats and return to the center of Fantasyland by the castle. Ride the King Arthur Carrousel.

12. Across from the King Arthur Carrousel, experience Pinocchio's Daring Journey (we recommend you skip the nearby Snow White's Scary Adventures).

13. Exit Pinocchio to your left, leave Fantasyland, and go into Frontierland.

Note: Because the needs of small children are so varied, we have not built specific instructions for eating into the touring plan. Simply stop for refreshments or a meal when you feel the urge. For best results, however, try to keep moving in the morning. In the afternoon, you can eat, rest often, and adjust the pace to your liking.

14. If you want, ride Big Thunder Mountain, taking advantage of the "switching-off" option.

15. Take a cruise on the Mark Twain Riverboat or the Sailing Ship *Columbia,* whichever departs first.

16. Keeping the waterfront on your right, proceed to the rafts for transportation to Tom Sawyer Island. Allow the children to explore the island.

17. Returning from Tom Sawyer Island, bear right into Critter Country and take in a show at the *Country Bear Playhouse.*

18. Leave Critter Country and pass through New Orleans Square into Adventureland. Explore the Swiss Family Treehouse.

19. See the show at the *Enchanted Tiki Room,* also in Adventureland.

20. This concludes the touring plan for Day Two. Use any time remaining to revisit favorite attractions, see attractions that were not included in the touring plan, or visit attractions you skipped because the lines were too long. Also, consult your daily entertainment schedule for parades, Fantasyland Theatre productions, or other live entertainment that might interest you. If the park is open in the evening, consider going back to your hotel for a nap and dinner, returning after 7 p.m. for a parade and *Fantasmic!*

TWO-DAY TOURING PLAN A, FOR DAYTIME TOURING OR FOR WHEN THE PARK CLOSES EARLY

For: Parties wishing to spread their Disneyland visit over two days and parties preferring to tour in the morning.

Assumes: Willingness to experience all major rides (including roller coasters) and shows.

Timing: The following Two-Day Touring Plan takes advantage of early morning touring and is the most efficient of all the touring plans for comprehensive touring with the least waiting in line. On each day you should complete the structured part of the plan by 3 p.m. or so. If you are visiting Disneyland during a period of the year when the park is open late (after 8 p.m.), you might prefer our Two-Day Touring Plan B, which offers morning touring on one day and late afternoon and evening touring on the other day. Another highly recommended option is to return to your hotel by midafternoon for a nap and an early dinner, and to come back to the park by 7:30 or 8 p.m. for the evening parade, fireworks, and live entertainment.

Note: The success of Day One of this touring plan hinges on your being among the first to enter the park when it opens. Do not use Day One of this plan when early admission (see explanation above) is in effect unless you have early admission privileges. If you are not eligible for early admission, use Day One of this plan on a day when early admission is not in effect (switching Day One and Day Two if necessary). To learn which days the early admission program is operating during your visit, call (714) 999-4560.

Day One

1. Arrive 30–40 minutes before the official opening time and purchase your admission, if necessary.

2. Line up in front of Gate 11, 12, or 13 (during busy periods of the year) or in front of any entrance gate with a short line.

3. When you are admitted to the park, move quickly to the far end of Main Street. If there is no rope barrier, continue without stopping to Tomorrowland and Space Mountain.

4. Ride Space Mountain.

5. Exit Space Mountain and bear left to Rocket Rods. Ride.

6. Exit Rocket Rods to the right and cross to Star Tours, then ride.

7. Exit Star Tours to the right and then turn left toward the Submarine Lagoon. Proceed to Fantasyland and ride the Matterhorn Bobsleds.

8. Return to Tomorrowland and experience the Submarine Voyage.

9. Exit the submarines to your right and ride Alice in Wonderland in Fantasyland, next to the Matterhorn.

10. Continue to move to your left and ride Mr. Toad's Wild Ride.

11. Exit to the left and ride Peter Pan's Flight.

12. Across the street from Peter Pan, ride Snow White's Scary Adventures.

13. On exiting Snow White's Scary Adventures, go next door and ride Pinocchio's Daring Journey.

14. Continuing to your left, proceed to Frontierland and ride the Big Thunder Mountain Railroad.

15. If you are hungry, try the Festival of Food (on the path back to Fantasyland) or Casa Mexicana, located across from the entrance to the Big Thunder Mountain Railroad.

16. While in Frontierland, ride the Mark Twain Riverboat or the Sailing Ship *Columbia* (whichever departs first).

Note: At this point check your daily entertainment schedule to see if there are any parades, fireworks, or live performances that interest you. Make note of the times and alter the touring plan accordingly. Since you have already seen all of the attractions for Day One that cause bottlenecks and have big lines, an interruption of the touring plan here will not cause you any problems. Simply pick up where you left off before the parade or show.

17. While in Frontierland, take a raft to Tom Sawyer Island.

18. After you return to the mainland, proceed through New Orleans Square to Adventureland. Tour the Swiss Family Treehouse.

19. Exit to your right and try to see the show at the *Enchanted Tiki Room.*

20. Return to Main Street via the central hub. See *The Walt Disney Story,* featuring "Great Moments with Mr. Lincoln."

21. This concludes Day One of the touring plan. If you have any energy left, backtrack to pick up attractions you may have missed or bypassed because the lines were too long. Check out any parades or live performances that interest you.

Day Two

1. Arrive 30–40 minutes before the official opening time and purchase your admission, if necessary. Once again, try to avoid early admission days unless you have early entry privileges.

2. Line up in front of Gate 11, 12, or 13 (during busy periods of the year) or in front of any entrance gate with a short line.

3. After passing through the turnstiles, continue to the end of Main Street. If there is no rope barrier, move as fast as you can to Adventureland and ride Indiana Jones.

4. Exit Indiana Jones to the left and pass through New Orleans Square to Critter Country. Ride Splash Mountain.

5. After you ride Splash Mountain, leave Critter Country and return to Adventureland. Ride the Jungle Cruise.

6. Exit the Jungle Cruise to the left and go to New Orleans Square. Ride Pirates of the Caribbean.

7. While in New Orleans Square, experience the Haunted Mansion.

8. Exit the Haunted Mansion to the left and return to Critter Country. See the show at the *Country Bear Playhouse.*

9. Returning to New Orleans Square, take the Disneyland Railroad to the Mickey's Toontown/Fantasyland Station, one stop down the line.

10. After you get off the train, bear to your left and cross under the railroad tracks to Mickey's Toontown.

11. In Mickey's Toontown, ride Roger Rabbit's Car Toon Spin.

12. If you have children in your party, tour Mickey's House and visit Mickey in his dressing room. Do the same at Minnie's House.

13. Leave Mickey's Toontown the same way you entered. Bear left after passing under the tracks and ride It's a Small World.

14. After It's a Small World, head toward the castle and the heart of Fantasyland. Ride the Storybook Land Canal Boats.

15. Passing between the Submarine Voyage and the Matterhorn, proceed to Tomorrowland and catch the Disneyland Monorail for a complete round trip. The loading platform for the Monorail is built over the docks for the Submarine Voyage. An escalator takes you up to the Monorail loading area. If you are hungry, consider getting off the Monorail at the Disneyland Hotel for lunch (don't forget to have your hand stamped for reentry).

16. Return to Tomorrowland on the Monorail.

17. This concludes the touring plan. Revisit your favorite attractions, or try any rides and shows you may have missed. Check your daily entertainment schedule to see if there are any parades or live performances that interest you.

TWO-DAY TOURING PLAN B, FOR MORNING AND EVENING TOURING OR FOR WHEN THE PARK IS OPEN LATE

For: Parties who want to enjoy Disneyland at different times of day, including evenings and early mornings.
Assumes: Willingness to experience all major rides (including roller coasters) and shows.

Timing: This Two-Day Touring Plan is for those visiting Disneyland on days when the park is open late (after 8 p.m.). The plan offers morning touring on one day and late afternoon and evening touring on the other day. If the park closes early, or if you prefer to do all of your touring during the morning and early afternoon, use the Two-Day Touring Plan A, for Daytime Touring or for When the Park Closes Early.

Note: The success of Day One of this touring plan hinges on your entering the park when it first opens. Do not use Day One of this plan when early admission is in effect unless you have early entry privileges. If you are not eligible for early admission, use Day One of this plan on a day when early admission is not in effect (switching Day One and Day Two if necessary). To learn which days the early admission program is operating during your visit, call (714) 999-4560.

Day One

1. Arrive 30 – 40 minutes before the official opening time and purchase your admission, if necessary.

2. Line up in front of Gate 11, 12, or 13 (during busy periods of the year) or in front of any entrance gate with a short line.

3. When you are admitted to the park, move posthaste to the far end of Main Street. If there is no rope barrier, continue quickly and without stopping to Adventureland and ride Indiana Jones. If there is a rope barrier, wait until the park opens and then race to Indiana Jones.

4. Bear left on exiting Indiana Jones and head for Critter Country. Ride Splash Mountain.

5. Next head to Tomorrowland as fast as your feet will carry you and ride Space Mountain. If the line looks long, be consoled by the fact that it will only get longer as the day wears on. Bite the bullet.

6. After exiting Space Mountain, bear left to Rocket Rods. Once again, expect to encounter a modest wait.

7. Exit Rocket Rods to the right and cross the street to ride Star Tours.

8. Return to Adventureland via the central hub and ride the Jungle Cruise. If you are a Disneyland veteran and wish to bypass the Jungle Cruise, skip ahead to Step 9.

9. Go to Fantasyland via the central hub and the walkway leading directly to the Matterhorn Mountain. As you pass alongside the Matterhorn, turn left into Fantasyland and ride Alice in Wonderland.

10. After you ride Alice in Wonderland, exit left past Mr. Toad's Wild Ride to Peter Pan's Flight. Ride Peter Pan's Flight.

11. Exit Peter Pan's Flight and proceed to Frontierland. The best route is to slip out of Fantasyland on the path running out of the back of the castle. In Frontierland, ride the Big Thunder Mountain Railroad.

Note: This is about as far as you can go on a busy day before the crowds catch up with you, but you will have experienced seven of the more popular rides and shows, and you will have cleared most of Disneyland's major traffic bottlenecks. Note also that you are doing a considerable amount of walking and some backtracking. Do not be dismayed; the extra walking will save you as much as two hours of standing in line. Remember, during the morning (through Step 11), keep moving. In the afternoon, adjust the pace to your liking.

12. After riding the Big Thunder Mountain Railroad, continue around the waterfront and see the Haunted Mansion.

13. Bear right after the Haunted Mansion to Pirates of the Caribbean. Ride.

14. Next, take a raft to Tom Sawyer Island for a little exploration.

Note: At this point check your daily entertainment schedule to see if there are any parades, fireworks, or live performances that interest you. Make note of the times and alter the touring plan accordingly. Since you have already seen all of the attractions for Day One that cause bottlenecks and have big lines, an interruption of the touring plan here will not cause you any problems. Simply pick up where you left off before the parade or show.

15. Go next to Adventureland and tour the Swiss Family Treehouse.

16. Exit the Treehouse to the right and see the show at the *Enchanted Tiki Room.*

17. Return to Main Street via the central hub. See *The Walt Disney Story,* featuring "Great Moments with Mr. Lincoln."

18. This concludes the touring plan for Day One.

Day Two

1. Eat an early dinner and arrive at the park about 5:30 p.m.

2. Proceed to Tomorrowland and see *Honey, I Shrunk the Audience.*

3. While in Tomorrowland, check out Innoventions in the big round building next to Space Mountain.

4. Next, go to Fantasyland and the Matterhorn Bobsleds. If the lines are too long, try again to ride just before the park closes.

5. Exit the Matterhorn Bobsleds to the left and head for Mickey's Toontown. Ride Roger Rabbit's Car Toon Spin.

6. Return to Fantasyland and ride It's a Small World.

Note: At this point check your daily entertainment schedule to see if there are any parades, fireworks, or live performances that interest you. Make note of the times and alter the touring plan accordingly. Since you have already seen all of the attractions for Day Two that cause bottlenecks and have big lines, an interruption of the touring plan here will not cause you any problems. Simply pick up where you left off before the parade or show. *Fantasmic!* is rated "not to be missed."

7. Exit It's a Small World to the right and proceed to the Fantasyland/ Mickey's Toontown Station. Take the Disneyland Railroad to the New Orleans Square/Frontierland Station.

8. Get off the train and turn left toward Critter Country. See a show at the *Country Bear Playhouse.*

9. This concludes Day Two of the touring plan. If you have some time left before closing, backtrack to pick up attractions you may have missed or bypassed because the lines were too long. Check out any parades, fireworks, or live performances that interest you. Grab a bite to eat. Save Main Street until last, since it remains open after the rest of the park closes.

Part Six

Universal Studios Hollywood

Universal Studios Hollywood was the first film and television studio to turn part of its facility into a modern theme park. By integrating shows and rides with behind-the-scenes presentations on movie making, Universal Studios Hollywood created a new genre of theme park, stimulating in the process a number of clone and competitor parks. First came the Disney-MGM Studios at Walt Disney World, followed shortly by Universal Studios Florida, also near Orlando. Where Universal Studios Hollywood, however, evolved from an established film and television venue, its cross-country imitators were launched primarily as theme parks, albeit with some production capability on the side. A fourth park, the disappointing MGM-Grand Adventures Theme Park in Las Vegas, offers rides and shows but does not have a studio component. Disney will soon challenge Universal in California with the opening of Disney's California Adventure sometime after the millennium. The new park, adjacent to Disneyland, will not have production facilities, but one of its theme areas will focus on Hollywood and the movies.

Located just off US 101 north of Hollywood, Universal Studios operates on a scale and with a quality standard rivaled only by the Disney, Sea World, and Busch parks. Unique among American theme parks for its topography, Universal Studios Hollywood is tucked on top of, below, and around a tall hill that in many states would pass for a mountain. The studios are divided into an open-access area and a controlled-access area. The controlled-access area contains the working soundstages, backlot, wardrobe, scenery, prop shops, postproduction, and administration. Guests can visit the controlled-access area only by taking the Backlot Tram Tour. The open-access area, which contains the park's rides, shows, restaurants, and services, is divided into two sections. The main entrance provides access to the upper section, the Upper Lot, on top of the hill. Five stage shows and one ride, as well as the loading area for the Backlot Tram Tour, are located in the Upper Lot. The Lower Lot, at the northeastern base of the hill, is accessible from the Upper Lot via a series of escalators. There are two rides, two shows, and two walk-through exhibits in the Lower Lot. All attractions, including rides, shows, tours, and exhibits, are fully profiled in the section "Universal Studios Hollywood Attractions."

The park offers all standard services and amenities, including stroller and wheelchair rental, lockers, diaper changing and infant nursing facilities, car assistance, and foreign language assistance. Most of the park is accessible to disabled guests, and TDDs are available for the hearing-impaired. Almost all services are in the Upper Lot, just inside the main entrance.

Gathering Information

The main Universal Studios information number is (818) 622-3801. Calling this number, however, often results in up to 20 minutes on hold or about 7 minutes on hold followed by a disconnect. If you have problems, try calling (818) 622-3735 or (818) 622-3750. Universal Studios Hollywood's Web address is **www.universalstudios.com** or **www.mca.com.**

WHAT MAKES UNIVERSAL STUDIOS HOLLYWOOD DIFFERENT

What make Universal Studios Hollywood different is that the attractions, with a couple of exceptions, are designed to minimize long waits in line. The centerpiece of the Universal Studios experience in the Backlot Tram Tour. While on the tram, you experience an earthquake, are attacked by the killer shark from *Jaws,* are grabbed by King Kong, and endure a simulated rain shower and a flash flood, among other things. In other parks, including Universal's sister park in Florida, each of these spectacles is presented as an individual attraction, and each has its own long queue. At Universal Studios Hollywood, by contrast, you suffer only one very manageable wait to board the tram and then experience all of these events as part of the tour.

In addition to the time savings and convenience provided by the tram tour, most of the live shows at Universal Studios Hollywood are performed in large theaters or stadiums. Instead of standing in line outside, guests are invited to enter the theater and wait in seated comfort for the production to begin.

Timing Your Visit

Crowds are largest during the summer (Memorial Day to Labor Day) and during specific holiday periods during the rest of the year. Christmas Day

Universal Studios

1. *Animal Actors Stage*
2. Back to the Future
3. *Backdraft*
4. Backlot Tram Tour

5. *Beetlejuice's Rockin' Graveyard Revue*
6. E.T. Adventure
7. Jurassic Park—The Ride

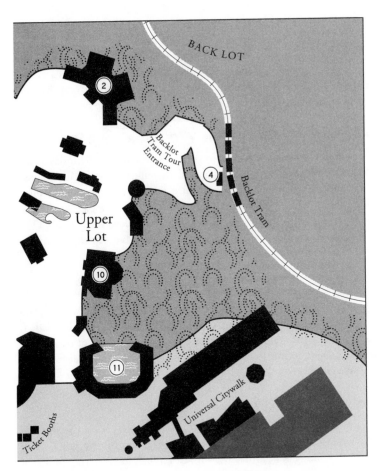

8. Lucy, A Tribute
9. *Terminator 2 3D*
10. *Totally Nickelodeon*
11. *Waterworld*

12. *Wild, Wild, Wild West*
    Stunt Show
13. *World of CineMagic*

through New Year's Day is extremely busy, as are Thanksgiving weekend, the week of Washington's Birthday, spring break for colleges, and the two weeks bracketing Easter. The least busy time is from after Thanksgiving weekend until the week before Christmas. The next slowest times are September through the weekend preceding Thanksgiving, January 4 through the first week of March, and the week following Easter to Memorial Day.

SELECTING THE DAY OF THE WEEK FOR YOUR VISIT

Weekends are more crowded than weekdays year-round. Saturday is the busiest day of the week. Sunday, particularly Sunday morning, is the best bet if you have to go on a weekend, but it is nevertheless extremely busy. During the summer, Friday is very busy; Monday, Wednesday, and Thursday are usually less so; and Tuesday is normally the slowest day of all. During the "off-season" (September–May, holiday periods excepted), Tuesday is usually the least crowded day, followed by Thursday.

HOW MUCH TIME TO ALLOCATE

Although there's a lot to see and do at Universal Studios Hollywood, you can (unlike at Disneyland) complete a comprehensive tour in one day. If you follow our touring plan, which calls for being on hand at park opening, you should be able to check out everything by mid- to late afternoon, even on a crowded day.

ENDURANCE LEVELS

Never mind that Universal Studios claims to cover 400 acres; the area you will have to traverse on foot is considerably smaller. In fact, you will do much less walking and, miracle of miracles, much less standing in line at Universal Studios than at Disneyland.

COST

Both one- and two-day tickets are available for about $38 and $48 respectively for adults, and about $28 and $38 for children ages 3 to 11. Even during the busier times of the year, however, it's easy to see everything in one day, so we do not recommend the two-day pass. Sometimes admission discounts are offered in area freebie publications available in hotels. Admission discounts are also periodically offered to AAA members. Vacation packages including lodging and park admission are available from Hilton and Sheraton, both of which offer accommodations close to the studios.

Arriving and Getting Oriented

Most folks access Universal Studios by taking US 101, also called the Hollywood Freeway, and following the signs to the park. If the freeway is gridlocked you can also get to the studios by taking Cahuenga Boulevard and then turning north toward Lankershim Boulevard. If you are coming from Burbank, take Barham Boulevard toward US 101, and then follow the signs.

Universal Studios has a big, multilevel parking garage at the top of the hill. Signs directing you to the garage are a bit confusing, so pay attention and stay to the far right when you come up the hill. Even after you have made it to the pay booth and shelled out $7 to park, it is still not exactly clear where you go next. Drive slowly, follow other cars proceeding from the pay booths, and avoid turns onto ramps marked "Exit." You may become a bit disoriented, but ultimately you will blunder into the garage. Once parked, make a note of your parking level and the location of your space.

Walk toward the opposite end of the garage from where you entered and exit into Universal CityWalk, a shopping, dining, and entertainment complex (no admission required) situated between the parking structure and the main entrance of the park. Bear left at CityWalk and continue for 100 yards or so to the Universal Studios ticket booths and turnstiles. If you need cash, an ATM is located outside and to the right of the main entrance. Nearby is a guest services window.

THE UPPER LOT

The Upper Lot is essentially a large, amorphously shaped pedestrian plaza. The freebie park map shows a number of street names such as New York Street and Baker Street, and place names like Cape Cod and Moulin Rouge, but on foot these theme distinctions are largely lost and placement of buildings appears almost random. In other words, do not expect the sort of thematic integrity that you find at Disneyland.

Inside the main entrance, stroller and wheelchair rentals are on the right, as are rental lockers. Straight ahead is a TV Audience Ticket Booth, where you can obtain free tickets to join the audience for any TV shows that are taping during your visit (subject to availability).

Attractions in the Upper Lot are situated around the perimeter of the plaza, except for the Wild, Wild, Wild West Stunt Show, which occupies a space in the middle of the lot. If you picture the Wild West show in the center of an imaginary clock and the main entrance as being 6 o'clock, then Animal Actors Stage is at 10 o'clock, Beetlejuice's Rockin' Graveyard Revue at 11 o'clock, Back to the Future—The Ride at 12 o'clock, the Backlot Tram Tour at 1 o'clock, Totally Nickelodeon at 3 o'clock, and Waterworld at 5 o'clock. Between Beetlejuice and Back to the Future (11 and 12 o'clock) are the escalators and stairs that lead to the Lower Lot. The Upper Lot attractions are described in detail below.

THE LOWER LOT

The Lower Lot is only accessible via the escalators and stairs descending from back left of the Upper Lot. Configured roughly in the shape of the letter **T**, the Lower Lot is home to Jurassic Park—The Ride, currently the headliner attraction at Universal Studios Hollywood. Stepping off the escalator, Jurassic Park is straight ahead. A hard right brings you to the E.T. Adventure ride. Moving down the stem of the **T**, Lucy, A Tribute is on your right and AT&T at the Movies is on your left. Both are walk-through, interactive exhibits. At the base of the **T** are two theater attractions. To your left is Backdraft, and to your right, the World of CineMagic. The Lower Lot attractions are described in detail below.

Universal Studios Hollywood Attractions

UPPER LOT ATTRACTIONS

Terminator 2 3D

Type of Attraction: 3D thriller mixed-media presentation

Scope & Scale: Super headliner

When to Go: Just after opening or after 4:30 p.m.

Special Comments: The nation's best theme-park attraction; very intense for some preschoolers and grade-schoolers

Author's Rating: Furiously paced high-tech experience; not to be missed; ★★★★★

Overall Appeal by Age Group:

Pre-school	Grade School	Teens	Young Adults	Over 30	Senior Citizens
★★★	★★★★★	★★★★★	★★★★★	★★★★★	★★★★

Duration of Presentation: 20 minutes, including an 8-minute preshow

Probable Waiting Time: 20–40 minutes

Description and Comments   The Terminator "cop" from *Terminator 2* morphs to life and battles Arnold Schwarzenegger's T-800 cyborg character. If you missed the *Terminator* flicks, here's the plot: A bad robot arrives from the future to kill a nice boy. Another bad robot (who has been reprogrammed to be good) pops up at the same time to save the boy. The bad robot chases the boy and the rehabilitated robot while menacing the audience in the process.

The attraction, like the films, is all action, and you really don't need to understand much. What's interesting is that it uses 3D film and a theater full of sophisticated technology to integrate the real with the imaginary. Images seem to move in and out of the film, not only in the manner of traditional 3D, but also in actuality. Remove your 3D glasses momentarily and you'll see that the guy on the motorcycle is actually on stage.

We've watched this type of presentation evolve, pioneered by Disney's *Captain EO, Honey, I Shrunk the Audience,* and *MuppetVision 4D. Terminator 2 3D,* however, goes way beyond lasers, with moving theater seats, blasts of hot air, and spraying mist. It creates a multidimensional space that blurs the boundary between entertainment and reality. Is it seamless? Not quite, but it's close. We rank *Terminator 2 3D* as "not to be missed" and consider it the absolute best theme-park attraction in the United States. If *Terminator 2 3D* is the only attraction you see at Universal Studios Hollywood, you'll have received your money's worth.

Touring Tips　The 700-seat theater changes audiences about every 19 minutes. Even so, because the show is new and hot, expect to wait about 30–45 minutes. The attraction, behind Marvel Mania, to the left of the park's entrance, receives much traffic during morning and early afternoon. By about 4 p.m., however, lines diminish somewhat. We recommend seeing the show first thing after the park opens or holding off until afternoon. If you can't stay until late afternoon, see the show first thing in the morning. Families with young children should know that the violence characteristic of the Terminator movies is largely absent from the attraction. There's suspense and action but not much blood and guts.

Back to the Future—The Ride

Motion Sickness

WARNING!

Type of Ride: Flight-simulator thrill ride

Scope & Scale: Super headliner

When to Go: First thing in the morning

Special Comments: Very rough ride; may induce motion sickness. Must be 3' 4" tall to ride. Switching off available (page 87).

Author's Rating: Not to be missed, if you have a strong stomach; ★★★★★

Overall Appeal by Age Group:

Pre-school	Grade School	Teens	Young Adults	Over 30	Senior Citizens
†	★★★★★	★★★★★	★★★★★	★★★★	★★½

† Sample size too small for an accurate rating

Duration of Ride: 4½ minutes
Loading Speed: Moderate

Description and Comments   This attraction is to Universal Studios Hollywood what Indiana Jones is to Disneyland: the most popular thrill ride in the park. Guests in Doc Brown's lab get caught up in a high-speed chase through time that spans a million years. An extremely intense simulator ride, Back to the Future is similar to Star Tours at Disneyland, but it is much rougher and more jerky. Though the story doesn't make much sense, the visual effects are wild and powerful. The vehicles (Delorean time machines) in Back to the Future are much smaller than those of Star Tours, so the ride feels more personal and less like a group experience.

In a survey of tourists who had experienced simulator rides in both Universal Studios and Disneyland, riders age 34 and under preferred Back to the Future to the Disney attraction by a seven-to-five margin. Older riders, however, stated a two-to-one preference for Star Tours over Back to the Future. The remarks of a woman from Mount Holly, New Jersey, are typical:

> *Our favorite [overall] attraction was Back to the Future at Universal. Comparing it to Star Tours, it was more realistic because the screen surrounds you.*

Most guests also find Back to the Future wilder than its Disney cousins. A Michigan woman writes:

> *Back to the Future was off the charts on the scary-o-meter. It made Splash and Big Thunder mountains seem like carnival kiddie rides.*

An English woman from Fleet Hants, who was tired of being jerked around, finally got mad (go girl!):

> *The simulators were fun, but they do seem to go out of their way to jerk you about, and the Back to the Future one was SO jerky that it made me quite angry.*

A man from Evansville, Indiana, reminds us that Back to the Future can humble even the most intrepid:

> *The Back to the Future ride at Universal was very rough and we are members of a roller-coaster club. We have seldom experienced such a rough ride and ridden over 300 coasters. If it was too strong for us, we shudder to think about mere mortals.*

Because the height requirement on Back to the Future has been lowered from 3' 10" to 3' 4", younger children are riding. Many of them require preparation. A Virginia mother suggests:

The five-year-old was apprehensive about the ride, but he liked it a lot. We assured him ahead of time that (1) it's only a movie, and (2) the car doesn't actually go anywhere, just shakes around. This seemed to increase his ability to enjoy that ride (rather than taking all the fun out of it).

Touring Tips As soon the park opens, guests stampede to Back to the Future. Our recommendation: be there when the park opens, and join the rush. If you don't ride before 10 a.m., your wait may be exceptionally long.

Note: Sitting in the rear seat of the car makes the ride more realistic.

Backlot Tram Tour

Type of Attraction: Indoor/outdoor tram tour of soundstages and backlot

Scope & Scale: Headliner

When to Go: After experiencing the other rides

Author's Rating: ★★★★½

Overall Appeal by Age Group:

Pre-school	Grade School	Teens	Young Adults	Over 30	Senior Citizens
★★★	★★★★	★★★★	★★★★	★★★★	★★★★

Duration of Ride: About 42 minutes

Load Speed: Fast

Description and Comments The Backlot Tram Tour is the centerpiece of Universal Studios Hollywood, and at 42 minutes, it is one of the longest attractions in American theme parks. The tour departs from the tram tour boarding facility to the *right* of Back to the Future and down the escalator. (Please note that there is also an escalator to the *left* of Back to the Future, so don't get confused).

The tram circulates though the various street scenes, lagoons, special effects venues, and storage areas of Universal's backlot. Recognizable scenery includes the house from *Psycho,* the town square from *Back to the Future,* and the Amity waterfront from *Jaws.* The tram passes several soundstages where current television shows and movies are being produced and actually enters three soundstages where action inspired by *Earthquake, Dante's Peak,* and *King Kong* is presented.

The great thing about the Backlot Tram Tour is that you see everything without leaving the tram—essentially the equivalent of experiencing four or five major attractions with only one wait.

Touring Tips   Though the wait to board might appear long, do not be discouraged. Each tram carries several hundred people and departures are frequent, so the line moves quickly. We recommend taking the tram tour after experiencing the other rides plus the two theater/soundstage presentations on the Lower Lot.

Including your wait to board and the duration of the tour, you will easily invest an hour or more at this attraction. Remember to take a rest room break before queuing up. Finally, be aware that several of the scenes may frighten small children.

Animal Actors Stage

Type of Attraction: Trained animals stadium performance
Scope & Scale: Major attraction
When to Go: After you have experienced all rides
Author's Rating: Warm and delightful; ★★★½
Overall Appeal by Age Group:

Pre-school	Grade School	Teens	Young Adults	Over 30	Senior Citizens
★★★★½	★★★★	★★★½	★★★½	★★★½	★★★½

Duration of Presentation: 20 minutes
Probable Waiting Time: 15 minutes

Description and Comments   Humorous demonstration of how animals are trained for films. Well-paced and informative, the show features cats, dogs, monkeys, birds, and other creatures. Sometimes, animals don't behave as expected, but that's half the fun. Often the animal stars are quite famous. In 1998, for example, the pig from the acclaimed movie *Babe* was featured.

Touring Tips   Presented five or more times daily, the program's schedule is in the daily entertainment guide. Go when it's convenient for you; queue about 15 minutes before show time.

Waterworld

Type of Attraction: Simulated stunt-scene filming
Scope & Scale: Major attraction
When to Go: After experiencing all of the rides and the tram tour
Author's Rating: Well done; ★★★★
Overall Appeal by Age Group:

Pre-school	Grade School	Teens	Young Adults	Over 30	Senior Citizens
★★★	★★★★	★★★★	★★★★	★★★½	★★★½

Duration of Presentation: 15 minutes
Probable Waiting Time: 15 minutes

Description and Comments   Drawn from the film *Waterworld,* starring Kevin Costner, this outdoor theater presentation features stunts and special effects performed on and around a small man-made lagoon. The action involves jet skis and various other craft, and of course, a lot of explosions and falling from high places into the water. Fast-paced and well-adapted to the theater, the production is in many ways more compelling than the film that inspired it.

Touring Tips   Wait until you have experienced all of the rides and the tram tour before checking out Waterworld. Because it is located near the main entrance, most performances are sold out. Arrive at the theater at least 15 minutes before the show time listed in the handout park map.

The Wild, Wild, Wild West Stunt Show

Type of Attraction: Stunt show with a Western theme
Scope & Scale: Major attraction
When to Go: After you have experienced all of the rides and the tram tour
Author's Rating: Solid and exciting; ★★★½
Overall Appeal by Age Group:

Pre-school	Grade School	Teens	Young Adults	Over 30	Senior Citizens
★★★★½	★★★★	★★★★	★★★★	★★★★	★★★★

Duration of Presentation: 18 minutes
Probable Waiting Time: 15 minutes

Description and Comments   The Wild West stunt show has shootouts, fist-fights, horse tricks, and high falls, all exciting and well executed. The fast-paced show is staged four to nine times daily in a large, horseshoe-shaped stadium. Somewhat on the corny side when compared to *Waterworld,* the stunt show depends as much on humor as on action.

Touring Tips   Show times are listed in the daily entertainment guide; go at your convenience after experiencing all of the rides and taking the tram tour.

Beetlejuice's Rockin' Graveyard Revue

Type of Attraction: Rock-and-roll stage show
Scope & Scale: Major attraction
When to Go: After experiencing all of the rides and the tram tour

Author's Rating: Outrageous; ★★★½
Overall Appeal by Age Group:

Pre-school	Grade School	Teens	Young Adults	Over 30	Senior Citizens
★★★★	★★★★	★★★★	★★★½	★★★½	★★★½

Duration of Presentation: 23 minutes
Probable Waiting Time: None

Description and Comments   High-powered rock-and-roll stage show stars Beetlejuice, Frankenstein, the Bride of Frankenstein, Wolfman, Dracula, and the Phantom of the Opera. In addition to fine vintage rock, the show features some of the most exuberant choreography found anywhere, plus impressive sets and special effects.

Touring Tips   Presented indoors, this energetic production runs four to eight times daily; consult the daily entertainment schedule in the handout park map. Check out Beetlejuice after enjoying the rides and the tram tour.

Totally Nickelodeon

Type of Attraction: Audience-participation game show
Scope & Scale: Major attraction
When to Go: After experiencing all of the rides and the tram tour
Author's Rating: ★★★
Overall Appeal by Age Group:

Pre-school	Grade School	Teens	Young Adults	Over 30	Senior Citizens
★★★½	★★★★	★★★	★★★	★★★	★★★

Duration of Show: About 26 minutes
Probable Waiting Time: About 15 minutes on busy days

Description and Comments   In this presentation, audience volunteers are divided into two teams that compete in a variety of strange games. Old-timers will recognize the mayhem as an elaborate, adolescent version of "Beat the Clock." Winners merit the dubious honor of being "slimed." If you don't understand this term, consult your children.

Touring Tips   While the insane games are fun to watch, this show is definitely expendable for groups touring without children or teens. If you go, see the show after experiencing all of the rides and the tram tour.

LOWER LOT ATTRACTIONS

E.T. Adventure

Type of Ride: Indoor adventure ride based on the move *E.T.*
Scope & Scale: Major attraction
When to Go: Before 10:30 a.m.
Author's Rating: ★★★★
Overall Appeal by Age Group:

Pre-school	Grade School	Teens	Young Adults	Over 30	Senior Citizens
★★★★	★★★★	★★★½	★★★½	★★★½	★★★½

Duration of Ride: 4½ minutes
Load Speed: Moderate

Description and Comments   Guests board a bicycle-like conveyance and escape with E.T. from earthly law enforcement officials, then journey to E.T.'s home planet. The attraction is similar to Peter Pan's Flight at Disneyland but is longer and has more elaborate special effects and a wilder ride.

Touring Tips   Most preschoolers and grade-school children love E.T. We think it worth a 20- to 30-minute wait, but nothing longer. Lines build quickly after 10 a.m., and waits can be more than two hours on busy days. Ride in the morning, right after Back to the Future. Guests who balk at sitting on the bicycle can ride in a more comfortable gondola.

A mother from Columbus, Ohio, writes about horrendous lines at E.T. Adventure:

> *The line for E.T. took two hours! The rest of the family waiting outside thought that we had gone to E.T.'s planet for real.*

Jurassic Park—The Ride

Type of Ride: Indoor/outdoor adventure ride based on the movie *Jurassic Park*
Scope & Scale: Super Headliner
When to Go: Before 10:30 a.m.
Author's Rating: ★★★★
Overall Appeal by Age Group:

Pre-school	Grade School	Teens	Young Adults	Over 30	Senior Citizens
★★★	★★★★½	★★★★½	★★★★	★★★★	★★★★

Duration of Ride: 6 minutes

Load Speed: Fast

Description and Comments   Guests board boats for a water tour of Jurassic Park. Everything is tranquil as the tour begins, and the boat floats among large herbivorous dinosaurs such as brontosaurus and stegosaurus. Then word is received that some of the carnivores have escaped their enclosure, and the tour boat is accidentally diverted into Jurassic Park's water treatment facility. Here the boat and its riders are menaced by an assortment of hungry meateaters led by the ubiquitous *T. Rex.* At the climactic moment the boat and its passengers escape by dropping over a waterfall.

Jurassic Park is impressive in its scale, but the number of dinosaurs is a little disappointing. The big herbivores are given short shrift to set up the plot for the carnivore encounter, which leads to floating around in what looks like a brewery. When the carnivores make their appearance, however, they definitely get your attention. The final drop down a three-story flume to safety is a dandy.

Touring Tips   You can get very wet on this ride. Even before the boat leaves the dock you must sit in the puddles left by previous riders. Once the boat is under way there's a little splashing, but nothing major until the big drop at the end of the ride. When you hit the bottom, enough water will cascade into the boat to extinguish a three-alarm fire. Our recommendation is to bring along an extra-large plastic garbage bag and (cutting holes for your head and arms) wear it like a sack dress. If you forget to bring a garbage bag, you can purchase a Universal Studios poncho for $7.50.

Young children must endure a double whammy on this ride. First, they are stalked by giant, salivating (sometimes spitting) reptiles, and then they are sent catapulting over the falls. Unless your children are fairly stalwart, wait a year or two before you spring Jurassic Park on them.

As the park's most hyped attraction, Jurassic Park stays jammed most of the day. Ride early in the morning after Back to the Future and E.T. Adventure.

The World of CineMagic

Type of Attraction: A minicourse on filming action sequences and a testimonial to the talents of Alfred Hitchcock

Scope & Scale: Major attraction

When to Go: Anytime

Special Comments: May frighten young children

Author's Rating: A little slow moving, but well done; ★★★½

Overall Appeal by Age Group:

Pre-school	Grade School	Teens	Young Adults	Over 30	Senior Citizens
★★½	★★★	★★★½	★★★½	★★★½	★★★½

Duration of Presentation: 30 minutes

Probable Waiting Time: 15 minutes

Description and Comments   Guests view a presentation on special effects and then go to an adjoining soundstage where the stabbing scene from *Psycho* is used to demonstrate camera angle and cinematic perspective. Audience members also participate in a demonstration showing how actors are filmed against a blue matte background in the studio, with the footage later superimposed onto film shot on location. The third and final installment is a sound effects stage where audience volunteers supply sound effects for a movie scene.

Touring Tips   This high-capacity attraction is in the most remote corner of the park. Its capacity for handling crowds combined with its isolated location usually add up to short waits. Visit after riding Back to the Future, E.T. Adventure, and Jurassic Park, and after experiencing *Backdraft* next door.

Backdraft

Type of Attraction: A multisequence minicourse on special effects

Scope & Scale: Major attraction

When to Go: After you have experienced all of the rides

Author's Rating: Sugar-coated education; ★★★★

Overall Appeal by Age Group:

Pre-school	Grade School	Teens	Young Adults	Over 30	Senior Citizens
★★★½	★★★★	★★★★	★★★★	★★★★	★★★★

Duration of Presentation: About 14 minutes

Probable Waiting Time: 20 minutes

Description and Comments   Guests move from theater to theater in this minicourse attraction. The presentation draws its inspiration from the movie *Backdraft*, which is about firemen fighting fires. Segments show the use of miniatures, demonstrate blue matte filming techniques, and discuss the precautions necessary for filming explosions and fire. The finale involves a "hot set" where a *Backdraft* scene involving a fire in a chemical warehouse is re-created. The entire presentation is nicely organized, well paced, and unexpectedly informative. In addition to learning something about how movies are made, you will gain some insight into the origin of fires and how firefighters extinguish them.

Touring Tips Consistently high-tech, this relatively short show packs quite a wallop. See it first thing after riding Back to the Future, E.T. Adventure, and Jurassic Park.

Lucy, a Tribute

Type of Attraction: Walk-through tribute to Lucille Ball
Scope & Scale: Diversion
When to Go: Anytime
Author's Rating: A touching remembrance; ★★★
Overall Appeal by Age Group:

Pre-school	Grade School	Teens	Young Adults	Over 30	Senior Citizens
★	★	★★	★★★	★★★	★★★

Probable Waiting Time: None

Description and Comments The life and career of comedienne Lucille Ball are spotlighted, with emphasis on her role as Lucy Ricardo in the long-running television series *I Love Lucy.* Well-designed and informative, the exhibit succeeds admirably in recalling the talent and temperament of the beloved redhead.

Touring Tips See Lucy during the hot, crowded midafternoon, or after you have seen all of the other Lower Lot attractions. Adults could easily stay 15–30 minutes. Children, however, get restless after a couple of minutes.

LIVE ENTERTAINMENT AT UNIVERSAL STUDIOS HOLLYWOOD

The theater and amphitheater attractions operate according to the entertainment schedule printed in the handout park map. The number of daily performances of each show varies from as few as three a day during less busy times of year to as many as ten a day during the summer and holiday periods. Also, according to the daily entertainment schedule, the Isla Nublar Jurassic Band entertains near the entrance to Jurassic Park in the Lower Lot. In the Upper Lot, look for the Doo Wop Singers belting out '50s and '60s harmonies near Mel's Diner. Performance times for the Doo Wop Singers are likewise listed in the daily entertainment schedule. In addition to the scheduled presentations, a number of street performers randomly work the park. These include Marvel Comic characters such as

Spiderman, cartoon characters such as Woody Woodpecker, and various film star impersonators.

DINING AT UNIVERSAL STUDIOS HOLLYWOOD

The counter-service food at Universal Studios runs the gamut from burgers and hot dogs to pizza, fried chicken, crepes, and Mexican specialties. We rank most selections marginally better than chain fast food. Prices are comparable to those at Disneyland, but on average the food at Universal is a little better.

If you are looking for full-service dining, try Marvel Mania in the park for American cuisine, or Wolfgang Puck's Cafe or the Hard Rock Cafe in the Universal CityWalk just outside the park entrance. If you leave the park for lunch, be sure to have your hand stamped for reentry.

UNIVERSAL STUDIOS HOLLYWOOD FOR YOUNG CHILDREN

We do not recommend Universal Studios Hollywood for preschoolers. Of 11 major attractions, all but 2 (Animals Actors Stage and Totally Nickelodeon) have the potential for flipping out sensitive little ones.

Universal Studios Hollywood Young Child Fright Potential Chart

Animal Actors Stage   Not frightening in any way.

Backdraft   Intense re-creation of fire terrifies many preschoolers.

Backlot Tram Tour   Certain parts of the tour are too frightening and too intense for many preschoolers.

Back to the Future   Intense, rough thrill ride. Potentially terrifying for people of any age. Switching-off available.

Beetlejuice's Rockin' Graveyard Revue   Creepy set, loud fireworks, performers in monster costumes. Most children ages 5 and up do fine.

E. T. Adventure   Moderately intense ride in the dark. Most children ages 5 years and up tolerate it well.

Jurassic Park—The Ride   Intense water flume ride. Potentially terrifying for people of any age. Switching-off available.

Terminator 2 3D   Extremely intense and potentially frightening for visitors of any age.

**Universal Studios Hollywood Young Child
Fright Potential Chart (continued)**

Totally Nickelodeon   Nothing frightening here beyond the screaming audience.

Waterworld   Fighting, gunplay, and explosions may frighten children ages 4 and under.

Wild, Wild, Wild West Stunt Show   Fighting, gunplay, and explosions may frighten children ages 4 and under.

World of CineMagic   Some intense special effects plus showing the shower murder scene from *Psycho*.

Universal Studios Hollywood One-Day Touring Plan

This plan is for groups of all sizes and ages and includes thrill rides that may induce motion sickness or get you wet. If the plan calls for you to experience an attraction that does not interest you, simply skip that attraction and proceed to the next step. Be aware that the plan calls for minimal backtracking. If you have young children in your party, consult the Universal Studios Hollywood Young Child Fright Potential Chart.

1. Call (818) 622-3801, the main information number, the day before your visit for the official opening time. If you can't get through or are put on hold, call (818) 622-3735 or (818) 622-3750.

2. On the day of your visit, eat breakfast and arrive at Universal Studios Hollywood 50 minutes before opening time. Park, buy your admission, and wait at the turnstiles. If you drive, you will save some time by dropping a member of your party off at the front entrance to purchase tickets while you park.

3. At the turnstile ask an attendant whether any rides or shows are closed that day. Adjust the touring plan accordingly.

4. When the park opens, turn left to *Terminator 2 3D* (opens summer of 1999). See the show.

5. Next, go straight through to the opposite end of the Upper Lot and ride Back to the Future.

6. Exit right and descend on the escalators to the Lower Lot. Take a hard right and ride E.T. Adventure.

7. Exit E.T. and cross the plaza and experience Jurassic Park—The Ride.

8. Retrace your steps back toward E.T. and take the street entering the plaza to *Backdraft.* See the show.

9. After *Backdraft,* go next door to the *World of CineMagic.*

10. Head back toward the escalators. Stop and see Lucy, A Tribute (on your right). Take a rest-room break before continuing.

11. Return to the Upper Lot. Cross in front of Back to the Future and descend on the escalator to the boarding area of the Backlot Tram Tour. Take the tour.

12. Return to the Upper Lot. Now is a good time for lunch if you are hungry.

13. At this point you have five major attractions, all theater presentations, to see:
    - *Waterworld*
    - *Totally Nickelodeon*
    - *Animal Actors Stage*
    - *The Wild, Wild, Wild West Stunt Show*
    - *Beetlejuice's Rockin' Graveyard Revue*

    All five shows are performed several times daily, as listed in the entertainment schedule. Plan the remainder of your itinerary according to the next listed shows for these presentations.

14. This concludes the touring plan. Spend the remainder of your day revisiting your favorite attractions or inspecting sets and street scenes you may have missed. Also, check your daily entertainment schedule for live performances that interest you.

Appendix

Readers' Questions to the Author

Q: When you do your research, are you admitted to the park free? Do the Disney people know you are there?
A: We pay the regular admission and usually the Disney people do not know we are on site. Both in and out of Disneyland, we pay for our own meals and lodging.

Q: How often is the Unofficial Guide *revised?*
A: We publish a new edition once a year, but make minor corrections every time we go to press.

Q: I have an old 1995 edition of the Unofficial Guide. *How much of the information [in it] is still correct?*
A: Veteran travel writers will acknowledge that 5-8% of the information in a guidebook is out of date by the time it comes off the press! Disneyland is always changing. If you are using an old edition of the *Unofficial Guide,* the descriptions of attractions existing when the guide was published should still be generally accurate. Many other things, however, particularly the Touring Plans and the hotel and restaurant reviews, change with every edition. Finally, and obviously, older editions of the *Unofficial Guide* do not include new attractions or developments.

Q: How many people have you interviewed or surveyed for your age group ratings on the attractions?
A: Since the publication of the first edition of the *Unofficial Guide* in 1985, we have interviewed or surveyed just over 6,500 Disneyland patrons. Even with such a large sample, however, we continue to have difficulty with certain age groups. Specifically, we love to hear from seniors concerning their experiences with Splash Mountain, Big Thunder Mountain Railroad, Space Mountain, the Matterhorn Bobsleds, Star Tours, Indiana Jones, and Rocket Rods.

Q: Do you write each new edition from scratch?
A: We do not. With a destination the size of Disneyland, it's hard enough keeping up with what is new. Moreover, we put great effort into communi-

cating the most salient and useful information in the clearest possible language. If an attraction or hotel has not changed, we are very reluctant to tinker with its coverage for the sake of freshening up the writing.

Q: *Do you stay at the Disneyland Hotel? If not, where do you stay?*
A: We do stay at the Disneyland Hotel from time to time, usually after a renovation or management change. Since we began writing about Disneyland in 1984 we have stayed in more than 20 different properties in various locations around Anaheim.

Q: *I laughed at the "When to Go" suggestions [for the attractions]. Too many were before 10 a.m. and after 5 p.m. What are we supposed to do between 10 a.m. and 5 p.m.?*
A: Our best advice is to go back to your hotel and take a nice nap. More in keeping with the spirit of your question, however, the attractions with the shortest waits between 10 a.m. and 5 p.m. are as follows:

- *The Walt Disney Story,* featuring "Great Moments with Mr. Lincoln"
- *Enchanted Tiki Room*
- Tom Sawyer Island
- *Country Bear Playhouse*
- Mark Twain Riverboat
- Sailing Ship *Columbia*
- It's a Small World
- Innoventions

Q: *Why are there no photographs of the theme parks in the* Unofficial Guide*?*
A: Disney has copyrighted many identifiable buildings and structures in Disneyland. Any recognizable photo of Disneyland that we publish without Disney's permission, even if we take the picture ourselves, could constitute copyright infringement according to Disney's legal representatives. Disneyland will not grant the *Unofficial Guide* permission to publish photographs because of Disney's relationship with Steve Birnbaum's *Official Guide to Disneyland.*

Q: *I have heard that when there are two lines to an attraction, the left line is faster. Is this true?*
A: In general, no. We have tested this theory many times and usually have not gained an advantage of even 90 seconds by getting in one line versus another. What *does* occasionally occur, however, is after a second line has *just been opened,* guests ignore the new line and persist in standing in the established line. As a rule of thumb, if you encounter a two-line waiting configuration with no barrier to entry for either and one of the lines is conspicuously less populated than the other, get in it.

Q: Can you recommend some good restaurants in the Disneyland area?
A: When working at Disneyland, we usually end up driving some distance for a decent meal. Our favorite restaurants within 12 minutes of the park are Granville's at the Disneyland Hotel; Tandoor Cuisine of India at 1132 E. Katella Avenue, east of I-5; and Peppers, a Mexican restaurant just west of the Hyatt Regency on Chapman Avenue. We have also had good meals at the Hungry Hunter, a steakhouse at 2438 E. Katella Avenue.

Readers' Comments

A Bloomington, Indiana, couple had this to say:

> *My wife and I are 42 years old. We took your advice on taking an afternoon break. That 2-3 hours rest time back at the [hotel] kept us refreshed for our entire stay. I think without the afternoon breaks we would have missed more and enjoyed less.*

Similarly, a Michigan woman wrote:

> *We were so glad we took the nap advice. At first we thought no way, but then thought about it and it was such good advice. I think the adults needed it more than the kids. We were all ready and willing for our afternoon naps, and had a great time when we returned [to the theme park].*

A dad from Plano, Texas, offered his insight to parents of small children:

> *While on the subject, some parents might benefit from two other things that we learned. First, from our use in conversation of your terms "switching off" or "baby swapping," our daughter quickly caught on to the fact that she was standing in line for a ride that was potentially terrifying for her. As a result, her own imagination-driven panic sometimes led to messy scenes in the anterooms of rides that Mom and Dad took turns experiencing but had no intention of forcing on her. Second, and more happily, it occurred to us that Dumbo, and the Mad Tea Party, which we experienced multiple times were, in effect, "thrill rides" for our five-year-old. If a flying elephant can give a small child the same gleeful exhilaration that her parents enjoy on Star Tours, then the wait in line is justified in both cases.*

A Chicago man questioned the *Unofficial Guide's* ratings, commenting:

> *One general comment about your age-ranged ratings. It seems that many adults must have rated the ride for its appeal to their children rather than for themselves. For example, do young adults really intend to encourage other young adults to ride Snow White by giving it three stars?*

A mom from Eugene, Oregon, found out about Saturday crowds the hard way, commenting:

> *My only parting remark is, people have got to be crazy to go to Disneyland on a Saturday, I don't care what time of year.*

Though this woman from Herndon, Virginia, didn't use the *Unofficial Guide* touring plans, she clearly got the main point of the book:

> *In all honesty, we didn't use any of your touring plans. After reading them I thought to myself, "you have to be kidding." Your plans did offer us hours of entertainment though. We imagined ourselves following them, and all that went through our minds was that we had to go, go, go, we can't stop. We have to run, jump, push, and shove to get to Space Mountain by 7:10 a.m.! Your plans are a great idea, but I'd rather go in the off-season and take my time.*

In contrast, a woman from Baltimore, Ohio, elevated planning to new heights, reporting:

> *I made up little laminated pocket-size cards to take with me to help pinpoint items of interest and where to find them. (My co-workers thought I was nuts when they saw my cards—but they were very handy!) I also had day-to-day plans (that matched the laminated cards) typed out and taped to the wall of my hotel room to check every night for the next day, i.e., phone numbers to call for lunch/dinner reservations, questions to ask, etc. Am I too organized?*

And a woman from Milford, Connecticut, learned something about letting the "tail wag the dog":

> *The plans we used didn't work out perfectly mainly because I am one of those compulsive agenda followers and my husband was the complete opposite (wanted to do what he wanted to do, when he wanted to do it). Our second day was the make-it-or-break-it day for us. I learned to lighten up a bit with the plans, my husband decided to give the plans a chance, and we decided to do a vote as a family on certain attractions, whether to see them or not. Everything was great after that!*

And finally, a father of two from Winnipeg, Manitoba, learned the quintessential Disney mantra from his young daughter:

> *Our six-year-old asks the same three questions about every attraction: Is it real? Will it eat me? and Can we go again?*

And so it goes.

Index

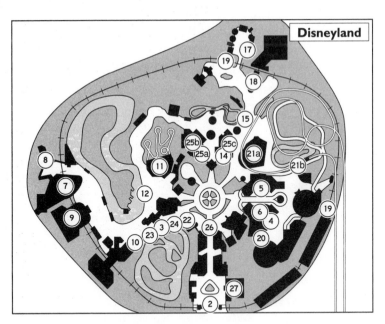

One-Day Touring Plan for Adults
Pocket Outline Version

For the detailed version of this Touring Plan, see page 186.

1. Arrive 30–40 min. prior to opening.
2. Line up at gate 11, 12, or 13.
3. Ride Indiana Jones.
4. Ride Space Mountain.
5. Ride Rocket Rods.
6. Ride Star Tours.
7. Ride Splash Mountain.
8. See the *Country Bear Playhouse* show.
9. See the Haunted Mansion.
10. Ride Pirates of the Caribbean.
11. Ride Big Thunder Mountain Rail-road.
12. Ride the Mark Twain Riverboat or the Sailing Ship *Columbia.*
13. Eat lunch.
14. Ride Peter Pan's Flight.
15. Ride the Storybook Land Canal Boats.
16. Check the daily schedule for live performances.
17. Ride Roger Rabbit's Car Toon Spin.

18. Ride It's a Small World.
19. Take the train from Mickey's Toontown once around the park and get off at Tomorrowland.
20. See *Honey, I Shrunk the Audience.* (If more than 15 minutes before the show, check out Innoventions first.)
21. Ride (a) Matterhorn Bobsleds and (b) Submarine Voyage.
22. See the show at the *Enchanted Tiki Room.*
23. Tour the Swiss Family Treehouse.
24. Ride the Jungle Cruise.
25. Ride (a) Snow White's Scary Adventures, (b) Pinocchio's Daring Journey, and (c) Alice in Wonderland.
26. See parades and live shows.
27. Browse Main Street and see *The Walt Disney Story.*

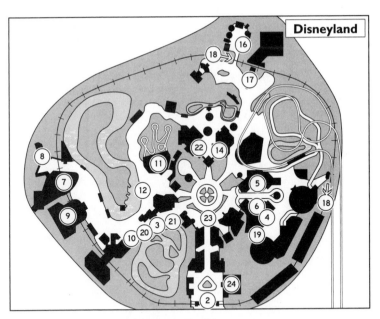

Disneyland

Author's Select One-Day Touring Plan
Pocket Outline Version

For the detailed version of this Touring Plan, see page 188.

1. Arrive 30–40 min. prior to opening.
2. Line up at gate 11, 12, or 13.
3. Ride Indiana Jones.
4. Ride Space Mountain.
5. Ride Rocket Rods.
6. Ride Star Tours.
7. Ride Splash Mountain.
8. See the *Country Bear Playhouse* show.
9. See the Haunted Mansion.
10. Ride Pirates of the Caribbean.
11. Ride Big Thunder Mountain Railroad.
12. Ride the Mark Twain Riverboat or the Sailing Ship *Columbia*.
13. Eat lunch.
14. Ride Peter Pan's Flight.
15. Check the daily schedule for live performances.
16. Ride Roger Rabbit's Car Toon Spin.
17. Ride It's a Small World.
18. Take the train from Mickey's Toontown once around the park and get off at Tomorrowland.
19. See *Honey, I Shrunk the Audience*. (If more than 15 minutes before the show, check out Innoventions first.)
20. Explore the Swiss Family Treehouse.
21. Ride the Jungle Cruise.
22. Ride Snow White's Scary Adventures.
23. See parades and live shows.
24. Browse Main Street and see *The Walt Disney Story*.

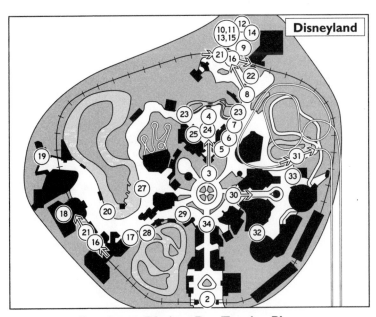

Dumbo-or-Die-in-a-Day Touring Plan,
for Adults with Small Children
Pocket Outline Version

For the detailed version of this Touring Plan, see page 190.
Review the Small Child Fright Potential Chart on pages 82–85.

1. Arrive 30–40 min. prior to opening.
2. Line up at gate 11, 12, or 13.
3. Go to Fantasyland via the castle.
4. Ride Dumbo, the Flying Elephant.
5. Ride Peter Pan's Flight.
6. Ride Alice in Wonderland.
7. Ride the Mad Tea Party.
8. Go to Mickey's Toontown.
9. Ride Roger Rabbit's Car Toon Spin.
10. Ride Gadget's Go-Coaster.
11. Try Goofy's Bounce House.
12. Tour Mickey's House.
13. Tour Chip 'n' Dale's Treehouse and Acorn Ball Crawl.
14. Tour Minnie's House.
15. See the *Miss Daisy*.
16. Take the train to New Orleans Square.
17. Ride Pirates of the Caribbean.
18. See the Haunted Mansion.
19. See the *Country Bear Playhouse* show.
20. Take a raft to Tom Sawyer Island.
21. Take the train from New Orleans Square to Fantasyland/Toontown.
22. Ride It's a Small World.
23. Ride the Casey Jr. Circus Train or the Storybook Land Canal Boats.
24. Ride the King Arthur Carrousel.
25. Ride Pinocchio's Daring Journey if the wait is less than 15 minutes.
26. Go to Frontierland.
27. Ride the Mark Twain Riverboat or the Sailing Ship *Columbia*.
28. Explore the Swiss Family Treehouse.
29. See the *Enchanted Tiki Room* show.
30. Go to Tomorrowland.
31. Take a round-trip monorail ride.
32. See *Honey, I Shrunk the Audience.* If there's 15 min. before the show, explore Innoventions first.
33. Ride the Tomorrowland Autopia.
34. See parades and live shows.

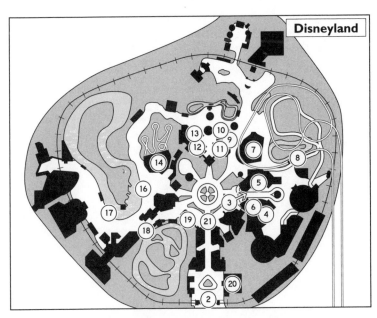

Two-Day Touring Plan A, for Daytime Touring or for When the Park Closes Early
Pocket Outline Version

For the detailed version of this Touring Plan, see page 198.

Day One

1. Arrive 30–40 min. prior to opening.
2. Line up at gate 11, 12, or 13.
3. Go to Tomorrowland.
4. Ride Space Mountain.
5. Ride Rocket Rods.
6. Ride Star Tours.
7. Ride the Matterhorn Bobsleds.
8. Ride the Submarine Voyage.
9. Ride Alice in Wonderland.
10. Ride Mr. Toad's Wild Ride.
11. Ride Peter Pan's Flight.
12. Ride Snow White's Scary Adventures.
13. Ride Pinocchio's Daring Journey.
14. Ride the Big Thunder Mountain Railroad.
15. Eat lunch.
16. Ride the Mark Twain Riverboat or the Sailing Ship *Columbia*. (Work live shows into Touring Plan.)
17. Take a raft to Tom Sawyer Island.
18. Tour the Swiss Family Treehouse.
19. See the *Enchanted Tiki Room* show.
20. See *The Walt Disney Story*.
21. See parades and live shows.

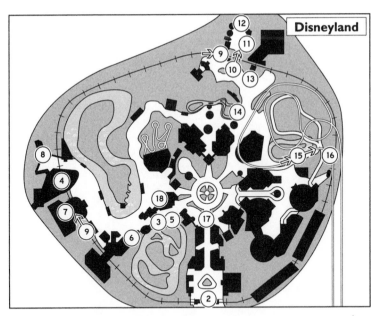

Two-Day Touring Plan A, for Daytime Touring
or for When the Park Closes Early
Pocket Outline Version

For the detailed version of this Touring Plan, see page 198.

Day Two

1. Arrive 30–40 min. prior to opening.
2. Line up at gate 11, 12, or 13.
3. Ride Indiana Jones.
4. Ride Splash Mountain.
5. Ride the Jungle Cruise.
6. Ride Pirates of the Caribbean.
7. See the Haunted Mansion.
8. See the *Country Bear Playhouse* show.
9. Take the train from New Orleans Square to the Fantasyland/Toontown Station.
10. Go to Mickey's Toontown.
11. Ride Roger Rabbit's Car Toon Spin.
12. Tour Mickey's and Minnie's Houses.
13. Ride It's a Small World.
14. Ride the Storybook Land Canal Boats.
15. Take a round-trip on the monorail.
16. Return to Tomorrowland on the monorail.
17. See parades and live shows.

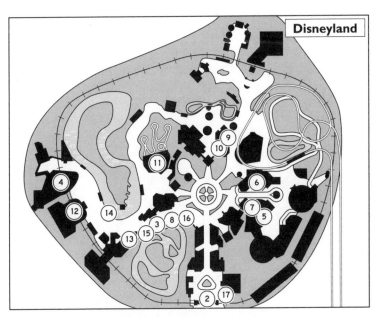

Two-Day Touring Plan B, for Morning and Evening Touring or for When the Park Is Open Late
Pocket Outline Version

For the detailed version of this Touring Plan, see page 201.

Day One

1. Arrive 30–40 min. prior to opening.
2. Line up at gate 11, 12, or 13.
3. Ride Indiana Jones.
4. Ride Splash Mountain.
5. Ride Space Mountain.
6. Ride Rocket Rods.
7. Ride Star Tours.
8. Ride the Jungle Cruise.
9. Ride Alice in Wonderland.
10. Ride Peter Pan's Flight.
11. Ride the Big Thunder Mountain Railroad.
12. See the Haunted Mansion.
13. Ride Pirates of the Caribbean.
14. Take a raft to Tom Sawyer Island. (Work live shows and parades into the Touring Plan.)
15. Tour the Swiss Family Treehouse.
16. See the *Enchanted Tiki Room* show.
17. See *The Walt Disney Story.*
18. Depart Disneyland.

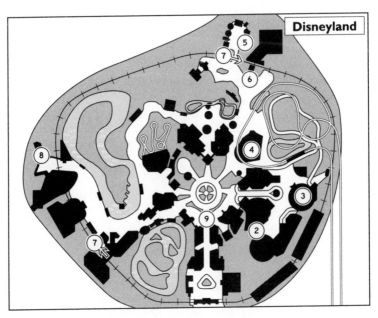

Two-Day Touring Plan B, for Morning and Evening Touring or for When the Park Is Open Late
Pocket Outline Version

For the detailed version of this Touring Plan, see page 201.

Day Two

1. Arrive at the park about 5:30 p.m.
2. See *Honey, I Shrunk the Audience*.
3. Explore Innoventions.
4. Ride the Matterhorn Bobsleds.
5. Ride Roger Rabbit's Car Toon Spin.
6. Ride It's a Small World. (Work live shows and parades into Touring Plan.)
7. Take the train from Fantasyland/Toontown to New Orleans Square/Frontierland.
8. See the *Country Bear Playhouse* show.
9. See parades and live shows.

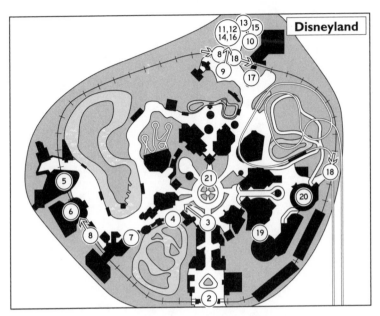

Two-Day Touring Plan for Adults with Small Children
Pocket Outline Version
For the detailed version of this Touring Plan, see page 193.
Review the Small Child Fright Potential Chart on pages 82–85.
Day One

1. Arrive 30–40 min. prior to opening.
2. Line up at gate 11, 12, or 13.
3. Go to Adventureland.
4. Ride the Jungle Cruise.
5. Ride Splash Mountain.
6. See the Haunted Mansion.
7. Ride Pirates of the Caribbean.
8. Take the train from New Orleans Square to Fantasyland/Toontown.
9. Go to Mickey's Toontown.
10. Ride Roger Rabbit's Car Toon Spin.
11. Ride Gadget's Go-Coaster.
12. Try Goofy's Bounce House.
13. Tour Mickey's House.
14. Tour Chip 'n' Dale's Treehouse and Acorn Ball Crawl.
15. Tour Minnie's House.
16. See the *Miss Daisy,* next to Goofy's Bounce House.
17. Ride It's a Small World.
18. Take the train from Fantasyland/Toontown around the park one time, then, get off at Tomorrowland.
19. See *Honey, I Shrunk the Audience.*
20. Check out Innoventions.
21. See parades and live shows.

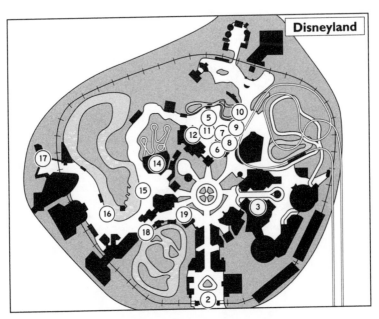

Two-Day Touring Plan for Adults with Small Children
Pocket Outline Version

For the detailed version of this Touring Plan, see page 193.
Review the Small Child Fright Potential Chart on pages 82–85.

Day Two

1. Arrive 30–40 min. prior to opening.
2. Line up at gate 11, 12, or 13.
3. Ride Star Tours.
4. Go to Fantasyland.
5. Ride Dumbo, the Flying Elephant.
6. Ride Peter Pan's Flight.
7. Ride Mr. Toad's Wild Ride.
8. Ride Alice in Wonderland.
9. Ride the Mad Tea Party.
10. Ride the Storybook Land Canal Boats.
11. Ride the King Arthur Carrousel.

12. Ride Pinocchio's Daring Journey.
13. Go to Frontierland.
14. Ride Big Thunder Mountain Railroad.
15. Ride the Mark Twain Riverboat or the Sailing Ship *Columbia*.
16. Take a raft to Tom Sawyer Island.
17. See the *Country Bear Playhouse* show.
18. Explore the Swiss Family Treehouse.
19. See the show at the *Enchanted Tiki Room*.
20. See parades and live shows.

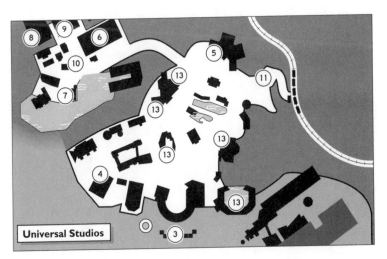

Universal Studios

Universal Studios Hollywood One-Day Touring Plan
Pocket Outline Version

For the detailed version of this Touring Plan, see page 222.
Review the Small Child Fright Potential Chart on pages 221–222.

1. Arrive 50 minutes prior to opening, buy your admission, and wait at the turnstiles.
2. Ask if any rides or shows are closed. Adjust your plan accordingly.
3. When the park opens, turn left to *Terminator 2 3D*. See the show.
4. Next, ride Back to the Future.
5. Ride E.T. Adventure.
6. Cross the plaza and experience Jurassic Park—The Ride.
7. See *Backdraft*.
8. Go next door to the *World of Cine-Magic*.

9. See Lucy, A Tribute.
10. Go to the boarding area of the Back-lot Tram Tour. Take the tour.
11. Eat lunch.
12. See (in any order) *Waterworld, Totally Nickelodeon, Animal Actors Stage, The Wild, Wild, Wild West Stunt Show,* and *Beetlejuice's Rockin' Graveyard Revue.*
13. Check the daily schedule for live performances.

1999 *Unofficial Guide* Reader Survey

If you would like to express your opinion about Disneyland or this guidebook, complete the following survey and mail it to:

> 1999 *Unofficial Guide* Reader Survey
> PO Box 43059
> Birmingham AL 35243

Inclusive dates of your visit: _____

Members of your party:

	Person 1	Person 2	Person 3	Person 4	Person 5
Gender:	M F	M F	M F	M F	M F
Age:					

How many times have you been to Disneyland? _____
On your most recent trip, where did you stay? _____

Concerning your accommodations, on a scale of 100 as best and 0 as worst, how would you rate:

The quality of your room? _____ The value of your room? _____
The quietness of your room? _____ Check-in/check-out efficiency? _____
Shuttle service to the parks? _____ Swimming pool facilities? _____

Did you rent a car? _____ From whom? _____

Concerning your rental car, on a scale of 100 as best and 0 as worst, how would you rate:

Pick-up processing efficiency? _____ Return processing efficiency? _____
Condition of the car? _____ Cleanliness of the car? _____
Airport shuttle efficiency? _____

Concerning your dining experiences:

Including fast-food, estimate your meals in restaurants per day? _____
Approximately how much did your party spend on meals per day? _____
Favorite restaurants outside of Disneyland: _____

_____

Did you buy this guide before leaving? ☐   while on your trip? ☐

How did you hear about this guide? (check all that apply)

Loaned or recommended by a friend ☐   Radio or TV ☐
Newspaper or magazine ☐   Bookstore salesperson ☐
Just picked it out on my own ☐   Library ☐
Internet ☐

Concerning your touring:

Who in your party was most responsible for planning the itinerary? _____

What time did you normally get started in the morning? _____

Did you usually arrive at the theme parks prior to opening? _____

Did you return to your hotel for rest during the day? _____

What time did you normally go to bed at night? _____

If a Disney Resort guest, did you participate in early entry? _____

On a scale of 100 as best and 0 as worst, rate the touring plans:
Name of plan   *Rating*

_____

_____

_____

What other guidebooks did you use on this trip? _____

_____

_____

_____

On a scale of 100 as best and 0 as worst, how would you rate them?

_____

_____

_____

Using the same scale, how would you rate *The Unofficial Guide(s)?*

_____

Are *Unofficial Guides* readily available at bookstores in your area? _____

Have you used other *Unofficial Guides?* _____

Which one(s)? _____

_____

_____

Comments about your Disneyland trip or *The Unofficial Guide(s):*

_____

_____

_____

_____

_____

_____